Ending Extreme Inequality

Ending Extreme Inequality

An Economic Bill of Rights
to Eliminate Poverty

Scott J. Myers-Lipton

Paradigm Publishers
Boulder • London

Copyright © 2015 by Scott J. Myers-Lipton

Published in the United States by Paradigm Publishers, 5589 Arapahoe Avenue, Boulder, CO 80303 USA.

Paradigm Publishers is the trade name of Birkenkamp & Company, LLC, Dean Birkenkamp, President and Publisher.

Library of Congress Cataloging-in-Publication Data

Myers-Lipton, Scott J.
    Ending extreme inequality : an economic bill of rights to eliminate poverty / Scott Myers-Lipton.
       pages cm
    Includes bibliographical references and index.
    ISBN 978-1-61205-727-9 (pbk. : alk. paper)
    ISBN 978-1-61205-896-2 (consumer ebook)
    1. Poverty—United States—History.   2. Social justice—United States—History.   3. Manpower policy—United States—History.   4. United States—Social policy—21st century.   5. Equality—United States—History—21st century.   I. Title.
    HC110.P6M9396 2014
    330—dc23
                                                                                      2014017343

Printed and bound in the United States of America on acid-free paper that meets the standards of the American National Standard for Permanence of Paper for Printed Library Materials.

19 18 17 16 15   1 2 3 4 5

To my students at San José State University, whose energy and commitment to ending extreme inequality are an inspiration to our community and beyond

Contents

Prologue

Today, poverty and inequality are at record levels. Forty-seven million Americans are living in poverty, the highest level since 1983. The median income has declined over the past several years, while the trend over the past thirty years has been one of anemic growth and stagnation. At the same time, growth for the top 1 percent of income earners has remained strong, with their net worth at 40 percent of all wealth, while the top 20 percent now control 89 percent of all the wealth, up from 81 percent in 1983. As a result of high poverty, middle-income stagnation, and the rich's increase of income and wealth, the United States is number one in income inequality in the industrialized world.

As a response to this situation, some people are calling for an Economic Bill of Rights, an American idea first proposed by presidents Franklin Roosevelt and Harry Truman, and later by Dr. Martin Luther King Jr. The Economic Bill of Rights has a clear and coherent vision and agenda on how to solve poverty and extreme economic inequality by proclaiming that there are certain "rights" that are needed to correct for the wrongs found in American society. These rights include the right to a job; to a living wage; to a decent home; to adequate medical care; to a good education; to adequate protection from economic fears of unemployment, sickness, and old age; and to fair competition.

This call for a second bill of rights has grown out of the American context, where high levels of poverty have been a major issue since the founding of the United States. In the late eighteenth century, over 30 percent of all Americans were living in poverty. With the rise of industrial capitalism in the mid-1800s, the nation's workers were confronted with eleven- to twelve-hour workdays and poverty wages for many. In response, workers fought back against this treatment, with the late nineteenth century being filled with labor strife. In the 1880s, there were over 500 strikes each year, as the working class struggled for decent pay and an eight-hour workday.

In the early twentieth century, progressives focused on youth poverty, as reformers addressed child labor, illiteracy, and malnutrition of the nation's youth. During the 1930s, poverty once again captured the nation's attention, as 24 percent of the nation was unemployed during the Great Depression. Thirty years later, poverty was once again the focus of the nation. After the passage of the Civil Rights Act and Voting Rights Act—which ended de jure racism in the United States—civil rights leaders turned their attention toward ending poverty. This reawakening to the plight of the poor inspired President Lyndon Johnson to declare a War on Poverty in order to put an end to it. While some have argued that the United States fought the War on Poverty, and poverty won, the reality was that there were some major gains made, particularly in senior poverty, which was reduced from 35 percent to 10 percent of the population, mostly through increased Social Security payments. Yet, after the murders of Dr. King and Robert Kennedy, and President Johnson's decision to not run for reelection, concerns of poverty and inequality moved to the back burner.

From 1980 to the early 2000s, while the nation was no longer focused on these issues, major structural changes to the economy were occurring, such as globalization and offshoring of jobs, as well as political changes, like tax policies that favored the 1 percent and public policies that kept the minimum wage stagnant. These economic and political changes of the late twentieth century led to large increases in poverty and inequality, as income from 1979 to 2006 for the middle class went up by 15 percent, whereas income for the bottom 20 percent actually decreased by 4 percent. At the same time, the income of the top 1 percent rose by 120 percent.

The nation awoke from its slumber in August 2005, when Hurricane Katrina struck the Gulf Coast and exposed to the nation and world that in the United States, poverty was alive and well. Then, the economic collapse of 2008 occurred, and the middle and working classes were hammered. From 2008 to 2012, foreclosures—a result of high-interest loans and the Great Recession's high unemployment—led to the loss of 8 million homes. For the middle class, unemployment reached 10 percent, but for people making under $20,000 a year the rate was double that, and it was triple that for folks making under $12,000. The result was that over the past four years, middle-class incomes decreased by 3 percent, while people making $40,000 or less had their incomes decrease by 10 percent. Importantly, this social suffering did not occur equally. Edward Wolff, an economist who studies inequality, recently reported that the median household income has dropped by 36.1 percent from the peak of the housing bubble in 2007, while the income of the top 1 percent dropped only 11.1 percent. Thus, the Great Recession actually increased income inequality.

I argue that this high level of poverty, in combination with the increasing gap in income and wealth inequality, is not good for democracy, and it is not a sustainable path for the nation. The social disruptions that it can cause became clearer in September 2011, when Occupy Wall Street physically occupied Zuccotti Park. With the catchy slogan "We are the 99%," Occupy Wall Street gripped the nation as it took over public spaces, first in New York City, and then around the country. And while Occupy did not offer clear policy solutions, it did focus clearly on the unequal distribution of income and wealth in the United States and the corrosive effect it has had on our democracy.

The question is why there has been, and continues to be, so much poverty and inequality in the United States. Answers to this question come from both the political right and left. I find the best answer to this question from two of our greatest Americans, President Franklin Delano Roosevelt and Dr. Martin Luther King Jr. When President Roosevelt took office in 1932, unemployment was at 15.9 percent and within a year it had jumped to almost 24 percent. In response, Roosevelt took bold action, creating three public works programs and implementing Social Security, unemployment insurance, and the Wagner Act, which legalized unions.

Underlying Roosevelt's solutions to the Great Depression was the analysis that the economic system was not providing security to working Americans. Roosevelt argued that capitalism, left to itself, created too much poverty since it was not providing enough jobs or creating jobs that provided an adequate income. This was of great concern to Roosevelt because the poverty created by capitalism made it impossible for many Americans to pursue happiness. As Roosevelt stated, "We have come to a clear realization of the fact that true individual freedom cannot exist without economic security and independence. 'Necessitous men are not free men.'" Roosevelt understood that American capitalism unleashed creativity and technology, but it also created too much economic insecurity and poverty. Therefore, the solution was to embrace capitalism's creativity but limit its tendency toward poverty and extreme inequality.

The second great American to provide an answer to the question of why there is so much poverty and inequality in the United States is Dr. Martin Luther King. Many of us are familiar with King's role as leader of the Montgomery Bus Boycott and his historic "I Have a Dream Speech" at the March on Washington. What many might not know is that Dr. King dedicated the last three years of his life to ending poverty. After helping to pass the 1964 Civil Rights Act and the 1965 Voter Rights Act, King realized that while these changes were important, they had done little to change the economic conditions of black Americans. King proclaimed,

> Now our struggle is for genuine equality, which means economic equality. For we know now, that it isn't enough to integrate lunch counters. What does it profit a man to be able to eat at an integrated lunch counter if he doesn't have enough money to buy a hamburger? What does it profit a man to be able to eat at the swankest integrated restaurant when he doesn't even earn enough money to take his wife out to dine? What does it profit one to have access to the hotels of our cities, and the hotels of our highways, when we don't earn

enough money to take our family on a vacation? What does it profit one to be able to attend an integrated school, when he doesn't earn enough money to buy his children school clothes?

To attempt to achieve economic justice, King began to focus his efforts on reforming the American capitalist system. King concluded that US capitalism was structurally flawed since it created too much poverty. American capitalism just didn't create enough good paying jobs, so there were always going to be millions of people in poverty. King stated, "In this other America, thousands and thousands of people, men in particular, walk the streets in search for jobs that do not exist." Importantly, King made this comment in 1968, in a time of strong economic growth. In other words, whether the economy is strong or in recession, there is still going to be poverty. As King stated, "No matter how dynamically the economy develops and expands it does not eliminate all poverty."

King's goal was to put an end to the "curious formula" that existed between whites and blacks. King said that the curious formula dated back to the founding of this country and the Constitution, when blacks were counted as 60 percent of whites when determining population size. King explained that the curious formula still existed since African Americans received one-half of all the good things in life and got twice the bad things in life. For example, in 1968 the unemployment rate for whites was 5 percent, but it was 10 percent for blacks. In 1970, 10 percent of white Americans lived in poverty, compared to 30 percent of blacks. This curious formula also existed in other areas as well, such as infant mortality, death rates on the battlefield, and loan denial rates. King wanted to put an end to this curious formula that existed between blacks and whites. Over time, King's vision expanded to include working-class and poor Latinos, Native Americans, and whites. King saw economic inequality as an issue that could unite these various groups, and he called on other ethnicities and races to "come together with us black people and let's gather ourselves together around this issue of poverty."

Clearly, both King and Roosevelt felt that since American capitalism had created poverty, it was the American government's responsibility to deal with it. Like Roosevelt, King felt that if a person was poor, he was not free. King stated, "If a man doesn't have a job or an income, he has neither life nor liberty nor the possibility for the pursuit of happiness. He merely exists." To King and Roosevelt, this was unacceptable.

SOLUTION

The solution advocated by both President Roosevelt and Dr. King was the Economic Bill of Rights. This second bill of rights was announced in

Roosevelt's 1944 State of the Union address. It was composed of the following "rights" or amendments, which Roosevelt outlined in his speech:

- The right to a useful and remunerative job in the industries or shops or farms or mines of the nation;
- The right to earn enough to provide adequate food and clothing and recreation;
- The right of every family to a decent home;
- The right to a good education;
- The right to adequate medical care and the opportunity to achieve and enjoy good health;
- The right to adequate protection from the economic fears of old age, sickness, accident, and unemployment.

Clearly, the Economic Bill of Rights is not a radical solution, since it is not calling for the overthrow of capitalism. Rather, it is a progressive American solution. Progressivism grew out of the slums and miserable factory conditions of the mid- to late nineteenth century. Importantly, progressives were not aligned to one political party or organization, but rather they were united in the belief that social and economic structures were responsible for the day's social problems, and that they could be solved through social reform. Progressives rejected laissez-faire policy and saw government as a positive force to improve society. Moreover, the Economic Bill of Rights is an American solution since it is based in the concept of the original Bill of Rights.

The idea for an Economic Bill of Rights can be found as early as 1932 in Roosevelt's speech to the Common Wealth Club. Here, Roosevelt states, "The task of Government in its relation to business is to assist the development of an economic declaration of rights, an economic constitutional order. . . . Every man has a right to life; and this means that he has also a right to make a comfortable living." Importantly, Roosevelt based his desire to eradicate poverty not in an egalitarian vision—that is, he did not believe that people should be paid more or less the same—but rather in liberty, as he believed strongly in free markets and private property. At the same time, since those same free markets created poverty and excessive inequality, Roosevelt believed that there should be a floor above the poverty line and a progressive tax structure to pay for it. In order to put into practice this liberty-based antipoverty vision, Roosevelt proposed a second bill of rights, but rather than focusing on political rights, as the first one had done, this bill would focus on economic rights. Most scholars agree that Roosevelt was not advocating for the literal passage of a second bill of rights but rather was promoting a set of constitutional commitments that would be carried out through a series of public policies passed by Congress.

Interestingly, Roosevelt expanded his vision to end poverty to the entire world. In his 1941 speech to Congress, he articulated Four Freedoms—the freedoms of speech and worship, and the freedoms from want and fear—which he thought were the essential freedoms that all nations should be founded upon. Roosevelt spelled out that *freedom from want* meant an "economic understanding which will secure to every nation a healthy peacetime life for its inhabitants—everywhere in the world."

A year after Roosevelt proposed the Economic Bill of Rights, he was dead. It was left to Roosevelt's successor, Harry Truman, to implement this set of public policies. In his 1946 State of the Union address, President Truman explained that an Economic Bill of Rights was the most effective way "to improve the welfare of the American people." Truman followed Roosevelt's lead in couching the Economic Bill of Rights in terms of freedom: "The new economic bill of rights to which I have referred on previous occasions is a charter of economic freedom which seeks to assure that all who will may work toward their own security and the general advancement; that we become a well-housed people, a well-nourished people, an educated people, a people socially and economically secure, an alert and responsible people."

In order to bring the Economic Bill of Rights into reality, Truman did three things: (1) he put forward a full employment bill declaring that all Americans were "entitled to an opportunity for useful and remunerative, regular, and full time employment" and that government should provide the expenditures to reach full employment; (2) he worked for the passage of a housing act, giving the federal government an active role in ensuring all Americans had a decent home since the free market did not build enough homes for low-income people; and (3) he sent a special message to Congress in 1945 calling on the nation to create a national health insurance plan run by the federal government, and while it would be optional, Americans could choose to pay into it a monthly fee, which would cover the cost of medical expenses.

Conservatives and businessmen opposed all of these efforts, and these bills were either defeated outright or greatly weakened. First, conservatives and businessmen watered down the employment act, so by the time it was passed in 1946, the idea that a job was a right had been removed, and "full employment" was changed to "promote" maximum employment. Second, the housing bill suffered a similar fate, as the provision to build hundreds of thousands of new low-income homes by the government was greatly weakened. Finally, they opposed and killed the national health insurance bill, arguing that the bill was socialistic.

The idea for a second bill of rights would remain dormant for almost twenty years until 1967, when Dr. Martin Luther King Jr. began using it to describe the direction in which the United States needed to go. King argued that the United States had made only surface changes up to 1966—including the passage of the Civil Rights Act of 1964 and the Voting Rights Act of 1965—and that more fundamental change was necessary to create the "Beloved Community." King called on the civil rights movement to transform itself into a human rights movement and push for the right to a job, a guaranteed annual income, and housing.

In the last years of his life, King dedicated his life to ending poverty and the curious formula, and he thought the best way to achieve this was through an Economic Bill of Rights that provided full employment through public works, a guaranteed income at middle-class-income levels, and the creation of 5 million low-income homes. In his last book King stated, "From a variety of different directions, the strands are drawing together for a contemporary social and economic Bill of Rights to supplement the Constitution's political Bill of Rights." In an article published eight days after his assassination, King stated emphatically, "We need an Economic Bill of Rights. This would guarantee a job to all people who want to work and are able to work. It would also guarantee an income for all who are not able to work."

BOOK OVERVIEW

Each chapter of this book will examine one of the rights or amendments of the Economic Bill of Rights. Clearly, these rights emerged out of wrongs. It is therefore important to understand the wrongs that have occurred in American history. Thus, a brief history of these wrongs will be discussed, as well as attempts from the nineteenth and twentieth centuries to right these wrongs. This will be followed by four to six twenty-first-century solutions offered by citizens, community groups, and politicians. The hope is that these contemporary and real-life solutions to poverty and inequality will inspire people to become involved, or stay involved, in these efforts, as well as frame our collective work in the context of a coherent vision offered by the Economic Bill of Rights.

Chapter 1 focuses on the "first amendment"—the right to a job. This opening chapter examines the history of public works, with a focus on Roosevelt's New Deal public works projects, Truman's Unemployment Act of 1946, King's call for public works, the passage of the Humphrey-Hawkins Full Employment Act, and the expansion of the Comprehensive Employment and Training Act (CETA) under President Jimmy Carter. More contemporaneously, President Barack Obama's stimulus plan is analyzed, with a focus on "shovel-ready" projects and the subsidized employment program. Chapter 1 will also discuss the Gulf Coast Civic Works Act, which was proposed to rebuild the Gulf Coast after Hurricane Katrina. The chapter concludes with a discussion of San Antonio 2020—a plan by Julian Castro, mayor of San Antonio, Texas, to create jobs through infrastructure projects such as roads, parks, and flood protection. This chapter will also consider the role of cooperatives in guaranteeing the right to a job.

Chapter 2 examines the "second amendment"—the right to a living wage. This chapter explores the long history of the living-wage movement, which includes the powerful roles workers and unions have played, as well as King's guaranteed income and President Richard Nixon's family income. Chapter 2 will also discuss the living-wage movement today, where it finds expression in efforts to raise the minimum wage, the idea for a basic income, the earned income tax credit, and cooperatives.

Chapter 3 explores the "third amendment"—the right to a decent home. This chapter provides a historic overview of efforts to create housing for all our people. It then looks at current efforts to build more affordable low-income housing and create a dedicated revenue source to fund the construction, as well as to provide rental assistance to fill the gap between the cost of housing and what people can afford. The chapter concludes with a discussion of how to stop the massive numbers of foreclosures, which has greatly reduced the number of Americans owning a home, and an examination of Rapid Re-Housing policies for people without homes.

Chapter 4 looks at the "fourth amendment"—the right to a good education. This chapter provides a historic overview of the nation's effort to provide a good education for all. Chapter 4 will explore how money, curriculum, and pedagogy affect whether students receive a decent education. Moreover, it will consider ways to provide a good education for all, which include equalizing school funding, attracting and retaining qualified teachers to high-need schools, reducing class size, providing a content-rich curriculum for all and teaching it with an active learning approach, providing universal preschool for four-year-olds, and encouraging integration.

Chapter 5 focuses on the "fifth amendment"—the right to adequate health care. This chapter examines the contributions of the Sheppard-Towner bill, Truman's push for a national health insurance bill, the community health clinics of the 1960s–1970s, and President Bill Clinton's failed efforts in the 1990s to achieve universal care. More recently, it will explore the federal government's Affordable Care Act, as well as Vermont's single-payer plan and the push for Medicare for All.

Chapter 6 considers the "sixth amendment"—the right to adequate protection from economic fears of old age and unemployment. It will explore the development of the Economic Security Act, which provides for the current rights we enjoy, as well as current efforts to strengthen Social Security.

Every effort has been made to ensure the accuracy of the documents and data in this book. Possible errors brought to the attention of the publisher and author will be researched, and if verified, will be corrected in future editions.

I would like to thank Rosie Mendoza and Lisa Mann, who helped format the citations; and my wife, Diane, and my two children, Gabriela and Josiah, for always inspiring and encouraging me.

Chapter 1

The Right to a Job

The First Amendment

PROBLEM

A difficult truth for both liberals and conservatives is that capitalism does not produce enough jobs to employ all the people who want to work. Liberals don't like to hear that capitalism does not produce enough jobs because their solution to reducing poverty and inequality focuses on equal opportunity. Over the past fifty years, liberals have argued that if you provide equal opportunity, all people, including the working class and poor, will have the ability to move up the economic ladder. In fact, almost all of the War on Poverty programs were based on equal opportunity. Underlying the War on Poverty was the belief that there was not something wrong with American-style capitalism, but rather extreme inequality and poverty could be solved if people were educated through projects such as Head Start, Follow Through, Upward Bound, Job Corps, and VISTA, while at the same time removing racist structures. For liberals, equal opportunity has been the panacea.

Yet, the problem with the economic opportunity model is that it fails to acknowledge that even in good economic times, the unemployment rate for Americans living in poverty tends to be much higher than those of the middle and upper classes. And when the economy is bad, like during the Great Recession of 2007–2009, this unemployment gap becomes even larger. For example, during that recession the unemployment rate was just 3.2 percent for

1

households making $150,000 or more and 4 percent for households making $100,000–$149,000, in comparison to a 19.1 percent unemployment rate for households making $12,500 to $20,000, and a staggering 30.8 percent for those under $12,499. Thus, while the unemployment rate of the upper middle class and rich was relatively low, the rate for working-class and poor Americans approached Great Depression levels. Interestingly, King's curious formula still applies, for in 2012 white unemployment was 7 percent, compared to 14 percent for black unemployment. Thus, no matter how much education people have or how many racial barriers are torn down, industrial capitalism does not produce enough jobs to employ all the people who would like to work.[1]

At the same time, conservatives don't like to hear that capitalism does not produce enough jobs. This is difficult for conservatives to accept because they have an undying belief in the power of the individual and personal responsibility. And while people need to take responsibility for their own lives and work hard to achieve their goals, it must also be recognized that there is a flaw in the American capitalist system, since no matter how hard one works, the unemployment rate for the working class and poor is high, as witnessed in the prior example. In addition, even when modern capitalism has been in "recovery," as in the early 1990s, early 2000s, and from 2010 to 2014, it has been a "jobless recovery" due to technological advances that have replaced humans with machines and the outsourcing of jobs. In June 2014, after more than four years of economic recovery, there are still 9.5 million Americans unemployed, with 3.8 million who have been out of work for six months or longer.[2]

This jobs crisis is hidden from public view due to the way in which the unemployment rate is calculated, which counts people as unemployed only if they don't have a job and have looked for employment in the past four weeks. For example, in June 2013, the overall unemployment rate was 7.6 percent, which is not great, but it is much better than the 10 percent unemployment rate during 2009 and 2010. However, if the unemployment rate took into account the people who want a job but haven't looked for the past four weeks or who took a part-time job because they couldn't find full-time employment, the unemployment rate almost doubles to 14.3 percent. Thus, the method for calculating the rate of unemployment underestimates the true nature of our jobs crisis.[3]

In the end, both liberals and conservatives do not see the flaw within the American capitalist system. To correct this wrong, there must be a new right, and it is the right to a job. Recognizing the principle of a right to a job does not undermine the nation's work ethic or the importance of education. However, these alone will not solve poverty and excessive inequality: a right to a job will. Only by recognizing that a job is a right will the United States take a major step in ending poverty and extreme inequality. Historically, this right to a job has been expressed through public works, where the government hires people directly or funds businesses to conduct public works projects. At the same time, the right to a job is different from the right to a living-wage job. This latter point will be discussed in Chapter 2.

As stated earlier, progressivism recognizes that economic and social structures are responsible for the social problems of the day, and that social reforms can solve them. The Economic Bill of Rights is within this historical tradition of progressivism since it moves beyond the liberal-conservative shortcomings stated earlier and potentially can unite Americans in the belief that in order to be able to pursue life, liberty, and happiness, the US democratic, capitalist system must be reformed because our current system does not produce enough jobs for all. Clearly, this right to a job through public works is something that both political parties can embrace, for not only the most famous Democrat of the twentieth century supported it, but also one of the most famous Republicans, Ronald Reagan. President Reagan supported public works because it provided socially useful projects and jobs, including one for his father during the Great Depression. Reagan stated, "Now a lot of people remember [the WPA] as boondoggles and raking leaves. . . . Maybe in some places it was. Maybe in the big city machines or something. But I can take you to our town and show you things, like a riverfront that I used to hike through once that was a swamp and is now a beautiful park-like place built by the WPA." Roosevelt's and Reagan's support shows that public works is perhaps the best solution to achieve full employment.[4]

SOLUTION

The solution to the "wrong" of not enough jobs is the right to a job. This right is based in the belief that there should be jobs for all Americans who want to work. The right to a job is not anticapitalistic, but rather it fixes capitalism's weakness of not producing enough jobs for all who want to work. In other words, it solves the problem of structural unemployment. The most common public policy that has been suggested to achieve this constitutional commitment of a right to a job has been public works.

THE HISTORY OF THE RIGHT TO A JOB
THROUGH PUBLIC WORKS PROJECTS

Public works has a long history in the United States. The term refers to when the government takes an active role in hiring people who are unemployed. Historically, Americans have turned to public works during an economic crisis when unemployment is high and the private sector has been unable to create enough jobs. However, in order to make a right to a job a reality, public works must be employed not just when the economy goes through cyclical levels of high unemployment; it must also be used to counteract the structural unemployment caused by capitalism.

In the late nineteenth century, cities created local jobs for the unemployed such as street paving, street cleaning, and sewer construction. Jacob Coxey took this idea to the national level when he called upon the United States in 1893 to employ the unemployed by building roads and civic buildings. Although Coxey and his followers were unsuccessful in convincing Congress to act, his idea found expression forty years later in Roosevelt's New Deal public works programs.

Historically, there have been two different types of public works projects. The first type was federally operated, which means that the government directly hired unemployed workers. Examples of this type of public works project are the Civilian Works Administration (CWA), which employed 4.3 million workers from 1933 to 1934; the Works Progress Administration (WPA), which employed 8.5 million workers from 1935 to 1943; and the Civilian Conservation Corps (CCC), which employed 3.5 million eighteen- to twenty-five-year-olds from 1933 to 1941. The other type of public works project was government funded but operated by private contractors. This was how the Public Works Administration (PWA) operated, which hired about 221,000 workers each year, or about one-eighth of all New Deal public workers. There has since been much analysis of which type of plan was more successful. While any modern-day public works agenda should consider both types, there is no question that if the goal is to hire the greatest number of people, the federally run program is more effective at hiring large numbers of the unemployed.[5]

New Deal public works of the CWA, PWA, WPA, and CCC—this alphabet soup of programs—injected $336 billion in 2008 dollars into the economy, hired over 10 million people, and in combination with other New Deal initiatives cut unemployment from almost 24 percent in 1933 to 10 percent by 1940. This 13.6 percent decrease was the single greatest drop in the unemployment rate in US history. In addition to reducing unemployment and poverty, New Deal public works built or repaired over 2,500 hospitals, 9,000 parks, 43,000 schools, 125,000 bridges, and almost 1 million miles of highways and roads, and they stocked 1 billion fish and planted 3 billion trees. Public workers literally built the infrastructure that we still utilize. Importantly, the New Deal public workers did more than build and repair infrastructure. Unemployed authors were hired to write books, actors were employed to put on play productions, educators were hired to teach literacy, and musicians were employed to play music. For many in the working class, the concerts held by the 238 WPA orchestras and bands were the first time they had ever heard live music.[6]

The impacts of Roosevelt's public works and other New Deal initiatives are striking. As stated earlier, unemployment was reduced from 23.6 percent in 1933 to 10 percent by 1940. In addition, the US economy began to grow at a rate of about 10 percent per year, with production doubling. Today, some claim that Roosevelt didn't solve the unemployment crisis because he didn't reduce it to 2 percent unemployment, which is where it was in 1942 during World War II. What these critics don't understand is that the over 13 percent cut in unemployment is the single greatest drop in the history of the country. Moreover, if Roosevelt and Congress would have provided more money to public works, as requested by WPA director Harry Hopkins, unemployment would have dropped even more.

After the death of Roosevelt, the new president, Harry Truman, tried to bring about FDR's first amendment to the Economic Bill of Rights by supporting the Full Employment Act of 1945. This bill, which was introduced by Sen. Robert Wagner (D-NY) and Sen. James Murray (D-MT) in January 1945, declared that all Americans were "entitled to an opportunity for useful and remunerative, regular, and full time employment" and that the government was to provide the investment and expenditures to achieve full employment. The Full Employment Act was supported by labor, civil rights, faith, and social welfare organizations. They argued that if full employment was achieved as a result of World War II, why couldn't full employment be achieved during peacetime. There was also concern that the private sector alone could not achieve full employment with the return of 12 million troops.[7]

The Full Employment Act stated that when the private sector failed to create jobs for all, the federal government would step in to create these jobs through federal investment and spending. The act went on to describe that the type of investment and spending that would be allowed included public works, as well as outlays for public services to home owners, veterans, business, agriculture, and consumers. Each quarter, the president would examine the jobs numbers and make alterations to the federal investment and expenditures to ensure jobs for all.

In September 1945 the act was passed, 71 to 10, in the Senate. However, in the House of Representatives, critics put forth an alternative bill entitled the Employment Protection Act. This second bill did not include the words *full employment* but rather promoted the idea of "maximum employment." Also, the Employment Protection Act removed the language of federal investment and spending and specifically took out any reference to public works. Conservative critics argued that the Senate bill would cost too much and cause inflation. They also argued that the bill was paternalistic and socialist, and perhaps even communist. After defeating the Full Employment Act, the alternative bill passed the House, 255 to 126. In the Senate Joint Conference Committee, the conservative alternative was also victorious, and

Truman signed it into law. Gone was any reference to public works, federal expenditures, and full employment.[8]

The idea of the right to a job remained dormant in the 1950s but reemerged after the great civil rights victories of the 1960s. With the Civil Rights Act of 1964 and the Voting Rights act of 1965, Dr. Martin Luther King Jr. and the civil rights movement had destroyed the legal apparatus supporting Jim Crow segregation and ensured the voting rights guaranteed in the 14th and 15th Amendments. However, the unemployment and underemployment caused by capitalism had not been dealt with. King thought that American-style capitalism was flawed, and he looked to FDR's Economic Bill of Rights as the solution. King believed that the most effective way to achieve full employment was to guarantee a job through public works. In one of his last interviews before his murder, King argued for an Economic Bill of Rights, which guaranteed "a job to all people who want to work and are able to work," carried out by "creating certain public works jobs." This would provide poor people of all races the money necessary to pay for housing, food, transportation, and health care. King recognized the program would cost money, but he felt that the richest nation in the world had the financial resources to provide full employment. King declared, "It didn't cost the nation one penny to integrate lunch counters. It didn't cost the nation one penny to guarantee the right to vote. But now we are dealing with issues that cannot be solved without the nation spending billions of dollars and undergoing a radical redistribution of economic power."[9]

In 1968, King was planning to lead a nonviolent army of 3,000 people from ten urban and five rural areas to Washington, DC, so as to shut down the city by disrupting the daily operation in order to force the nation to respond to his demands to end poverty through public works, a guaranteed income, and construction of low-income housing. King's vision to end poverty in America was shattered when he was tragically murdered in Memphis, Tennessee, where he had gone to support striking garbage workers.

Yet, the idea of public works as a way to bring about jobs for all would not die. In 1974, six years after King's death, his widow, Coretta, formed and co-chaired the National Committee for Full Employment. The committee was a coalition of forty labor, civil rights, religious, and civic organizations. This committee argued that there was not a welfare problem in this country, but rather an unemployment crisis. Coretta King reached out to then governor of Georgia Jimmy Carter and sent him the committee's material calling for development of full employment legislation. Carter joined the committee, and four years later, when he was president, he signed into law the Full Employment and Balanced Growth Act.[10]

This law, which is also known as the Humphrey-Hawkins Full Employment Act, strengthened the 1946 employment act by committing the nation to full employment for the first time. Although the act recognized that private enterprise was still the main sector for American employment, it asserted that the federal government had the responsibility "to use all practicable programs and policies to promote full employment." The act also made clear that if a person was willing to work, he or she had a right to a job. As proclaimed in the opening paragraph of the legislation, the goal of the Humphrey-Hawkins Full Employment Act was "to translate into practical reality the right of all Americans who are able, willing, and seeking to work to full opportunity for useful paid employment at fair rates of compensation." The act based its call for full employment on the fact that the United States had a long history of structural and cyclical unemployment, and that monetary and fiscal policies alone have been unable to achieve full employment. The act stated that "Congress finds the Nation has suffered substantial unemployment and underemployment ... over long periods of time" and "recognizes that general economic policies alone have been unable to achieve the goals set forth in this Act related to full employment."[11]

Importantly, the Humphrey-Hawkins Full Employment Act provided clear goals to cap the unemployment rate. Specifically, it stated that by 1983, the unemployment rate should not be higher than 3 percent for anyone over age twenty, and that for sixteen- to nineteen-year-olds, it should not be higher than 4 percent. Moreover, it required the president to act if the unemployment rate exceeded these limits, stating that it is "the purpose of this title to require the President to initiate, as the President deems appropriate, with recommendations to Congress when necessary, supplemental programs and policies to the extent that the President finds such action necessary to achieve these goals, including the goals and timetable for the reduction of unemployment." The act then clearly defined what type of employment policies the president can initiate, which included (1) accelerated public works (including the creation of standby public works projects), (2) public service employment, (3) youth employment programs, and (4) training programs, as well as other federal expenditures, including employment tax credits and wage vouchers. Last, the president was instructed to consider "a triggering mechanism" that would implement these programs during recessions, when unemployment rose above 3 percent and 4 percent, and phase them out when unemployment was reduced below these levels. Using the above goals and timetables, the president's actions would create "reservoirs of public employment and private nonprofit employment projects."[12]

It should also be noted that the Full Employment and Balanced Growth Act had a strong focus on youth unemployment. This originated in the National Committee for Full Employment, which had highlighted that the unemployment rate for youths of color was triple the level of the overall unemployment rate. Accordingly, the Humphrey Hawkins Full Employment Act included individuals aged sixteen and over in the public works projects, and called for the creation of youth jobs "through the use of targeted employment tax credits, wage vouchers and other incentives to private sector business."[13]

Some critics complained that the Full Employment Act decentered full employment as the primary national economic goal since it also committed the nation to control inflation and balance the budget. However, proponents argued that this bill was a major accomplishment as it changed the nation's employment goal from "maximum employment" to "full employment," set specific targets for unemployment to stay below, and required the federal government to create public works jobs in order to reduce it to that level.

At the signing ceremony, Coretta King said that the Full Employment and Balanced Growth Act was perhaps as significant as the Civil Rights Act of 1964 and the Voting Rights Act of 1965, adding that it was "a tribute to Martin Luther King, Jr., because in 1968, he started a crusade calling for a job and income for all people who needed a job." Unfortunately, the Full Employment Act didn't turn out the way Coretta King had hoped, as presidents from both the Democratic and Republican parties disregarded most of its provisions regarding full employment. The one major program that was expanded during the Carter administration was the Comprehensive Employment and Training Act (CETA), which had started under President Richard Nixon. Initially, CETA provided public service jobs, but President Carter changed it so that it would be federally funded jobs but with a private contractor. At its height, CETA employed 725,000 people and provided 1 million summer jobs for youth at a cost of $10 billion, which cut 1 percentage point off the unemployment rate. However, with the budget deficit climbing, Carter began cutting back CETA, and by 1981, it employed just 300,000. CETA was abolished during the Reagan administration, replaced by state grants for job training, with a focus on youth. Reagan's plan also offered a very limited number of summer youth jobs.[14]

With President Reagan's election in 1980, the nation's politics turned much more conservative, and there was no longer talk of a "right to a job" through public works. This held true through the presidencies of George H. W. Bush, Bill Clinton, and George W. Bush. However, the Great Recession changed everything.[15]

THE HISTORY OF THE RIGHT TO A JOB THROUGH COOPERATIVES

Another enterprise that furthers the idea of a right to a living job is *cooperatives*. From the beginning of human society, people have cooperated and provided mutual aid to one another in order to increase fishing, hunting, gathering food, or meeting other basic needs. In fact, the creation of an agriculture society would not have been possible without the mutual aid provided by farmers to one another as they picked crops, constructed barns, and shared equipment. These early examples of informal cooperation would form the basis of the modern-day cooperative.

Cooperative businesses developed as a result of industrial capitalism. In the nineteenth century, people in both Europe and the United States were moving from the rural areas to the cities in search of employment in the new factories. Once there, they had little control of their working and living conditions, as well as their food. Many workers were paid in "chits," which were redeemed only at the factory store. In many places, the factory store charged high prices and provided substandard groceries and clothes. In 1843 a group of millworkers in Rochdale, England, created the first successful cooperative store. The millworkers had recently gone on strike, and when their demands were not met they looked for other ways to improve their lives. They focused their attention on the company store, deciding to create a worker-owned store that would provide higher-quality food at lower prices. Twenty-eight people came together and in the spirit of mutual aid created the Rochdale Society of Equitable Pioneers. Each person had invested one British pound—two weeks of wages—to join. This new store, which was owned and operated by the "worker-owners," began by selling flour, oatmeal, butter, and sugar. It soon added candles, which were used to light the building, as the gas company refused to provide the new store with gas.[16]

To run their new business, the members of the Rochdale cooperative developed the following eight principles: (1) open, voluntary membership; (2) democratic control; (3) limited return, if any, on capital; (4) net surplus belongs to owners; (5) honest business practice; (6) ultimate aim is to advance the common good; (7) educate members and general public about cooperatives; and (8) cooperation among cooperatives. These cooperative principles, with a focus on economic democracy and profits going to the worker-owners, allowed the workers to make higher wages.[17]

First, the cooperative model provided each member a vote; in other words, democracy was not just for the political realm but for the economic realm as well. Worker-owners ran the company; there was no boss. This principle of economic democracy allowed a cooperative to pay higher wages since the worker-owners were the ones to set wages, and naturally, they were willing to vote for themselves to be paid a decent wage. This idea of economic democracy mirrored the workers' demand for political democracy, as many of them were "Chartists," a British movement that was petitioning Parliament to allow all men the right to vote for their political leaders, and not just property owners. At that time, only 1,000 of the 24,423 residents of Rochdale were allowed to vote. Thus, economic and political democracy had developed together.[18]

Second, the net surplus or profits went to the worker-owners rather than to a boss or an investor. Thus, there was more money to go for workers' wages, since the boss and investors generally receive the lion's share of the surplus. This principle that profits belong to the worker-owners, along with the other co-op principles that were developed 170 years ago, still guide cooperative businesses today. Interestingly, cooperatives both operate within the capitalist system and, at the same time, challenge it. Benjamin Franklin helped create one of the first American cooperatives, an insurance company. In 1730 a devastating fire had destroyed many buildings in Philadelphia, and Franklin's response was to recommend the development of a volunteer fire department, which was created in 1736, and an insurance company owned and operated by community members who contributed to it. In 1752 the Philadelphia Contributionship for the Insuring of Houses from Loss by Fire was created and run by its subscribers, which shared equally "in the losses as well as the gains."[19]

In 1865 Michigan became the first state to enact a cooperative statute allowing for their development. In the next five years, Massachusetts, New York, Pennsylvania, Connecticut, and Minnesota enacted laws permitting the establishment of cooperatives. By 1911, twelve US states had enacted cooperative laws, and today all fifty states allow cooperatives. The federal government initially opposed cooperatives, banning them in the late nineteenth century since it believed they violated antitrust laws. However, in 1922 the federal government reversed course and passed the Capper Volstead Act, which allowed for cooperative enterprises. During the New Deal, agricultural and farming cooperatives received loans from the government, and interest in cooperatives spread to rural electrification, as Congress created loans that exclusively went to cooperatives that supplied electricity to rural areas that were not being served by capitalist suppliers. In 1934 Upton Sinclair ran for governor of California, and almost won on a platform that embraced cooperatives as a means to employ the 750,000 unemployed in the state. Sinclair's plan was entitled End Poverty in California (EPIC), and it focused on taking over idle factories and agricultural land that had been shut down, and to turn them over to the workers to be run as cooperatives.[20]

In the 1950s, the most successful cooperative ever developed began humbly in the Basque region of Spain. After the end of World War II, Spain was divided into two worlds, that of the rich (particularly the landowners in this mostly agrarian nation) and the poor, who were forced to live with high unemployment, low wages, and horrible working conditions, including workdays of ten to twelve hours. It was within this context that Father Jose Maria Arizmendiarrieta—along with five students from the polytechnic school that he had created in the previous decade—launched ULGOR, a worker-owned manufacturing business that made heaters and ovens in Mondragon. In 1959, Father Arizmendiarrieta and the worker-owners created a bank, Caja Laboral Popular, which was instrumental in providing capital for additional cooperatives to start, and in 1969, a co-op supermarket, Eroski, was founded. Based on the values of cooperation, empowerment, innovation, and social responsibility, the Mondragon worker-owner model has created tens of thousands of needed jobs and has paid living wages. Over the next fifty years, the Mondragon Cooperative would become the largest worker-owner cooperative in the world.[21]

Back in the United States, Huey Newton of the Black Panther Party was working to achieve complete control of the institutions in the community. By the mid-1960s, Newton had concluded that there were not enough jobs in the black community and that cooperatives were the best alternative to create them. As Newton stated, "The most important element in controlling our own institutions would be to organize them into cooperatives, which would end all forms of exploitation. Then the profits, or surplus, from the cooperatives would be returned to the community, expanding opportunities on all levels, and enriching life." For Newton, cooperatives were less exploitive since the workers controlled and operated the businesses.[22]

In 1978, Congress expanded this idea of providing loans to all cooperatives by creating the National Consumer Cooperative Bank (NCCB). Today, the bank has $1.6 billion in assets and is dedicated to providing loans to cooperatives in the areas of education, grocery, health care, and housing.[23]

As can be seen by this history, cooperatives have worked within the capitalist structure, particularly creating jobs and serving needs that capitalists have ignored. At the same time, cooperatives challenge capitalism's basic tenet of owners being separate from workers. In a country that emphasizes individualism and private ownership as the means to economic advancement, the idea of running a business in a spirit of mutual aid provides a powerful alternative to organize commerce, markets, and the community. American workers have always maintained a spirit of mutual aid in times of crisis, but this extension of co-ops into business provides people with an alternative model of economic development that is neither capitalist nor socialist, but something new. It also provides people the opportunity to take the initiative themselves rather than wait for a public policy to change.

THE RIGHT TO A JOB: CURRENT APPROACHES

In the waning days of George W. Bush's presidency, the economy went into a free fall because toxic loans had been created through subprime mortgages (i.e., high interest loans) and "guaranteed" through credit default swaps. In March 2008, assets began to become toxic (i.e., worthless), and JP Morgan Chase was provided a $29 billion bailout to cover the toxic assets of Bear Stearns, which the former mega-firm had just recently purchased. In September 2008, toxic assets forced Freddie Mac and Fannie Mae, the two largest mortgage lenders, to borrow $200 billion from the federal government. Ten days later, American International Group (AIG) was given an $85 billion bailout. This financial crisis crippled the US economy, with employers dumping 800,000 jobs a month by late 2008 and through the spring of 2009.[24]

This bailout of Wall Street led some Americans to call for a bailout of Main Street. With the election of Barack Obama as president, there was great interest in whether he was going to create a national public works program to deal with the unemployment crisis that followed the financial crisis. From January 2008 to February 2009, the US economy lost 8.8 million jobs, or 6 percent of all workers. This contraction led to an increase in the nation's unemployment to 10 percent in 2009, with some communities reaching as high as 27 percent. Some thought a *"New* New Deal" was in the works, as *Time* magazine superimposed President Obama on an iconoclastic image of President Franklin Roosevelt, and David Demerjian of *Wired* called for a modern-day Works Progress Administration.[25]

What President Obama ended up doing was something quite different. He worked to enact the American Recovery and Reinvestment Act, which was a $787 billion stimulus package focusing on tax cuts, expenditures to states to support essential services (education, public safety, health care), extension of unemployment benefits, and infrastructure projects. The largest amount of the stimulus package—$288 billion—went to tax breaks, while $180 billion went to aid the states, with just $105 billion going to infrastructure projects. President Obama has been given credit that his stimulus package averted a second Great Depression, but critics charge that it has not led to a sharp reduction in unemployment since he avoided a large-scale public works project. And while the federal stimulus can hardly be described as focusing on public works, there were two key components of the bill that are important for the future of public works—the "shovel-ready" infrastructure projects and the subsidized employment program—for they provide insights into how to ensure the right to a job.[26]

In 2009, President Obama said he was going to create 675,000 infrastructure jobs, and that many of these jobs were "shovel-ready." These jobs could be loosely categorized as public works since they were similar to the PWA model of building and repairing infrastructure through the private sector. As stated earlier, the record number of unemployed desperately needed jobs, and the US infrastructure was, and still is, in dire need of rebuilding. According to the American Society of Civil Engineers, the United States received an overall rating of a "D" on their 2009 report card, and they estimated that the cost to rebuild the national public infrastructure was $2.2 trillion over a five-year period. And while some regional planners called Obama's infrastructure spending a drop in the bucket, it is important to know whether these projects were successful at creating jobs.[27]

In December 2009, the US Conference of Mayors gave President-Elect Obama a list of 11,391 "ready to go" infrastructure projects, and the American Association of State Highway and Transportation Officials provided a list of 9,800 projects. Two months later, President Obama signed into law the Recovery Act. By the summer of 2009, 1,000 transportation projects were under way; by that September, there were 4,500 projects in motion, and one year later, 14,000 projects were active. Unfortunately, many of these projects didn't start in the 90 to 120 days that Obama targeted but took over a year to begin. For example, in August 2009, over one-half of the $5 billion to states had been disbursed to weatherize homes, but more than one-half the states hadn't even started these projects. In addition, neither the states nor nonprofit groups were ready to handle the large amount of money approved for the program, which was twenty to thirty times the usual. This was due in part to the funding structure, which required the federal government to give the money to the states, and then the states to hire the local contractors or nonprofits. In addition, resistance by contractors to pay local prevailing wages as required by the 1931 Davis-Bacon Act delayed projects.[28]

By 2011, Obama distanced himself from the idea of "shovel ready" projects since it took time to get the jobs started. Obama infamously stated, "But the problem is ... that spending it out takes a long time, because there's really nothing—there's no such thing as shovel-ready projects." However, there were some cases where jobs were in fact "shovel ready." For example, in Aiken, South Carolina, at the Savannah River Site, which is a "nuclear reservation" spanning 310 miles, $1.6 billion of stimulus money was immediately spent in the summer of 2009, as thousands of workers were hired to decommission Cold War nuclear reactors, install pumps, and transport barrels of waste to the Southwest. This hiring led to a dramatic drop in unemployment in the county, from 10.2 percent to 8.5 percent, in just a few months. The key was that it was a well-developed plan that had all the contractors in place, and all that was necessary was the financing.[29]

All in all, the Recovery Act created over 100,000 projects, including the repair or building of roads, bridges, bus and fire stations, and water pipes. Yet, in comparison to the New Deal, there was much more repair than building. For example, in the first year, road improvements were made to 22,000 miles of roads, while only 230 miles of new roads were built. Partly this had to do with the fact that repairs were more shovel ready than building something new. In 2010, at the height of the spending for the Recovery Act, the Congressional Budget Office estimated that in the area of construction, 1 million jobs had been created or saved, and overall stimulus spending had saved or created 1.4 to 3.6 million jobs. Importantly, these numbers include jobs both directly created and indirectly created (through such things as consumer spending), something not done in the New Deal, which counted only jobs directly created.[30]

Public infrastructure jobs will continue to be an important component of rebuilding America, particularly in light of our inferior infrastructure and structural and cyclical unemployment. However, there are other areas where jobs can be created, particularly in human services, which do not require a great deal of education. As Dr. King noted, "The human services—medical attention, social services, neighborhood amenities of various kinds—are in scarce supply in this country, especially in localities of poverty." King argued for the expansion of human services since it is an industry that is "labor intensive, requiring manpower immediately rather than heavy capital investment as in construction or other fields; it fills a great need not met by private enterprise; it involves labor that can be trained and developed on the job." In addition, King argued that "the policy of the government should be to subsidize American business to employ individuals whose education is limited." The key thing is to get people into jobs first. In fact, King's motto was "Jobs First, Training Later."[31]

This focus on subsidizing jobs in human services and business was incorporated into Obama's stimulus plan through the $1.3 billion of emergency funding to Temporary Assistance to Needy Families (TANF). The TANF Emergency Fund was started in 2009, and in just under two years, 260,000 subsidized jobs for adults and youth in thirty-three states had been created. These subsidized employment jobs were in nonprofits, local government agencies, and businesses. States were given great latitude to determine how to best structure the subsidized employment programs. For example, some states ran the programs directly, while other states had the counties operate them. States and counties had control over what level the job would be subsidized at, what the maximum and minimum pay would be (but not lower than federal minimum wage), and how many hours would be allowed. For example, while most states and counties subsidized 100 percent of the wages for a year-round adult job, a few states subsidized 80 percent of the wages, with the other 20 percent coming from the employer. With regard to wages, Los Angeles paid $10 an hour while South Carolina paid $7.25 an hour. In addition, many programs allowed ex-offenders to participate, giving hope to many who have an extremely difficult time finding work because of the stigma of having been incarcerated.[32]

This subsidized job program was very successful at employing the unemployed quickly. Take for example Perry County, Tennessee, which had a rural population of 7,600 people and the second-highest unemployment rate in the nation. In December 2008, unemployment was at 27 percent, and Governor Phil Bredesen decided to focus on Perry County and other areas of high unemployment within Tennessee. The governor supported the overall stimulus package, but he thought, "So much of that stuff is kind of stratospheric. When you've got 27 percent unemployment, that is a full-fledged depression down in Perry County, and let's just see if we can't figure out how to do something that's just much more on the ground and direct, that actually gets people jobs." With the governor's embrace of the subsidized employment program created within TANF, Perry County cut its unemployment from

27 percent to under 14 percent in less than two years. Two-thirds of these subsidized jobs were in the private sector at such places as a trucking company, a hotel, a pie company, and a milkshake place. People also worked in the public sector, at such offices as the Department of Transportation, the sheriff's department, and the local school board. In addition to these adult jobs, Perry County created 150 youth summer jobs. Taking a page out of the New Deal, young people worked with local artists to paint murals onto main street buildings. In total, the TANF emergency fund created 138,050 jobs for youth (up to age twenty-four) during the summer and year-round.[33]

The impact of the subsidized job program cannot be overstated; according to several locals from Perry County, it "saved their community." It put food on the table and kept people in their homes. Frank Smith, age forty-one, lost his job as a truck driver and was about to be evicted when he obtained an employer-subsidized job with the Transportation Department. "The day I came from my interview here, I was sitting in the court up here where I was being evicted. . . . Luckily I'm still in the same place."[34]

Subsidized employment programs were also successful in larger counties, such as in Los Angeles, where it was used to create 10,458 adult jobs and 18,131 summer youth jobs. San Francisco created 4,127 adult jobs and over 1,000 summer youth jobs. Laundry Locker, an eco-friendly dry cleaning business, participated in San Francisco's JOBS NOW! Program and hired four subsidized workers, which made it possible to free up money to spend on marketing. According to the owner, "This has enabled us to substantially grow our business, doubling our revenue in the last year and turning the corner to profitability. . . . Without the JOBS NOW! program, there is a good chance we would be another casualty of the recession, which would have meant 21 more people on unemployment or other social services." Positively, 82 percent of the participating businesses thought that the JOBS NOW! program helped their companies operate more efficiently, with 72 percent of them reporting increased sales.[35]

States too were successful at implementing job programs, as Illinois created the most jobs of any state in the nation. An intermediary nonprofit called Put Illinois to Work ran the program and employed 31,293 people. Again, the results were dramatic. For example, the program put J. D. of Chicago to work after a year of being unemployed. He worked at a nonprofit where he learned new skills in office administration. J. D. states, "Put Illinois to Work has helped me become more of a responsible father to my kids. . . . I now can say without hesitation that I can pay the bills for my family and keep a solid roof over our heads."[36]

What is hopeful is that these subsidized job programs received bipartisan support. For example, Haley Barbour, the Republican governor of Mississippi, developed an innovative jobs program that hired 3,200 unemployed individuals. The program was unique in that it focused on creating jobs in small businesses (under twenty-five workers) and had a sliding scale approach to the subsidies, with the state paying 100 percent of wages in the first two months and then only 25 percent by the sixth month. After six months, the business paid all wages, with the hope that the sliding scale made it possible for the worker to keep his or her job at the conclusion of the subsidy.[37]

The subsidized employment program was a success for both employees and employers. Caronina Grimble, senior project manager from the Illinois Department of Human Services, summed it up when she stated that her state's subsidized employment program exceeded all expectations: "Our worker-trainees are thrilled to be earning a paycheck that allows them to meet their basic needs and learn new skills. Our employers are grateful for the opportunity to expand their workforce during a time of economic uncertainty." Many workers retained their jobs after the subsidy ended; for example, Florida showed that 41 percent of its employees were retained in their jobs after the end of the subsidy. Some states and counties tried to encourage job retention by providing various incentives. Oklahoma reimbursed employers for 100 percent of wages paid for the first month and 50 percent of wages paid for the next three months; employers who retained employees for six months *beyond* this four-month subsidy period received an additional 50 percent reimbursement for the final three months of the subsidy period. This means that employers who retained employees for ten months received a subsidy for 100 percent of the wage for four months. In addition, Oklahoma reimbursed employers for wages up to $12 per hour.[38]

The subsidized employment program from the Obama stimulus showed that it was possible to create jobs quickly, effectively, and economically. This program also showed that the unemployed wanted to work, and that small businesses were willing to hire the unemployed when given subsidies. Furthermore, studies have shown that many former TANF recipients who had been hired through this program transitioned to unsubsidized work, either at the same job or in the same field. And while people were employed in government, nonprofits, and businesses, the majority of hires were at small businesses. This focus on small business was a defining aspect of this jobs program, and it is what differentiates it from other public works projects, which historically have focused on community projects. This win-win program was supported strongly by the American public, with 79 percent agreeing that the subsidized employment program should be extended. Unfortunately, Senate Republicans did not agree, rejecting a one-year extension and letting the program expire in September 2012.[39]

The evidence above demonstrates that a PWA-style public works infrastructure project and a subsidized work program can help fulfill the goal of the right to a job. In addition to these two models, there have been other modern-day public works attempts, most notably in the Gulf Coast following Hurricane Katrina. After Hurricane Katrina struck, and exposed to the nation and world that the United States still had a large-scale problem with poverty and racism, a group of students and community leaders worked to rebuild the Gulf through a new New Deal. The Gulf Coast Civic Work Act, or House Resolution 2269, would have created 100,000 jobs to rebuild public infrastructure and restore the environment. More specifically, the act would have created (1) a minimum of 100,000 jobs and training opportunities for local and displaced workers to rebuild hospitals, roads, parks, police and fire stations, schools, sewer and water systems, and workforce housing; (2) a civic conservation corps for seventeen- to twenty-four-year-olds to focus on wetland restoration, forestation, and urban greenery; (3) summer and after-school employment and training opportunities for twelve- to nineteen-year-olds; (4) Local Advisory Boards to provide oversight and transparency; and (5) grants for artistic projects to highlight Gulf Coast history and culture and to chronicle the stories from the hurricane. The Gulf Coast Civic Works Act was designed to be a pilot project, and the hope was that if it worked in the Gulf Coast, it could be used as a model for the rest of the nation. The bill received forty-three congressional co-sponsors but did not obtain the backing of the Republican or Democratic leadership, and it died in committee.[40]

In addition to the above regional approach, cities have responded with new initiatives to create jobs and build infrastructure. For example, Mayor Julian Castro of San Antonio, Texas, developed the San Antonio 2020 plan by using an extensive community engagement process that involved thousands of citizens. The plan calls for the transforming of San Antonio into a world-class city by 2020, with the goal of increasing public safety, reducing car usage, tripling public transportation ridership, doubling green jobs, and doubling the attendance of publicly funded arts programs. This community input led to the easy passage of the largest bond measure in the city's history, a $596 million bond measure in 2012 to support 140 infrastructure projects, including roads, libraries, museums, parks, public safety facilities, and flood protection. It is hoped that these projects will create thousands of new jobs. Other cities also passed bond measures in 2012, including nearby Houston, which plans to create 12,000 jobs by rebuilding schools, parks, fire stations, and job training sites.[41]

These city and regional public works approaches are important for they serve as models and pilot projects for the nation. However, if a right to a job is to be a reality for all Americans, eventually there must be federal action commensurate with the problem. Structural unemployment leaves millions unemployed, and billions of dollars will need to be spent to employ them through federal direct hiring, through federal contracts with private business, or via subsidized employment in nonprofits, as well as by the private and public sectors. Cyclical unemployment can be dealt with when it occurs, increasing or decreasing funding as dictated by the changing economy.

Some are still calling on President Obama to initiate a New Deal jobs program. Occupy Detroit has recently asked Obama to sign an executive order "to implement a massive WPA style public works program under authority of the Full Employment Act" so as to guarantee our right to work. In addition, Marjorie Cohen, the past president of the National Lawyers Guild, wrote in 2010 that President Obama should sign an executive order creating a WPA program, just as FDR had done, arguing that he could legally use the $700 billion that has already been appropriated by Congress for the Troubled Asset Relief Program (TARP), since it was given to preserve home ownership, create jobs, and encourage economic growth. She argues that since the money has mostly been paid back, $300 billion could create 6 million jobs paying $50,000, or $600 billion could create 12 million jobs. And Representative John Conyers of Michigan has introduced the Humphrey-Hawkins 21st Century Full Employment and Training Act (HR 870), which would create specific funds for job creation and training, and would be paid for by a 0.25 percent tax on securities transactions on US stock and commodity exchanges.[42]

In addition to public works, another contemporary example that contributes to the goal of a right to a job is cooperatives. Today, there are more than 29,000 cooperatives, with 120 million members, and they employ 850,000 people. Interest in cooperatives has increased since the economic crisis of 2008, as the Great Recession has caused some people to lose faith in banks, corporations, and financial institutions, and people are searching for alternative models to organize work. There are several types of cooperatives, including consumer, producer, and worker models. A consumer cooperative is an enterprise owned by consumers and managed by them democratically with the goal of fulfilling the needs of its members. Consumer cooperatives are the largest type of co-op, composing 92 percent of all co-ops. Two examples of consumer cooperatives are credit unions and food co-ops. Credit unions differ from banks in that they are owned by members rather than stockholders, are exempt from most taxes since they are not-for-profits, which in turn allows them to provide better rates, and depositors buy shares in the credit union rather than providing a "loan" to a bank. Today, there are over 92 million credit union members. There are approximately 350 food co-ops in the United States; they provide organic, locally grown food, consumer education, and discounts or rebates to their members. Importantly, food co-ops were the originators of both organic food and locally grown food.[43]

Another type of a co-op is a producing cooperative, an example of which is the Cooperative Regions of Organic Producer Pools (CROPP). Marketing its products under the Organic Valley Family of Farms brand, CROPP is a network of 1,814 organic family farmer-owners in thirty-three states that produce similar products (cheese, eggs, juice, milk, and soy products). CROPP consolidates its product sales in order to ensure decent prices and access to larger markets. In September 2012, George Siemon, one of the producer cooperative founders, stated, "The success of Organic Valley proves that organic agriculture can be a lifeline for America's struggling family farms. . . . In an era of rising and falling agricultural prices, Organic Valley farmer-owners can count on a stable, living wage to stay in business on their land." Producing cooperatives compose 5 percent of all co-ops.[44]

A third co-op model is the worker-owner cooperative, and even though it is the smallest of the cooperative models, at just 1 percent of all co-ops, it is important to this discussion on wages since the worker-owner model has perhaps the greatest potential to change the workplace. Today, there are 223 US worker-owner co-op firms, with an average of eleven employees, and they are involved in all types of businesses, including a taxi service, laundry service, and solar panel installation. Here are a few examples: In Madison, Wisconsin, Union Cab is the largest taxi service in that city, with sixty-five cabs, $7 million in revenue, and 230 drivers, dispatchers, and mechanics as members. Union Cab started in 1979 after a protracted labor struggle with Checker Cab. After the workers realized that Checker was not going to enforce the union contract, and the filing of twenty-five grievances with no resolution, some of the workers decided to open up a cooperative taxi service. Union Cab operates under the Rochdale principle of "one member, one vote," which ensures that the worker-members are involved in making business decisions, including pay scale. Union Cab does have managers, but they are overseen by a board of directors, which are chosen by the worker-members. Thus, the workers supervise management, rather than the other way around, with the result being a more humane workplace.[45]

A major development in the cooperative movement has been the creation of the Evergreen Cooperative Initiative in 2008 by a group of university, foundation, hospital, and local government leaders in Cleveland, Ohio. The vision of Evergreen Cooperative is to replicate the Mondragon model, with the goal of transforming the Greater University Circle, home to 43,000 residents whose average household income is $18,500. The working group made a commitment to take a portion of its $2 billion worth of goods and services it buys each year and drive it to the Evergreen Cooperative in order to create living-wage jobs. In 2009 the initiative launched its first two green businesses: the Evergreen Cooperative Laundry and Evergreen Cooperative Solar.[46]

The Evergreen Cooperative Laundry is equipped with $2.5 million of Energy Star–efficient laundry machinery, and the building it is housed in has had $1.3 million of modifications in order to achieve a LEED Silver certification, which means it has reduced energy and water bills by 30 percent to 50 percent. However, Evergreen has not trained people for green jobs with the hope they get hired; rather, Evergreen has created the jobs, and then hired the workers to do the jobs. At the same time, Evergreen employees are also worker-owners, so they are having the opportunity to shape the business. When talking about Evergreen Laundry, Medrick Anderson, one of the worker-owners, stated, "You help it grow, you nurture it, you are instrumental in what it becomes, and that's the difference between working at Evergreen and someplace else." At Evergreen, workers go through a six-month trial period, and then the other members of the co-op decide democratically to accept (or not) the probationary worker as a worker-owner.[47]

In 2009, Evergreen Cooperative Solar was launched, and today, the company operates under the name Evergreen Energy Solutions (E2S). The company installs photovoltaic panels that transfer sunlight into electrical power. Solar panels are installed on buildings at no cost to the owners of the building, and then E2S sells the energy it generates back to them. The upkeep of the panels is also taken care of by E2S. Solar panels have been installed on buildings at Case Western Reserve University, Cleveland Clinic, University Hospitals, the Cleveland Housing Network, and the cities of Cleveland and Euclid. In addition, E2S does installation and weatherization of individual homes. This green weatherization service, which can cut home energy bills by 30 percent, allows the worker-owners to have employment during the four to five months that E2S can't install solar panels because of the weather. As James Harris, an E2S worker-owner, states, "If it wasn't for Evergreen, and the cooperative, I don't know where I'd be right now. It is hard getting a job now, and having the opportunity to have a career, it is just great. They changed my life in a lot of ways." Currently, there are twenty-one laundry worker-owners and twenty solar workers, and the goal is to have fifty workers at each cooperative.[48]

In 2011 Evergreen launched its third business, a 3.25-acre hydroponic greenhouse. The greenhouse, which uses only mineral nutrient solutions in water and no soil, was completed in November 2012, and the first seeds were planted the following month, with the first plants harvested in early 2013. Each year, the greenhouse will produce 3 million heads of lettuce and 300,000 pounds of herbs, to be sold to Case Western Reserve University and the Cleveland Clinics, as well as to local supermarkets. Twenty-five people have been hired initially. In the next several years, Evergreen plans to develop a total of ten businesses, which will employ 500 worker-owners.[49]

Union Cab and Evergreen Cooperatives are just two business examples operating under the co-op model. Others include Cooperative Home Care in New York—which provides 1,600 living-wage jobs to home-care providers who normally receive poverty wages—and Alvarado Street Bakery in Sonoma, California, which has ninety-one worker-owners producing organic bread. There is also a new joint project between the US Steelworkers Union and Mondragon Cooperative in Spain, with the goal of creating worker-owner factories within the labor movement. In addition, there are regional organizations forming, like the Network of Bay Area Worker Cooperatives

(NoBAWC, pronounced "No Boss") in San Francisco, which includes over thirty worker cooperatives with 1,000-plus members.[50]

Outside the United States, the worker-owner co-op model is perhaps even stronger. For example, South Africa has 17,000 worker-owner co-ops, Italy has 8,000, France has 1,700, and Argentina has over 200 co-ops. While the average co-op worldwide has twenty workers, Mondragon Cooperative Corporation, the largest and most successful worker co-op, has 83,000 worker-owners (43 percent women) and is composed of over 100 cooperatives with $20 billion in total sales, making it the largest business enterprise in the Basque region, and the second-largest in Spain. In addition to creating living-wage jobs, the values of the cooperative ensure that extreme inequality does not occur, with the Mondragon worker-owners setting caps on the ratio between the highest-paid workers' salary and the lowest, which on average is 5 to 1. This 5 to 1 ratio is far different than the US corporate model, where CEO pay is 350 times the average worker and 770 times the minimum-wage worker.[51]

To encourage even more interest in co-ops around the globe as a way to create jobs and reduce poverty, the United Nations made 2102 "the International Year of the Cooperatives." At the UN, panel sessions were held throughout 2012 that brought cooperatives and national governments together to encourage dialogue and discuss how governments can better support the development and maintenance of the co-op sector.[52]

SUMMARY

In this chapter, President Barack Obama's shovel-ready projects and subsidized employment programs have been analyzed, as well as contemporary public works projects such as the Gulf Coast Civic Works Act and the San Antonio 2020 plan. While recognizing that private enterprise is the main sector for employment in the United States, public works programs must be developed in order to guarantee the first amendment right to a job since American-style capitalism does not produce enough jobs for all. Moreover, cooperatives have become a powerful approach in the effort to guarantee the right to a job.

Chapter 2

The Right to a Living Wage

The Second Amendment

PROBLEM

While unemployment—both structural and cyclical—is one reason for the high level of poverty and inequality in the United States, another major reason is the amount of low-paying jobs that modern American capitalism creates. Currently, 28 percent of US jobs pay poverty wages, which is defined as earning less than what it takes for a full-time worker to lift a family of four out of poverty ($11.06 an hour, or $23,005 a year). Looking into the future, the economy in 2020 is scheduled to generate this same level of poverty jobs. Thus, there is not just a problem with finding a job, but with the quality of the job.[1]

Today, we live in a globalized world where products are manufactured and transported anywhere in the world. This shift began in the 1970s when multinational corporations capitalized on transportation and communication improvements and began to move factories and plants to the Southern Hemisphere and to other regions where labor was cheap and unions were weak. This offshoring of jobs, combined with increased automation, devastated the American working class, as good-paying union jobs were reduced sharply. For example, in the manufacturing sector, where workers earned on average $77,505 in 2012, the overall percentage of jobs decreased from 26 percent in 1969 to 9 percent by 2012. As jobs were shipped abroad, unions were weakened at home. Add to that a business community that has fought union efforts to organize, and the result has been a precipitous drop in union membership from 35 percent of the overall workforce in the 1950s to 11.3 percent in 2013, and 6.7 percent in the private sector.[2]

What replaced many of these union jobs have been low-paying service jobs. *Low-wage work* is defined as work that earns an income below twice the poverty line. Earning twice the poverty rate the worker is not poor, but he or she struggles to make ends meet. Today, 103 million Americans, or one-third of the US population, live in a family with a household income below $36,000, or twice the poverty rate for a family of three. Incredibly, one-half of all jobs in the United States pay less than $36,000 a year, while one-fourth of all jobs pay less than $22,000, which is the poverty line for a family of four. Even the recovery that began in 2009 has not helped, as 58 percent of the jobs created over the past several years have been low paying. Today, the United States has the largest proportion of low-wage work in the industrialized world.[3]

Another reason that poverty level jobs have increased is that the minimum wage has not kept pace with inflation. If the minimum wage had been indexed to inflation in 1968, today's national minimum wage would be $10.55; instead, it is $7.25. Minimum wage has not been increased because conservatives and business interests like the Chamber of Commerce have worked against it in Congress. Over the past forty years, inflation kept rising, but years would go by without any increase in the minimum wage. During the ten-year stretch from 1997 to 2007, Congress did not raise the minimum wage at all, while over the past three years since the most recent federal increase, minimum wage has lost 50 cents in value.[4]

The overall result of the above changes has been devastating to the working and lower classes. In 1973, poverty was at 11 percent or 23 million people, which was the lowest level since measuring the federal poverty rate. By 2012, poverty hit a fifty-three-year high, with the numbers of people in poverty at their highest level since the collection of poverty statistics began. Today, 47 million people, or 15 percent of the population, live in poverty, including 16 million kids, which is more than one out of five. This high poverty rate ranks the United States second-highest in the industrialized world for childhood poverty, with only Romania having a higher percentage of poverty for kids. Dr. King's curious formula still works, as blacks in the United States have almost three times the poverty rate as whites. Today, 28 percent of African Americans live in poverty, compared to 10 percent of whites. Not surprisingly, King's curious formula also applies to Native Americans and Latinos, as their poverty rates are 26 percent and 25 percent, respectively.[5]

The poor and working class are not the only groups that are hurting. In 2011, median household incomes fell 1.5 percent from 2010, to $50,054 a year; from 2007 to 2011, median household income had declined by 8 percent. These changes have created a situation where all but the top incomes suffer. In 2011, the bottom 80 percent of incomes fell while the top 20 percent rose, with the top 1 percent increasing its household income by 6 percent. The income gap between poor and rich people is now at its widest margin in more than forty years.[6]

SOLUTION

The solution to the "wrong" of poverty jobs is the right to a living-wage job. This right is based on the belief that if you work hard and play by the rules, you deserve a fair wage. Today, wages are not fair because many Americans who work full time still find it difficult to pay for the basics of rent, food, clothing, and transportation. If full-time workers are not able to pay for these basics, they are forced into government programs, such as food stamps and Medicaid. The right to a living-wage job is not anticapitalistic; rather, it fixes capitalism's weakness of not producing enough living-wage jobs for all who want to work, helping to solve the problem of poverty and excessive income inequality.

Some of the public policies that have been suggested to achieve this constitutional commitment of a right to a living wage have been collective bargaining, increasing the minimum wage, public works projects, guaranteed income programs, earned income tax credits, and cooperatives.

THE HISTORY OF THE RIGHT TO A LIVING WAGE

Capitalism has always had difficulty creating enough good-paying jobs. From the founding of the country, people gave thought to what wages were necessary for the working class and poor to be able to purchase indispensable commodities (e.g., food, clothing, housing). They also considered what was a moral standard necessary for a person to possess so as not to be stigmatized as indecent. In the same year that the US Constitution was ratified, Adam Smith in his treatise *The Wealth of Nations* argued that people of "the lowest rank" should have both "the commodities which are indispensably necessary for the support of life" and "whatever the custom of the country renders it indecent for [a] creditable person ... to be without."[7]

Matthew Carey, one of the early republic's most renowned printers and editors, elaborated on this concept of the "indispensable necessities of life." In 1829, Carey argued that it was impossible to purchase life's necessities on the wages of an industrial worker because a month's work for a couple garnered $143 while monthly expenses were $146. He concluded that poverty was the result not of personal failure but of an unjust distribution of wealth. Carey stated, "We must never forget, that *the low rate of wages is the root of the mischief*; and that unless we can succeed in raising the price of labour, our utmost efforts will do little towards bettering the condition of the industrious classes." Carey's solution was to pay workers enough to secure the indispensable necessaries of life.[8]

In 1869, a national market was formed with the completion of the transcontinental railroad, and industrial capitalism thrived with the federal government taking a hands-off, laissez-faire approach. Soon, merchants, farmers, and small-town artisans no longer controlled the destiny of the country, as they were replaced by a new capitalist elite. Of course, along with the development of a capital class came the working class. By 1900, the number of factory workers had grown to 5.5 million, up from 1.3 million in just forty years. Together, the capitalists and workers were producing more manufactured goods than England, France, and Germany combined. And while great wealth was made for the capitalists, life was not as grand for the working class. Wages for factory workers were low and the workday was long, with the average worker toiling eleven hours a day, six days a week. In addition, living conditions for the working class were deplorable, with three to four families living in a single room and the children freezing and facing starvation.[9]

In addition, early capitalist development was highly unstable, going through a series of booms and busts, with the latter devastating to the working class. In 1873, a depression caused the unemployment of 1 million workers, and many faced starvation. The following year, 90,000 workers slept in police stations because they had lost their housing. Depression again hit from 1882 to 1885, and this time 2 million were unemployed. And while the busts were catastrophic, the booms were not all great for the working class, as factory workers were forced to work and live in miserable conditions.[10]

Labor advocates pushed for structural solutions to the capitalist system, with one of their key demands being an increase in pay through collective bargaining. For example, the Knights of Labor, which was created in 1869 and had a membership of 702,000 members by 1886, worked to humanize the capitalist system. The organization's preamble cautioned against "the recent alarming development and aggression of aggregated wealth, which, unless checked, will inevitably lead to the pauperization and hopeless degradation of the toiling masses." The Knights of Labor advocated for a system "which will secure to the laborer the fruits of his toil" and "to secure for the workers a proper share of the wealth that they created." During this time, labor's position can be summed up in this banner: "'Each for himself is the bosses' plea; Union for all will make you free."[11]

At the turn of the century, Americans began to quantify what it meant to be poor. In 1899, W. E. B. Du Bois was one of the first US scholars to connect an actual dollar amount to poverty. In *The Philadelphia Negro,* Du Bois argued that a family of five living in the black areas of Philadelphia was poor if it made less than $5 a week, or $260 a year, and was very poor if it made $150 or less. Basing his calculations on the work of British poverty scholar Charles Booth, Du Bois described poverty as a state where a family was barely sufficient for a decent independent life, while a family was considered "very poor" if it was incapable of a decent independent life. In 1904 Robert Hunter, a social worker, expanded on this idea of connecting a dollar amount to poverty and created the first national poverty line. In Hunter's book *Poverty*, he determined that the poverty line for a family of five living in the North was $460 and for the South it was $300.[12]

In addition to quantifying poverty, others began to make a distinction between a poverty wage and a living wage. In 1906 Father John Ryan wrote a book entitled *Living Wage*, which argued that adult male workers should make $600 a year in order to provide for a "decent livelihood." For Ryan, this meant they would make enough income to provide food, clothing, a five-room apartment or house, education for four to five children, recreation, and savings for sickness and retirement. This idea of a living wage rather than a subsistence wage would influence reformers and scholars throughout the twentieth century. For example, in 1962, the preeminent economist Alice Bourneuf wrote, "We believe that every man has a right to earn a living wage, a wage which will enable him to provide medical care, decent housing, good food, and which will leave a margin for savings for old age and emergencies, and for the acquisition of property."[13]

A key policy change to ensure workers made a subsistence wage was the development of *minimum-wage laws*. In 1912, Massachusetts became the first state to pass such a law, with the Commonwealth's Commission on Minimum Wage Boards arguing that if businesses did not pay the minimum wage, they were "parasitic" since they were unrightfully taking "the working energy of a human being." Other states followed, and by 1923, fourteen states and the District of Columbia had passed minimum-wage laws. Initially, minimum-wage laws were restricted to women and were justified as a way to discourage prostitution. At the same time, businesses were opposed to the minimum-wage laws and worked to overturn them. Businesses believed the laws impeded employers from setting the price for their workforce. In 1923, the Supreme Court overturned the minimum-wage laws, arguing that they were unconstitutional since women enjoyed the same constitutional protections that men possessed regarding the ability to negotiate a contract.[14]

With the election of Franklin Roosevelt as president in 1932, a federal minimum-wage law was created for all workers. However, the Supreme Court struck it down in 1935. The following year, President Roosevelt won reelection with the promise to find a constitutional way to protect the rights of workers. In that same year, the Supreme Court on a 5 to 4 vote once again held that these minimum-wage laws were unconstitutional. Interestingly, when FDR threatened to add six more justices to the Supreme Court, the court reversed course, and in the following year it ruled that statewide minimum-wage laws were constitutional. In addition, Congress enacted the Fair Labor Standards Act in 1938, which provided a federal minimum wage of 25 cents an hour for all workers, as well as capped the work week at forty-four hours and banned child labor. Roosevelt called this federal law "the most far-sighted program for the benefit of workers ever adopted." Over the next seventy-five years, the federal minimum wage has been increased twenty-seven times, since it is not indexed to inflation.[15]

Public works, another major policy that Roosevelt had pushed, also has had an impact on the right to a living wage. Clearly, the second amendment's right to a living wage and the first amendment's right to a job are interconnected since public works provides a wage floor. Jacob Coxey, who led the march on Washington in 1894 to urge Congress to develop a national public works program, realized this interconnection when he said that "no employer of labor outside of the government will be able to employ a single man for less than one dollar and fifty cents per day of eight hours." In 1890, the average wage for a worker was $1.50 a day for ten hours of work. Coxey's goal was to use public works jobs as a wage floor, so as to increase wages while at the same time reducing the number of hours worked per day.[16]

This idea of public works serving as a wage floor was carried into Roosevelt's New Deal. Both the Public Works Administration (PWA) and the Civilian Works Administration (CWA) paid workers a prevailing wage, which was the rate paid to union workers for that area. However, when the Works Progress Administration (WPA) was started several years after the PWA and CWA, it paid "sustainable wages," which were a bit more than what the government paid for "home relief" welfare programs. Upset by this decision to not pay living wages, some workers fought back, leading several strikes at WPA offices and job sites. Under pressure, the federal government backed down and agreed to pay wages closer to the prevailing wage. After the New Deal and World War II, there was no longer any large public works agency overseen by the executive branch. Yes, there were infrastructure projects, such as the interstate highway system that was promoted by President Dwight Eisenhower, but the government contracts developed out of the Federal Highway Act of 1956 were given to private contractors with no antipoverty focus. A decade later, Dr. Martin Luther King Jr. rekindled the idea of using public works to help poor people pay for adequate housing, food, clothing, and health care.[17]

Another policy that focused on the right to a living wage was the *guaranteed income.* Although the idea for a guaranteed income dates back to the 1940s, it was conservative economist Milton Friedman who helped popularize it in the 1960s. The plan was simple: Provide a sufficient income to all households that were in need of it. The guaranteed income was designed to be universal, so that all citizens who lacked income would receive it. A basic income would be provided to the long-term unemployed, the recently unemployed, the underemployed, the low-wage worker, the divorced mom who had been out of the labor market for years, and so on. The only criterion was a lack of income.[18]

Other guaranteed income models were proposed during this era. Some provided enough income for subsistence, while others were pegged at middle income. Some required no work to receive the income, while others required some work or community service. Some models made payments yearly and used a sliding scale—decreasing the amount awarded when more money was made—while others were offered monthly payments that were not dependent on the amount a person made.

Conservatives and liberals alike supported the guaranteed income as both were unhappy with the welfare system. The guaranteed income appealed to conservatives because it eliminated many government workers, as there was no need to check eligibility or to make a decision about the size of the welfare based on special circumstances. The guaranteed income also appealed to conservatives since the recipients were allowed to choose where and how to spend the money rather than have this determined by some government bureaucrat. In addition, conservatives hoped that a guaranteed income would be more supportive of marriage, since they believed welfare undermined families by providing support when the man was absent.

The guaranteed income appealed to liberals since it did not stigmatize the poor in the ways that Aid to Families with Dependent Children (AFDC) had done. AFDC had solidified nineteenth-century poorhouse thinking into twentieth-century welfare policy by categorizing the poor as unworthy. Welfare recipients complained that they were made to feel badly about receiving financial support at the welfare office and were treated inhumanely. Liberals supported the guaranteed income program as it eliminated these categories of the "worthy" and "unworthy" poor, as well as the demeaning process recipients received at the welfare office. Moreover, liberals also hoped that the guaranteed income could not just reduce but end poverty, something that welfare had been unable to do. In 1967, Dr. King stated, "I am now convinced that the simplest approach will prove to be the most effective—the solution to poverty is to abolish it directly by a now widely discussed measure: the guaranteed income." King argued that a guaranteed income tied to middle-class income levels, along with a public works program ensuring full employment, would allow poor people, regardless of race, to have the money to pay for adequate food, clothing, housing, and health care. In arguing for a guaranteed income, King stated, "Some people are too young, some are too old, some are physically disabled, and yet in order to live, they need income."[19]

The War on Poverty planners were interested in the guaranteed income, but they didn't include it as part of their overall strategy. However, as urban riots broke out in major cities throughout the nation from 1964 to 1968, there was a realization among the Johnson administration that a more ambitious plan was necessary to combat poverty. In response, the Office of Economic Opportunity, which was responsible for the oversight of the War on Poverty, launched pilot projects around the country in 1967 in order to study the impact of a guaranteed income. These pilot projects took place from 1968 to 1979 in several states, including Iowa, New Jersey, Pennsylvania, and South Carolina, as well as in the cities of Denver, Colorado; Gary, Indiana; and Seattle, Washington. Families were placed in experimental groups (i.e., a guaranteed income provided) and control groups (i.e., no guaranteed income provided), with the former groups getting different levels of money to determine the impact of generous and less generous payments. Workers in the experimental groups were given a negative income tax ranging from 50 percent, 75 percent, 100 percent, and 250 percent of the poverty line, as well as different tax rates on the income they earned through work. For example, some families had their guaranteed income reduced 70 cents for every dollar earned, while others had it reduced 50 cents. The results from these pilot projects showed that families in the experimental group, in comparison to the control group, increased expenditures on housing and home ownership. Positive results were also found for the children in the experimental group, as they received higher test scores in elementary school and had reduced dropout rates in high school. There was no change in marital status of the families, except in the Seattle-Denver study, where there was a marked increase in divorce. Researchers were surprised by this finding and were unsure if it was an aberration or it was caused by an increase in economic freedom.[20]

The Seattle-Denver study was the largest and most diverse, with 2,063 white families, 1,960 black families, and 856 Latino families participating. This pilot project was consistent with the others, showing a small decrease in hours worked. No workers left their jobs, but some reduced their work hours modestly. Married men's hourly work week decreased by 5 percent, while married women and single mothers reduced their work by 17 percent and 12 percent, respectively. This modest decrease might be construed as negative, but researchers learned that people used this extra time to look for a higher paying job and to obtain more training, as well as to spend more time with the children. The researchers concluded, "Cash assistance programs would not cause a massive withdrawal of workers from the labor force, as some have feared."[21]

As these studies were being conducted, President Nixon, a Republican, put forward the Family Assistance Program (FAP) in 1972. Nixon didn't wait for the results of these studies to be completed; rather, he put forward the radical idea to end the New Deal welfare programs and replace them with a guaranteed income through a negative income tax. Nixon's plan was bold and visionary since for the first time in US history, the government would provide a guaranteed income for all low-income households. Nixon's plan would provide a family of four with $1,600 annually plus $800 for food stamps (the poverty rate was $3,000). All adults would need to work or be in job training programs with the exception of single mothers with children under the age of six. The penalty rate for working was cut from two-thirds under the AFDC welfare system to one-half of every dollar, and recipients would lose $500 annually if they did not sign up for work. Nixon's plan passed the House of Representatives but stalled in the more liberal Senate. Opposition came from liberals, who said $1,600 a year was not enough money to survive on, particularly for low-income people in the cities, while conservatives didn't want to extend support for the "able-bodied" poor. The bill was defeated in the Senate Finance Committee and never made it to the full Senate.[22]

An idea closely related to the guaranteed income was the earned income tax credit (EITC). The EITC, which was signed into law by President Gerald Ford in 1975 with bipartisan support, is similar to the guaranteed income model in that it provides a tax credit to low-income people, but instead of being a universal program, it is focused solely on people who work. The EITC was designed to encourage and reward work by giving low-wage workers a tax credit, thus guaranteeing that these workers make a minimum annual salary. It is a refundable tax credit that either lowers the federal tax owed or comes as cash back. Initially, the EITC started small, providing a $400 annual benefit to 6 million families. However, President Reagan, the father of the modern conservative movement, expanded the EITC in 1985, calling it "the best anti-poverty bill, the best pro-family measure, and the best job-creation program ever to come out of the Congress of the United States." Republicans liked it because it cut the welfare rolls, while Democrats liked it because it put more dollars into the working poor's wallets.[23]

The EITC continued to garner bipartisan support, and in 1993, President Bill Clinton made the program more generous to parents with two or more children. As a part of Clinton's plan to "end welfare as we know it" and to make work pay, he argued that the EITC expansion "will reward the work of millions of working, poor Americans by realizing the principle that if you work 40 hours a week and you've got a child in the house, you will no longer be in poverty." President George W. Bush again expanded it by adding a child tax credit. By 2004, 21 million low- and moderate-income working families were receiving an average annual refund of $1,500, which moved close to 5 million people out of poverty.[24]

Last, as mentioned in Chapter 1, cooperatives were developed in the 1840s in England and took a major step forward in the 1950s in Spain under the leadership of Father Jose Maria Arizmendiarrieta as a way to address high unemployment. The Mondragon cooperatives that he initiated also address capitalism's tendency to pay poverty wages to many workers. The cooperative, with its focus on economic democracy and profits going to the "worker-owners," ensures that people earn a living wage. The Mondragon worker-owner model has created tens of thousands of needed jobs and has allowed living wages to be paid, which are on average 13 percent higher than those paid by traditional businesses. Importantly, the Mondragon model has provided a new vision to create living-wage jobs within modern capitalism.

THE RIGHT TO A LIVING WAGE: CURRENT APPROACHES

Let's now turn our attention to modern-day examples of people and organizations whose work contributes to the goal of a right to a living-wage job. Modern-day examples to be explored include efforts to (1) bargain collectively, (2) increase the minimum wage, (3) develop public works projects, (4) create guaranteed income programs, (5) expand the earned income tax credit, and (6) develop cooperatives.

Collective bargaining continues to be one of the most effective ways for low-wage workers to increase their pay from poverty wages toward a living wage. In 2012, union jobs paid on average $943 a week in comparison to $742 a month for nonunionized workers, a 21 percent difference. Today, there are union efforts to increase wages at McDonald's, Yum! Brands (owners of KFC, Pizza Hut, and Taco Bell), and Walmart, which are the nation's top three businesses that employ low-wage employers. Fast-food workers are predominantly women (accounting for two-thirds of workers) and people of color, and the average age is twenty-eight. Fast-food restaurants and Walmart limit the hours that employees work, so that legal protections are not triggered (e.g., health insurance), and up to now, fast-food restaurants and Walmart have been union free. However, there are major efforts afoot to change the conditions of these workers. In New York City, an organizing effort has begun to unionize fast-food workers. Fast Food Forward was created in early 2012 by a group of organizations (NY Communities for Change, Service Employees International Union, and the Black Institute) in order to unionize fast-food workers at McDonald's, Burger King, Dominos, KFC, Taco Bell, and Wendy's. Fast Food Forward is hoping to capitalize on a series of 2011 labor victories in New York, when NY Communities for Change successfully won unionization at six supermarkets and four carwashes.[25]

Fast Food Forward's objective is to raise the wages of New York City's fast-food workers to $15 an hour; currently, the average wage is $9 an hour, or $18,500 a year. Jonathan Westin, organizing director at NY Communities for Change, states, "The fast-food industry employs tens of thousands of workers in New York and pays them poverty wages. . . . A lot of them can't afford to get by. A lot have to rely on public assistance, and taxpayers are often footing the bill because these companies are not paying a living wage."[26]

To kick off their campaign, Fast Food Forward held a one-day strike on November 29, 2012. It was the largest set of labor actions in the history of the fast-food industry. At a McDonald's restaurant on Madison Avenue, fourteen of the seventeen employees scheduled to work that morning did not show up for their shift; rather, the workers rallied outside with hundreds of supporters. At the protest, Pamela Waldron, who has worked at the KFC in Pennsylvania Station for eight years, stated that she cannot afford to feed her family on her $7.75 hourly wage. Pamela asserted, "I'm protesting for better pay. . . . I have two kids under 6, and I don't earn enough to buy food for them."[27]

A strategy that Fast Food Forward is utilizing to win higher wages is to dramatize the income inequality that exists within the industry. The organization points out that the fast-food industry grosses $200 billion annually and pays its CEOs on average $25,000 a day, while at the same time, the workers in their restaurants earn on average $11,000 a year. This average fast-food salary amounts to just 25 percent of the money needed to survive in New York City. At the same time that worker's salaries are so low, company profits continue to rise: Yum! Brands is up 45 percent, and McDonald's is up 130 percent since the end of the Great Recession. With this growth in profits, the number of food preparation workers has continued to grow, increasing 55 percent since 2000.[28]

In the same month that Fast Food Forward began its campaign in New York, another group, the Workers Organizing Committee of Chicago (WOCC), started a similar effort in Chicago. WOCC is a union of fast-food and retail workers fighting for a union contract for its workers that would pay $15 an hour. During the Christmas shopping season of 2011, on a cold December day, hundreds of WOCC supporters marched through Chicago's Magnificent Mile shopping district, culminating in a sit-down blockade of Macy's, where twenty-four supporters were arrested. WOCC points out that downtown Chicago stores and restaurants bring in over $4 billion but the workers have hardly benefited at all from the profits while the executives and investors have enriched themselves. Brittany Smith, a WOCC member who is a college student and who works for Urban Outfitters for $8.75 an hour, states, "Some of the time I luck out and I can eat two meals a day ... but most of the time, I'm eating one." In April 2013, WOCC workers walked off their jobs, and their strike led to some major victories, with Whole Foods in East Lakeview raising its average hourly pay for workers from $10 to $12, and with the Nordstrom Rack and Macy's raising pay 25 cents an hour, from $11 to $11.25 and $8.25 to $8.50, respectively. Even McDonald's raised its pay for a number of employees by 10 cents an hour. According to WOCC spokesman Deivid Rojas, it is a "huge deal to them" to get these raises. Yet, as Macy's worker Krystal Maxie-Collins stated, "I'm proud to receive it, but it's still not a living wage. It's still not ... enough money to cover everything." WOCC now claims 1,000 members and hopes to use these wildcat strikes to build a workers' movement strong enough to win its demand of $15 an hour through a negotiated contract.[29]

The largest low-wage employer in the nation, Walmart, which employs 1.4 million workers, or one out of every ten retail workers in the United States, is not surprisingly also the target of a movement to pay higher wages. The Organization United for Respect at Walmart (OUR Walmart) has created a twelve-point declaration, which has the goal to increase the pay of workers to $13 an hour and expand full-time work so that no worker would be forced on government services (food stamps, Medicaid), as well as to stop retaliation for workers who speak out. OUR Walmart is composed of thousands of Walmart employees, or "associates," and is supported by the United Food and Commercial Workers (UFCW). In a change of strategy, OUR Walmart is not calling for unionization or collective bargaining, as Walmart has successfully defeated earlier attempts to organize workers. In 2011, OUR Walmart traveled to Walmart headquarters in Bentonville, Arkansas, with ninety-seven associates and presented their twelve-point declaration to Karen Casey, the senior vice president for global labor relations, in the parking lot. The following year, OUR Walmart led its first strike against the company in Pico Rivera, California, when over thirty associates walked off their morning shift and held a rally in front of the store to denounce management's retaliation against workers who spoke out against poor working conditions. Manuela Rosales, a twenty-five-year-old Walmart associate who worked in the cell phone department, left her shift because "when we speak out, they cut my hours in retaliation and they have me pull pallets, which is very hard work. . . . I'm a single mom and I can't afford them cutting my hours."[30]

One month later, on November 23, 2012, on Black Friday—one of the busiest shopping days of the year—OUR Walmart called a one-day strike at stores across the nation. This nationwide strike and protest took place at about 400 Walmart stores in forty-six states, and over 500 Walmart workers participated in them, along with many thousands of community supporters and faith leaders. While Walmart management denied the strikes had any effect on business, OUR Walmart celebrated the first time Walmart stores experienced collective action by workers across the nation. This Black Friday protest was followed by an even larger protest in November 2013, with actions at 1,500 Walmart stores, which led to 111 arrests.[31]

The battle to increase wages for low-wage employers has just begun and will continue in the years to come. What is at stake is the US economy: Will it be an economy that benefits everyone, or just the folks at the upper ends, with a large segment of the population in low-wage, no-benefit "McJobs"? If things don't change, the answer is clearly the latter, as seven out of the ten fields where the fastest employment growth is occurring are in low-wage work. However, if change is brought about by the efforts of workers, the nation will move closer to the vision laid out in the Economic Bill of Rights' second amendment. This vision is supported by a recent study that showed that if the retail industry paid its workers $25,000 a year ($13 an hour), 734,000 workers in the United States would be lifted out of poverty. The report notes that this increase in wages would cost $20.8 billion, or just 1 percent of the $2.2 trillion in annual sales by large retailers. This represents a 10 percent increase in payroll for firms with 1,000 employees, or a 6 percent payroll increase for the overall retail sector. This could be paid for out of the retail industries' $35 billion profits (2012); it could also be paid for with a small increase in the cost of goods. If the retail businesses passed the whole cost on to consumers, the price of goods would increase by just 1 percent. If the retailers passed one-half of the wage cost onto customers, the average household would pay $17.73 more a year. At the same time, the extra money in the economy would increase the gross domestic product (GDP) by $12–$15 billion a year, and 100,000 to 132,000 jobs would be added.[32]

Another modern-day example that contributes to the right to a living wage is the minimum-wage campaigns that are currently taking place. In the face of little action at the federal level, cities and states are taking matters into their own hands. In 2012, community groups in two cities—San Jose, California, and Albuquerque, New Mexico—led successful campaigns to increase their minimum wage; in San Jose, voters passed a minimum-wage initiative on the November ballot, raising the minimum wage in the city from $8 to $10; and in Albuquerque, they raised it from $7.50 to $8.50.

The San Jose campaign emerged out of a sociology class at San Jose State University. In the fall of 2010, Marisela Castro, a student in a college course titled Wealth, Poverty, and Privilege came up with the idea of starting a campaign to increase the minimum wage in Silicon Valley. Marisela was moved to action because she could no longer stand the injustice she was witnessing at the after-school program where she was working. Kids were sneaking food into their backpacks because their parents were making just $8 an hour, which wasn't enough to ensure food at home. In addition, parents had to work two jobs, making it difficult to provide the necessary support structure for their children to be successful in school. This social injustice drove Marisela to act, and the following semester, Marisela took a course called Social Action with the goal of increasing the minimum wage to $10 an hour in Silicon Valley.

In the spring Social Action course, three students (Leila McCabe, Heather Paulson, and Saul Gonzalez) joined forces with Marisela and conducted background research. As part of their research, they found that three cities had already significantly increased their citywide minimum wage: San Francisco ($10.24 an hour); Santa Fe, New Mexico ($10.29 an hour); and Washington, DC ($8.25 an hour). Importantly, the latest social scientific research showed that an increase in a citywide minimum wage did not increase the unemployment rate. In March 2011, the Center for Economic and Policy Research released its study on citywide minimum wages in San Francisco (implemented in 2004), Santa Fe (implemented in 2004), and Washington, DC (implemented in 1993). The center found that "the results for fast food,

food services, retail, and low-wage establishments in San Francisco and Santa Fe support the view that a citywide minimum wage can raise the earnings of low-wage workers, without a discernible impact on their employment." This study also found that there was little to no negative impact on small businesses because they generally passed on the cost by raising prices slightly. In fact, the researchers argued that there was a positive impact on businesses since minimum-wage workers stayed in their jobs longer.[33]

Another study, conducted by economists and regional planners, looked at minimum-wage laws where counties from different states straddled each other but had different minimum wages. The researchers found that there were "no detectable employment losses." A third study, by the Fiscal Policy Institute, showed that "states with minimum wages above the federal level have had faster small business and retail job growth." What is clear is that minimum-wage laws, while they definitely help low-wage workers, show little to no impact on businesses or the unemployment rate. A *New York Times* editorial in January 2011 put it this way: "Studies have not been able to determine definitively whether the employment impact of a higher wage is positive or negative, just that it is small." At the same time, minimum-wage laws have the positive effect of providing low-wage workers with a bit more money and an increased retention rate.[34]

That spring semester, Marisela and her classmates created the Campus Alliance for Economic Justice (CAFÉ J), and their first project was the minimum-wage campaign. During the summer, CAFÉ J students began meeting regularly with the directors of Sacred Heart Community Services, the largest antipoverty center in San Jose; Step Up Silicon Valley, the campaign to cut poverty in one-half in Santa Clara County; and several other community leaders about a citywide minimum-wage campaign in San Jose. That fall, the students raised money to conduct a poll, and then actually helped to conduct it. With the poll numbers showing that San Joseans overwhelmingly supported a $2 increase to the hourly minimum wage, the South Bay Labor Council joined the leadership team and became an extremely important ally. Other organizations became involved as well, including the United Way, Catholic Charities, Jewish Federal of Silicon Valley, the NAACP, and the Silicon Valley Council of Non Profits.

In the spring of 2012, students in collaboration with other allies helped to gather 36,000 signatures (19,200 were required) to put the measure on the November 2012 ballot. In the summer and fall, the coalition took multiple actions to convey three messages to the voters: (1) If you work hard and play by the rules, you deserve a fair wage; (2) $8 is not fair since a full-time minimum-wage worker can't pay for the basics on that salary; and (3) increasing the minimum wage encourages self-sufficiency and reduces the need for government services. Though the campaign was outspent by at least 5 to 1, San Jose voters passed the minimum-wage increase by 60 percent to

40 percent to enact a $10 citywide minimum wage, with an annual increase based on the consumer price index.

A year after implementation of San Jose's $10 minimum wage, the results have been very positive, as unemployment has been reduced, the number of businesses has grown, the number of minimum-wage jobs has expanded, and the average employee hours have remained constant. First, the unemployment rate has dropped in the San Jose metro area from 7.6 percent in February 2013—right before the implementation of the $10 minimum wage—to 5.9 percent in April 2014. Part of the reason for this almost 2-point drop in unemployment is that the 40,000 minimum-wage workers in San Jose have pumped into the local economy over $100 million this past year, helping to stimulate the economic growth of Silicon Valley. Second, overall business growth is up, with 84,000 businesses registered at the start of 2014, in comparison to 75,000 in the previous year. Importantly, the leisure and hospitality industry—the sector that includes food services, and where many minimum-wage employees work—experienced a net increase of 4,000 jobs in San Jose in 2013. In the city center, businesses grew by 3 percent in the past year, with the retail sector, which includes restaurants, increasing to 19 percent of all downtown businesses, up from 15 percent in 2012. Third and finally, the average number of hours worked in the San Jose metro area in 2013 is nearly the exact amount that it was in 2012 (36.5 hours in 2013 vs. 36.9 hours in 2012).

These positive results in San Jose have given support to civic leaders and politicians in other California cities trying to "raise the wage," including the 2014 successful efforts in Berkeley ($12.53 by 2016) and Richmond ($13 by 2018, then will rise with a CPI). In November 2014 the citizens of Eureka, San Francisco, and Oakland will vote on minimum-wage increases.[35]

This trend to increase the minimum wage is occurring outside of California as well. In November 2013, the small city of SeaTac, a suburb of Seattle, voted to increase the minimum wage to $15 an hour for travel and hospitality workers in large businesses (e.g., in hotels with 100 rooms or more and in businesses that have a minimum of thirty nonmanagerial employees). This was followed by the unanimous vote of the Seattle City Council in 2014 to raise the minimum wage to $15 over the following three years for businesses with more than 500 workers and over the next seven years for businesses with fewer than 500 workers. Also, Bernalillo County in New Mexico extended Albuquerque's minimum-wage increase to $8.50 an hour for 10,000 workers in the unincorporated areas of the county.[36]

San Jose's success also provided energy to California Assembly Member Luis Alejo's minimum-wage bill. After seeing his own minimum-wage bill defeated several times, Alejo convinced the California State Legislature to pass a graduated $10 minimum wage. In July 2014, California's minimum wage increased by $1 to $9 an hour, and in midyear 2015, it will increase to $10 an hour. California is one of twenty-two states that has a higher minimum wage than the federal government's $7.25 an hour. Of course, all of this is happening in the context of President Obama's endorsement of Sen. Tom Harkin's (D-IA) and Rep. George Miller's (D-CA) $10.10 minimum-wage bill at the national level.[37]

A third contemporary example contributing to the right to a living-wage job is increasing wages through public works jobs. Chapter 1 showed how public works benefited US families and communities in earlier times. In addition to the direct benefit to workers' pocketbooks, public works has a positive effect on private sector wages. This is due to supply and demand. If there is less supply of labor, with demand being equal, the price of labor will increase. Unfortunately, there is little to no recent research in the United States on how public works increases wages; however, there is evidence from other countries. For example, in May 2012, the Centre for the Study of African Economics released a report that examined India's large-scale public works programs and its impact on wages. In 2005, India passed the Employment Guarantee Act, which guaranteed 100 days of work for rural residents in soil and water conservation, forestry, flood control, and other infrastructure projects. In its first two and one-half years, 30 million households received public works jobs and workers put in 3.5 billion days of work. The report explored public works in 249 districts in nineteen Indian states and concluded that the public works program had increased the overall rural wage rate by 5 percent. Importantly, the Employment Guarantee Act requires one-third of the public workers must be women, so both women and men had their wages increased. In Zambia, those with public works jobs increased their access to health services by 13 percent as a result of the ability to pay, while their kids increased school attendance by 15 percent.[38]

A fourth current example that contributes to the right to a living wage is the guaranteed income. There is once again scant research, but this time it is due to the fact that no guaranteed income plan has been attempted since the four pilot projects were implemented as part of President Johnson's War on Poverty. The main advocate for a guaranteed income in the United States is the US Basic Income Guarantee (USBIG) Network. USBIG's 300-plus members are advocating for the federal government to guarantee a citizen's income at some minimal level, which it will not fall below for any reason. While there is discussion about what this basic income should be, it is agreed that it would be above the poverty line, and that it would be high enough to pay for necessities; additional income would be necessary for luxury items. Thus, work would still be incentivized and no harm would be done to the work effort.

This basic income model proposed by USBIG differentiates itself from President Nixon's Family Assistance Plan in several ways: first, it would be universal, meaning that all people would receive it, not just the poor or working class; second, it would be given unconditionally and not means tested; and third, there would be no work requirement. USBIG supporters argue that a universal basic income should be seen like the right of an education for all children. It is given to rich and poor alike as citizens of our democracy. Advocates point to the example of the Alaska Permanent Fund, which has provided every individual in the state of Alaska a cash dividend each year that comes from the sale of oil by the state-owned oil business. Cash payments go to all Alaskans who have been in the state for one year or more, including children. This amount has ranged from a low of $331 in 1984 (in the early years of the oil fund) to a high of $2,069 in 2008. Early studies showed that Alaskans have not used the money on frivolous things: over 50 percent was spent on day-to-day expenses, one-third was allotted to savings or debt reduction, and only 10 to 15 percent went to special large purchases.[39]

Advocates of a basic income also think it is an effective response to poverty since it simplifies government policy and increases individual autonomy, as people are freed up to pursue activities they truly desire. They argue that the poverty rate could be cut in half without increasing taxes and that the basic income would replace traditional welfare spending, thus eliminating programs like Temporary Assistance to Needy Families (TANF), unemployment insurance, and food stamps. Each spring since 2002, basic income supporters have met on the East Coast to discuss and promote their plan.

The idea for a basic income entered into the larger public dialogue during the Occupy Wall Street protests in 2011, when some Occupy protestors called for a guaranteed income to deal with the excessive income inequality in US society. Yet, it was the Swiss-based Generation Basic Income group that has catapulted this idea into the public consciousness. Generation Basic Income gathered 100,000 signatures in 2013, enough to put the basic income on a national referendum, which will take place soon. The Swiss plan is simple: provide every adult citizen of Switzerland approximately $2,800 a month from the state. The supporters of this initiative argue that it will wipe out poverty, as well as change people's relationship to money. No longer will people be forced to work at a job because they need the money; rather, people will be free to pursue jobs that they are truly interested in. Enno Schmidt, one of the key organizers for the Swiss basic income, puts it this way:

> Income from labour will be renegotiated. With a basic income, I can say no to a bad deal. And yes to what I really want. With a basic income I already bring an income to employment. Earned income is supplemented with the amount of income that secures my existence. Good work that people like to do, will be cheaper. Poor work that people do not like to do, will be better paid, because no-one can be blackmailed with their existence to do it. Basic income does not necessarily mean more money. It is the *unconditional* nature

of the income that is important. Only someone who has little today will have more money in their pocket with a basic income.[40]

The Swiss plan is supported by BIEN, a large European advocacy group founded in 1986 under the name of the Basic Income European Network and since renamed the Basic Income Earth Network. BIEN currently has "networks" in twenty countries (mostly in Europe, but also in Australia, Argentina, Japan, Mexico, and South Korea) working to establish a basic income. BIEN differentiates itself from the European model of welfare in that its basic income is provided (1) to individuals and not households, (2) regardless of income status, and (3) without requiring an individual to work or accept a job if it is offered. This last stipulation is included so as to prevent anyone from taking a dead-end poverty job. BIEN draws its support from liberals (since it focuses on the alleviation of poverty), conservatives (since it eliminates bureaucracy by eliminating program administrators), and libertarians (since it provides individuals more freedom and keeps in place the beneficial parts of market capitalism). Every two years, BIEN holds an international conference to promote the idea of a universal basic income.

A fifth modern example that contributes to the goal of a right to a living wage is the earned income tax credit (EITC). As was discussed earlier, the EITC was created by President Ford to encourage and reward work by providing a tax credit to low-wage workers, and the program had been expanded under Presidents Reagan, Clinton, and Bush. More recently, President Obama delivered on a 2008 campaign promise to expand the EITC for families with three or more children and to increase the credit for married couples to eliminate a "marriage penalty." These changes increased the EITC so that by 2011, over 27 million low- and moderate-income families (married couples earning under $49,078 and singles earning under $43,998) received a total of $56 billion in tax credits, moving 6.6 million people out of poverty. Interestingly, the EITC is much more accessible than the other programs serving low- and moderate-income families since 75 percent of the families eligible for this credit claim it, whereas 66 percent of eligible families claim food stamps (now called the Supplemental Nutrition Assistance Program) and only 40 percent of eligible families claim TANF. The EITC program was to be cut as part of the 2012 "fiscal cliff," but it was restored under pressure from President Obama and has been extended until 2017. Currently, families with three or more children can receive a tax credit of $5,891, families with two children can receive $5,236, families with one child can receive $3,169, and families with no children can receive $475. President Obama tried to raise the amount for families with no children but was unsuccessful.[41]

A sixth, and last, contemporary example that contributes to the goal of a right to a living wage is cooperatives. Evergreen Cooperative, as discussed previously, has adopted the Mondragon model and applied it in Cleveland.

At Evergreen, after the six-month probationary period, employees are voted in as worker-owners, at which point they receive a raise and health benefits at no cost. Workers start off at $10 an hour and can make up to $16 an hour. In addition, the new worker-owner uses part of the raise to buy his or her initial ownership stake in the co-op, and then each year thereafter if the company makes a profit, a percentage of the earnings are deposited into a "capital account" owned by the worker. When the workers leave the company or retire, they give up ownership in the company, and the equity stake they have built up in their capital account is given to them. It is estimated that after eight years, the worker's equity stake will be $65,000.[42]

Living wages are also a part of the Union Cab model in Madison. Under the guiding principle that "a living wage at a 40-hour work week is a priority," first-year cab drivers make $10–$12 an hour, whereas senior workers make $18–$20. Drivers are paid by commission, starting out at 36 percent commission, which increases by 1 percent for every 2,500 hours they drive. Senior drivers and managers are paid about $40,000 a year, and they receive health care.[43]

SUMMARY

In Chapter 2, six ideas have been discussed to achieve this constitutional commitment of a right to a living wage: collective bargaining, increasing the minimum wage, earned income tax credits, public works, a guaranteed income, and cooperatives. If the United States is to guarantee the right to a living wage, surely many of these six ideas will play a major role.

Chapter 3

The Right to a Decent Home

The Third Amendment

PROBLEM

Affordable and decent housing is a challenge for many Americans. The problem is that the cost of rent is high and one-third of Americans are poor or nearly poor. The 2012 poverty rate for a family of four was $23,021 a year, which means the family earned $1,918 a month before taxes. With the average monthly rent in 2012 being $1,008 (an all-time high), families are left with less than $1,000 to pay for all other basic necessities. This combination of high rents and high poverty causes 42 million American households to pay more than 30 percent of their income for housing—30 percent being the accepted standard for affordability. Incredibly, 20 million US households pay more than 50 percent of their income for housing. Research shows that the lack of affordable housing produces a host of negative social outcomes, which include childhood health problems such as anemia, asthma, stunted growth, and viral infections, as well as lower academic achievement and behavioral problems in school.[1]

Exacerbating the problem of affordability is the lack of housing units available for moderate- to low-income families. The reality is that our nation does not produce enough housing units for the working class and poor. Consider very low-income people, which by definition means they make 50 percent of an area's median income (AMI). In Connecticut, the

43

median yearly income is $64,247, so a family is considered very low income if the household makes below $32,124, while in New Mexico the median income is $43,424, so a family is considered very low income if it makes below $21,712. Currently, 18 million American households are considered very low income; at the same time, there are only 11.6 million rental units affordable and available for them. Furthermore, for every 100 households whose income is in the bottom 30 percent, there are only thirty rental units affordable and available for them.[2]

There are many reasons why the supply gap exists, but a critical factor has been the lack of commitment to affordable housing by the federal government. First, the United States does not spend very much money on affordable housing in comparison to the overall budget. In 2012, the United States spent about $29 billion on housing assistance (mostly through vouchers) for 3.3 million people. This level of funding serves only one out of four eligible renters and is only 1 percent of the overall federal budget. Second, the United States operates and maintains a minimal amount of publicly owned housing, just 1.2 million units. Third, US housing policy generally demolishes more housing units than it builds. Just look at the HOPE VI program, the most recent US housing policy, which has demolished 96,200 low-income housing units over the past fifteen years, while building 56,800 units. This combination of a lack of government funding for housing, a supply gap of affordable units, and a high poverty rate has led to many people becoming homeless. In 2012, the annual national survey counted 633,782 people as homeless. This makes the United States a leader in the industrialized world in homelessness.[3]

The final housing challenge has been the negative effect of the Great Recession. Over the past six years, foreclosures and repossessions have risen sharply. From 2007 to 2012, 16.3 million households received foreclosure notices and the banks repossessed 5 million homes, the majority of which were due to the loss of jobs. In comparison, 4.2 million households received foreclosure notices from 2000 to 2006, with only 300,000 households having their homes repossessed. More recently, as the economy has improved, the number of foreclosures has begun to slow, as 812,000 homes were in some stage of foreclosure by the end of 2013—which is a 34 percent drop from the previous year, and the lowest level since 2006. In addition to losing their homes, people have also lost their wealth, since a home represents the greatest single asset of many American households. In 2013, roughly 7 million home owners were still "underwater" (i.e., they owed more than their house was worth). And while all income groups have suffered a loss of wealth as a result of the Great Recession, the effect on the poor has been the greatest. In 2007, the bottom 20 percent had $32,000 of wealth; two years later, it was reduced to $3,000, a drop of 91 percent.[4]

The growth of the American middle class after World War II owed a lot to the establishment of the Federal Housing Authority in 1934 and to generous entitlements offered by the GI Bill, including access to higher education. However, these government programs were not race neutral in their effects. Racism encouraged neighborhood redlining and thus limited black and Latino access to mortgage loans. Discriminatory mortgage practices prevented people of color from developing assets through home ownership, creating a significant wealth gap. More recently, blacks and Latinos gained greater access to home ownership, but it was through predatory home loans that inflated the housing bubble. The Great Recession wiped out the gains made by people of color through home ownership, with Latinos losing 66 percent and blacks losing 53 percent of their wealth from 2005 to 2009, in comparison to whites, who lost 16 percent. In 2005, the average white household had $134,992 in wealth, whereas the average Latino household had only $18,359 and the average black household had $12,124. By 2009, the average white household had $113,149 in wealth, whereas the average Latino household had $6,325 and the average black household had $5,677. The median wealth of white households is now nineteen times that of black households and fifteen times that of Hispanic households, which is twice the prevailing disparity of the previous two decades.[5]

SOLUTION

Housing is a necessary part of human survival. Without it, people are left to the elements, and in many parts of the country, this is life threatening. At the same time, housing is more than where someone sleeps; it is where most of a person's time is spent, and it is where people feel safe, supported, and secure. In addition, housing impacts many other aspects of our lives, as it determines the quality of the schools our children attend, whether good jobs are close by, whether grocery stores and banks are in the community, and whether one lives in a segregated or integrated community.

The solution to the "wrong" of not having enough affordable, decent housing is the right to housing. This right is based on the belief that there should be affordable, decent housing for all in the United States. This right was clearly articulated by President Roosevelt when he declared that every family had a right to a decent home. For Roosevelt, the wrong that needed to be righted was the fact that "many millions of Americans still live in habitations which not only fail to provide the physical benefits of modern civilization but breed disease and impair the health of future generations. The menace exists not only in the slum areas of the very large cities, but in many smaller cities as well. It exists on tens of thousands of farms, in varying degrees, in every part of the country." While Roosevelt proposed this right to decent housing, it was left up to President Truman to develop a federal housing policy that would secure this right. Truman argued that a federal policy was necessary because the free market was not going to build enough homes for all Americans since developers build where the most profit can be made. For Truman, the way to ensure a decent home for all Americans was for the government to become directly involved in the creation of housing. Seen in this way, the right to housing fixes capitalism's weakness of not producing enough affordable housing units.[6]

Following is a discussion of the history behind the right to decent housing, as well as modern-day approaches to achieve this constitutional commitment. These modern-day approaches include guaranteeing the right to a job and living wage; building more affordable, low-income housing and creating a dedicated revenue source to fund the construction; providing rental assistance to fill the gap between the cost of housing and what people can afford; stopping foreclosures; and enacting Rapid Re-Housing policies for people without homes.

THE HISTORY OF THE RIGHT TO A DECENT HOME

In the early years of the United States there was little support for the idea of the right to decent housing. In the nineteenth century, a common response for people unable to afford housing was to have them go live in a poorhouse. Poorhouses were built on farmland and were seen by the wealthy as a cost-effective way to deal with poverty. The goals of the poorhouse were to provide housing for the "worthy poor," encourage the work ethic of the "able-bodied poor," and reduce taxes on the wealthy since giving people money for food and rent, which was the English and colonial tradition, was more expensive. However, there were some early American thinkers, such as Thomas Paine, who asked the nation to provide meaning to the words that "all men are created equal." Inspired by the lack of poverty that existed in Native American communities, Paine argued that since the land was once owned in common by all, a 10 percent tax on inheritance should be levied in order to provide all men and women turning twenty-one years of age a grant of £15 so they could purchase a farm. If Paine's "agrarian justice" would have been enacted, it would have gone a long way to achieve the right to housing.[7]

By the mid-1800s, there was growing concern that poorhouses were unsuccessful at providing decent housing and at reducing poverty. At the same time, the nation's economy was shifting from agriculture to factories, where goods once made by hand by artisans and apprentices were now made by machine. The new manufacturing jobs were located in the cities, and people moved to work in the factories from within the United States and from abroad. As a result, the number of people living in American cities jumped from 6.2 million in 1860 to 42 million in 1915. Sadly, Anglo-Saxon racism forced African Americans, Chinese, Italians, Japanese, Jews, and Poles into ethnically segregated ghettos.[8]

The factory workers worked between ten and twelve hours a day at low wages, and the living conditions for the working class were deplorable. People lived in houses with no heating, obtained water from unreliable public hydrants, received light from kerosene lamps, and cooked on stoves that were heated by scraps of scavenged wood and coal. The high infant mortality rate reflected the poor living conditions, with some cities experiencing 135 infant deaths out of 1,000. This social suffering of the urban working class was highlighted in a series of books in the late nineteenth century. In one of these books, entitled *How the Other Half Lives,* Jacob Riis describes the living conditions: "That was a woman filling her pail by the hydrant you just bumped against. The sinks are in the hallway, that all the tenants may have access—and all be poisoned alike by their summer stenches. Hear the pump squeak! It is the lullaby of tenement-house babes. In summer, when a thousand thirsty throats pant for a cooling drink in this block, it is worked in vain. But the saloon, whose open door you passed in the hall, is always there." Jacob Riis's exposé and the work of progressive reformers did inspire some local reforms, like providing construction regulations for tenement houses that provided access to light, fire escapes, and improved sanitary conditions (e.g., one toilet per twenty people). However, not all city-dwellers lived like this. The homes of the factory owners and their benefactors had such amenities as central heating, electricity, indoor plumbing, natural gas, and telephones.[9]

Up through 1930, there was no national response on housing. The Great Depression changed everything. In the early 1930s, thousands of home owners were threatened with foreclosure since their loans were short-term and nonamortized (i.e., paying interest only). Every few years, these loans needed to be refinanced at prevailing interest rates from the local banks or investors. With the collapse of the banking system and the lack of available capital to finance these short-term loans, millions of Americans faced foreclosure. In order to stabilize the housing market and stop foreclosures, Roosevelt created the Home Owners' Loan Corporation (HOLC) in 1933 to provide mortgage relief for families under the threat of foreclosure. Loans were provided for up to 80 percent of the value of the home at 5 percent interest for twenty-five years.[10]

These HOLC loans became so popular that Roosevelt took the next step in the following year to help pass the 1934 National Housing Act, which provided insurance to lenders if they made available thirty-year loans at 5 percent interest through the newly created Federal Housing Administration (FHA). These New Deal efforts created the market for local lenders to sell long-term and amortizing loans (i.e., where part of the payment goes to reducing the principal and part goes to interest). This shift to long-term and amortizing loans moved the nation away from renting and toward home ownership; it also encouraged the building of new homes and the repair of existing homes. However, there was a harmful side to Roosevelt's housing policy, as the practice of "redlining" was introduced: whole areas on maps were marked with red lines indicating that the federal government would not lend based on race since it was seen as "too risky." This practice of demarcating white sections of the city as "low risk" and black areas of the city as "high risk" was begun by the HOLC and continued by the FHA. The result was that whites obtained 98 percent of the FHA loans between 1934 and 1962. Moreover, the FHA policies promoted white flight, as neighborhoods with even a small black population were seen as "hazardous." These New Deal programs would also not lend money to a black person wanting to live in a white area, and vice versa. For example, a 1938 FHA manual encouraged officials to not mix "inharmonious racial or nationality groups" and "the occupancy of properties except by the race for which they are intended."[11]

In addition to stabilizing the private housing market—at least for some—Roosevelt had the federal government construct publicly owned housing since he believed that the nation's housing stock was substandard. Roosevelt used his bully pulpit to draw attention to the housing crisis, stating, "I see one-third of a nation ill-housed, ill-clad, ill-nourished. . . . The test of our progress is not whether we add more to the abundance of those who have much; it is whether we provide enough for those who have too little." In order to meet this test, Roosevelt had the national government build housing. Initially, the Public Works Administration—one of the public works projects mentioned in Chapter 2—built 22,000 housing units from 1934 to 1936. To build even more federal housing, Roosevelt signed the Wagner-Steagall Housing Act in 1937, which created the US Housing Authority (USHA). USHA lent $650 million to states and local housing authorities in order to build publicly owned housing projects that were rent-subsidized (i.e., 50 percent of the rent came from tenants, 33 percent from the federal government, and 17 percent from local authorities). USHA gave low-interest, long-term loans of up to 90 percent of the project costs. The goal was to house the working and middle classes who were suffering in the Great Depression. By late 1940, over 500 USHA projects were completed or were in progress, building 122,000 units, with 41,000 units (33 percent) designated for African Americans. By 1942, some 53,000 additional apartment units were completed.[12]

These efforts by USHA demonstrated that the federal government could effectively build low-income housing. At the same time, the Wagner-Steagall Housing Act had been weakened by many compromises. For example, the federal government was required to destroy an equal amount of substandard slum units before the public units were built. This nod to the real estate interests ensured that while the quality of housing went up, the number of housing units did not. Thus, there would be no decrease in overall housing prices. It also caused great hardship for the people living in the units, since many of them had no place to go as the new housing was built. In addition, the Wagner-Steagall Housing Act was crafted so that while the money was federal, the control was local through a public housing authority. This allowed for the local public housing authority to determine where the projects were to be built, how they were to be maintained, and where the different ethnic and racial groups would live in order to maintain segregation.[13]

The next major step in housing policy came in support of the soldiers returning from World War II. In 1944, the federal government enacted the GI Bill of Rights, which provided the returning soldiers, many of whom were working class, the opportunity to purchase a home with a low-interest loan that required no down payment. From 1944 to 1954, the GI Bill allowed veterans to purchase 4.2 million homes, many of which were in the newly created suburbs. By 1956, 42 percent of veterans had become home owners as a result of the GI Bill, in comparison to 34 percent of nonveterans of the same age. Positively, the GI Bill created the wealth that allowed for a stable middle class, which endured through the 1970s. Negatively, the GI Bill primarily helped white soldiers and their families purchase homes, whereas African American, Latino, and Native American soldiers were denied access to the GI benefits at nearly every step of the process. This institutionalized racism, which was supported by the Federal Housing Administration, limited people of color to less than 2 percent of all GI home loans. For example, many black soldiers were not told about the GI benefits. If the soldiers did find out, and they accessed them through the Veterans Administration, the local banks would still deny them a loan. Furthermore, black soldiers were denied mortgage insurance when they wanted to buy in white neighborhoods because the FHA wanted to maintain segregation. Black soldiers were also denied mortgage insurance when they wanted to buy in black neighborhoods since the FHA deemed these areas "too high risk." As one black veteran from Texas put it, "The financial backers of the GI Bill have so divided locations and placed restrictions on certain areas that as it is. . . . NO NEGRO VETERAN is eligible for a loan." All in all, the GI Bill provided whites with $95 billion, plus the wealth it created through appreciation. This wealth creation was denied to African Americans and other people of color, and has set up the racialized inequality the nation experiences today.[14]

The GI Bill of Rights was enacted in the same year Roosevelt put forward the Economic Bill of Rights. As stated earlier, it was Roosevelt who had called for "the right to decent housing," but after the death of FDR, it was Truman who was left to enact a public policy to achieve this constitutional commitment. Truman's attempt was the 1949 Housing Act, which established as a national objective "the achievement as soon as feasible of a decent home and a suitable living environment for every American family." In that year, there were still 5 million American families living in slums and 3 million families sharing their homes with others. At the signing ceremony, Truman proclaimed that the 1949 Housing Act "opens up the prospect of decent homes in wholesome surroundings for low-income families now living in the squalor of the slums." Specifically, the bill called for federal funds for slum clearance and the construction of 810,000 low-income housing units in six years, as well as financing for rural home owners. At this time, the focus was on eliminating slum conditions and replacing slums with decent housing.[15]

Unfortunately, Congress never provided the necessary resources to attain the goals of the 1949 Housing Act. By 1954, only 263,800 units had been built, one-third of the goal set in the bill, and many of these units were part of large-scale housing projects. Not surprisingly, the bill did not include statutory declarations to provide the basis for a lawsuit to compel allocation of the necessary resources by the courts. In 1954, Congress reaffirmed its "commitment" to housing, and 179,000 public housing units were built over the next four years. However, ten years after Truman's clarion call for decent housing for all, a total of 442,000 new units were built, just 55 percent of Truman's goal. At the same time, urban projects continued to destroy more housing than they built. For example, in New York, the Lincoln Center project built 4,400 apartment units but destroyed 7,000 units. To make matters worse, large-scale public housing was becoming stigmatized as a segregated space with high crime rates, with critics calling them "vertical ghettos."[16]

In the following decade, the civil rights movement captured the nation's attention. After achieving the end of Jim Crow segregation by the mid-1960s, the civil rights movement turned its attention to human rights, and housing emerged as a central issue. As part of this movement, residents, faith-based groups, and small businesses in cities around the nation came together and created local nonprofit organizations, also known as community development corporations (CDCs), with the goal of revitalizing local communities. CDCs offered a variety of services, but they have always had housing as a central focus. As a result of their strong commitment to build and maintain low-income housing, CDCs have become the main alternative to government-owned public housing for low-income people.

At the national level, the federal government created the Department of Housing and Urban Development (HUD) in 1965 as part of President Johnson's War on Poverty. The goal of HUD was to provide "a decent, safe, and sanitary home and suitable living environment for every American," and the secretary of HUD was given a seat on the president's cabinet. Three years later, President Johnson and Congress felt compelled to respond to the murder of Dr. Martin Luther King Jr., and within seven days of his assassination, they enacted the Civil Rights Act of 1968. In the months before his assassination, Dr. King was planning to bring 4,000 nonviolent protestors to Washington, DC, as part of the Poor People's Campaign, with the demand of 5 million new housing units to be built in ten years. When King was murdered, civil disturbances and riots broke out in over

100 cities across the nation, and in response, Johnson and Congress passed the Civil Rights Act of 1968.[17]

This bill, also known as the Fair Housing Act, ended discrimination in housing, making it illegal to refuse to sell or rent a dwelling to a person because of his or her race, color, or national origin. As George Romney, the HUD secretary from 1969 to 1973, stated in a confidential memo to his aides, there was a "high-income white noose" that was placed around the inner city where black and brown people lived, and it was the hope of Romney to use this new bill to remake America's housing patterns. Romney's efforts, known as "open communities," used the Fair Housing Act's language to "affirmatively further" fair housing by withholding HUD funding to white neighborhoods unless discriminatory zoning practices were ended and more low-income housing was built in white communities. President Nixon did not support Romney's effort to integrate the suburbs, stating to his aides that they needed to "stop this one." Nixon called on HUD to end "open communities," and eventually Romney decided that his services were no longer needed as secretary of HUD since Nixon was "no longer interested in my counsel and advice."[18]

In addition, the Fair Housing Act set a ten-year target of constructing or rehabilitating 26 million housing units, with 6 million of them for the poor. A key difference with these low-income units was that they would be constructed using a more market-based approach. By the early 1970s, conservatives and the housing industry successfully shifted the nation's housing policy away from a supply-based model of large-scale housing projects that were government owned and toward a demand-based model that was privately owned but federally subsidized. This new public-private partnership built new housing units through tax incentives, low-cost mortgages, and rent subsidies to private developers. In exchange, the private developers were required to rent these new housing units to low- and moderate-income people for twenty years, after which they could rent the units on the open market. President Nixon promoted this market approach to housing, and it led to the development of 1 million units of affordable housing between 1974 and 1983.

The other component of this demand-based model was to increase the number of people who could afford housing, which was now seen as the number-one housing problem. In 1974, President Nixon created a housing voucher plan—informally known as Section 8—which provided low-income households the ability to obtain affordable housing in privately owned apartments. This program now serves 2 million people and is one of the nation's main initiatives to provide low-income housing. As part of Section 8, tenants pay 30 percent of their income to landlords, and the federal housing vouchers cover the difference so that landlords still receive market value. The voucher program serves adults with children (41 percent), disabled adults (29 percent), seniors (19 percent), and childless adults (10 percent). Seventy-five percent of voucher recipients are extremely low income households (i.e., earning 30 percent or below the average median income). However, instead of fixing the nation's housing policy, the demand-based model came with its own set of problems. First, the actual number of housing units built was 1 million, which did not come close to the lofty goal of 6 million set by the Fair Housing Act. Congress learned its lesson and would never again put actual targets on the number of houses to be built. Second, the privatized model led to large-scale corruption. By 1975, hundreds of private developers, appraisers, and government agents were charged with bribery, kickbacks, and falsification of government statements regarding a building's value, and almost 500 people were convicted.[19] These housing abuses, which continued into the 1980s, weakened support for public housing, even though the recipients of public housing were not involved. Yet, in many ways, the mid- to late-1970s was the nadir for federal investment in housing for low- and moderate-income people. From 1970 to 1980, the number of low- and moderate-income households receiving federal assistance rose from 1 million to 3 million. In 1977, HUD's budget authority for subsidized housing programs—which are commitments made on future housing assistance—was $78.2 billion, and HUD made housing commitments to 392,103 new renters. In that same year, Congress passed the Community Reinvestment Act, which was enacted to encourage banks to invest in low- and moderate-income communities, many of which were communities of color since banks had historically redlined these communities by not providing them loans.[20]

Up to this point, the right to decent housing had been the nation's guiding principle; with the election of President Reagan in 1980, all of this changed. For the previous fifty years, conservatives and liberals may have argued over what was the most effective housing policy (e.g., demand-based or supply-based models), but both parties agreed that the federal government had a role to play in securing this right. Under Reagan, there was little to no support for the right to housing, or for any federal housing policy whatsoever. Reagan's deputy secretary for HUD summed up this change of policy when he stated, "We're basically backing out of the business of housing, period." These words were backed by action, as HUD's budget authority for subsidized housing programs was cut 80 percent to $13.7 billion by 1989. In addition, new housing commitments made to renters were cut by 310,397, and entire projects, such as the project-based housing program, were eliminated. In many ways, Reagan's philosophy was to return to the pre–New Deal Era, with no federal support for housing.[21]

In response, housing advocates and congressional Democrats fought back. In 1987, Congress passed the Low Income Housing Tax Credit of 1987, a market-based model to increase production of low-income housing units by private developers and nonprofit organizations by providing a dollar-for-dollar reduction in taxes for ten years. Since its inception, it has become one of the main sources of funding for low-income housing, providing money for about 100,000 low-income units per year. Unfortunately, this increase in units has not kept pace with the number of units lost per year, as over 2 million units were lost due to demolition or removal from the rental market between 1993 and 2003. These units were demolished or withdrawn because the owners could charge higher rents outside the program or because they lacked enough capital to make the necessary repairs.[22]

Congress also passed in 1987 the McKinney-Vento Homeless Assistance Act, which arranged for grants to states to provide emergency shelter for the burgeoning homeless population, which many housing advocates blamed on the Reagan budget cuts. The early approaches focused on providing for the immediate needs of the people, so soup kitchens and shelters were opened. As the homeless crisis continued into the late 1980s and mid-1990s, over 40,000 programs were developed, and they offered a variety of services, but only a handful of them concentrated on housing.[23]

By 1992, housing advocates were able to restore some of the housing cuts from the Reagan era. The number of federally subsidized rental units had increased to 4.7 million in 1992, up from 2.9 million in 1980. In addition, HUD's actual outlays of housing assistance had increased from $15 billion in 1980 to $20 billion in 1992. And while the 1990s saw an increase in total funding for housing assistance—up to $30 billion in 2000—spending as part of the percent of the federal deficit was flat, rising just 1 percent. In fact, commitments made to new renters for housing assistance dropped in this decade, from 68,737 to 27,285. At the same time, President Clinton did initiate a major new program, HOPE VI, which was a public-private venture based on the New Urbanism model of building mixed-income housing that was friendly to pedestrians, accessible to transit, and dense. This mixed-income housing model was designed to eliminate the worst of the public housing projects with rental housing of townhomes, duplexes, and detached row-style homes, which would allow for daily interaction with people on the street. According to Michael Kelly, the executive director of the Philadelphia Housing Authority, the goal was to "have the welfare recipient next to the school teacher next to the doctor, and you can't tell who's who from the outside." From 1996 to 2010, HOPE VI grants produced 107,800 new housing units, with 56,800 units affordable for low-income people. HOPE VI grants also demolished 96,200 "severely distressed" public housing units. Some housing activists and residents did not oppose the demolition; rather, they opposed HUD's decision not to replace the units at a one-to-one ratio. Once again, the nation's housing policy destroyed more housing units than it built.[24]

On the positive, HOPE VI has improved housing quality and sense of safety. For example, in Philadelphia's HOPE VI housing, crime rates fell 63 percent and the drug problems that were connected with the six housing projects that were demolished and replaced have been greatly reduced. On the negative, HOPE VI did not replace housing units on a one-to-one ratio, so there is less affordable housing than before. In Philadelphia, one HOPE VI development has less than 50 percent of the units it used to have, and another development has less than 33 percent of the residents it originally had. This pattern in HOPE VI projects has been replicated across the nation. Furthermore, HOPE VI has not helped residents move off of rental assistance, as only 5 percent of the recipients no longer require housing assistance. HOPE VI might provide a new home to some, but it has not solved the other issues of poverty, such as a living-wage job.[25]

Another goal of President Clinton's New Urbanism was that more people would have the ability to purchase single-family homes. As a part of this effort, Clinton worked to loosen the standards to which low- and moderate-income people could access credit. While this did increase the amount of housing available to people with low to moderate incomes in the late 1990s and early 2000s, it would have negative consequences during the Great Recession, as these are the people who lost their homes in record numbers during the foreclosure crises.[26]

In the past decade, it has been a fight to just maintain the status quo. During 2001–2008, Congress rejected most of President George W. Bush's proposed housing cuts. More recently, President Obama has put forward more money for housing assistance, but he has been continually rebuffed by Congress. In 2013, the nation was left with 1.2 million public housing units, where the government covers operating expenses, as well as two types of Section 8 rental assistance programs covering 3.3 million families that subsidize units that are privately owned. The vast majority of these 5 million households are extremely low income (making one-third of the AMI), over one-half are disabled or elderly, and more than one-third have children. Sadly, Congress cut federal housing assistance by $2.5 billion, or 6 percent, from 2010 to 2012. This lack of investment in low-income housing makes it possible for only one-quarter of all eligible families to receive federal housing assistance. Thus, while 5 million low-income families currently receive federal housing assistance, 15 million eligible low-income families received no assistance.[27]

It should be noted that the federal government does have a strong housing policy for people in the middle to upper classes, and it is mostly carried out through the home mortgage deduction. This tax deduction allows home owners the ability to subtract the interest payments on their home mortgages directly from their gross income, providing home owners a tax break worth thousands of dollars. In total, this deduction equals almost $90 billion, which is three times the amount spent on affordable housing assistance. Incredibly, home owners in the top income brackets receive the majority of this housing support, with more than 50 percent going to annual incomes above $100,000. In addition, if you include the other tax breaks (i.e., capital gains exclusion, real estate tax deductions, and other tax benefits), the federal expenditure for home ownership is almost $200 billion. This disparity has led to a situation where high-income families ($200,000 or more) are receiving $7,014 a year, in comparison to low-income families ($20,000 or less), who are receiving just $1,471 a year.[28]

THE RIGHT TO A DECENT HOME: CURRENT APPROACHES

On some level, the solution to housing is straightforward: abolish poverty through public works and a guaranteed income, and pay a living wage so that working-class and poor Americans can afford housing. As Dr. King noted, "We are likely to find that the problems of housing and education, instead of preceding the elimination of poverty, will themselves be affected if poverty is first abolished. The poor transformed into purchasers will do a great deal on their own to alter housing decay." Thus, in order to have decent housing for all, the United States must create policies that guarantee a job, an income, and a living wage.[29]

King's perspective is also in alignment with today's advocates who say that the United States doesn't have a housing crisis since there are enough units right now for all Americans to live in. Cathy Albisa, executive director of the National Economic and Social Rights Initiative, argues this point when she states, "This crisis is not a housing crisis, because we have excess housing in this country, but a human rights crisis." The facts on the ground bear this out. According to the 2012 US Census Bureau, the United States has 132 million housing units available, with 114 million units occupied, which leaves 18.4 million units open. If poverty were abolished as suggested by Dr. King, millions would be able to pay for their own rent or mortgage, and the "housing crisis" would be solved.[30]

Yet, not all advocates are working on the right to decent housing through a guaranteed job and a living wage. Others approach this issue by working specifically on housing. These approaches include (1) building more affordable, low-income housing; (2) creating a dedicated revenue source to fund this construction; (3) providing rental assistance to fill the gap between the cost of housing and what people can afford; (4) stopping foreclosures; and (5) enacting Rapid Re-Housing policies for people without homes. What connects many of these efforts is that they operate from the principle that all Americans have a right to decent, affordable housing.

Today, many community groups and organizations are working to build more affordable housing units. They utilize both for-profit developers and nonprofit organizations, and generally have adopted the mixed-income model. On the positive, the mixed-income model has provided quality housing for tens of thousands of households throughout the nation. At the same time, some housing advocates are concerned that not enough of these units are targeted at extremely low-income and very low-income people (30 to 50 percent AMI). Generally, a housing development will offer only a handful of the units to these groups. Deborah Austin, representing the National Low Income Housing Coalition, is concerned that the low-income and extremely low-income groups do not get the same access to units in a mixed-income development as moderate-income families (80 to 120 percent AMI) since the latter may receive preferential treatment. Austin states that her organization is not opposed to utilizing mixed-income housing as one of the solutions to affordable housing but has "always stood for the proposition that when you have scarce resources, you want to get the money out to those with the greatest need."[31]

As stated earlier, community development corporations provide the greatest opportunities for low-income people since they have a strong commitment to build and maintain low-income housing. Currently, there are 4,600 CDCs, and on average, they are building 87,000 housing units a year. The average CDC staff size is ten, and the average length of time they have been in business is eighteen years. Over the past forty years, they have built or rehabilitated 1.25 million units, or about one-third of all the affordable housing in the nation. In addition to building affordable housing, CDCs have created more than 750,000 jobs. This increase of housing, jobs, and services has enhanced low-income communities across the nation, as 65 percent of the people that CDCs work with are very low-income or extremely low-income. In a study of twenty-three cities, CDCs have significantly improved multiple neighborhoods in eight cities, greatly improved one neighborhood in eleven cities, and had a block-by-block impact in the other four cities. Most of the CDC funding comes from the federal government, but they also receive funding from state and local governments, as well as from local banks as part of the Community Reinvestment Act.[32]

Two of the most successful CDCs are the New Community Corporation and Chicanos Por La Causa. The New Community Corporation (NCC) was founded in Newark, New Jersey, after the 1967 urban riots that killed twenty-six people and damaged $15 million worth of property. The underlying cause of the riots was the deplorable housing conditions and poverty faced by the predominantly African American community in Newark. After the riots, William Linder, a Catholic priest, and a group of Newark residents conducted a needs assessment in the community. Their work led to the creation of the NCC, which decided to focus on rebuilding the housing units that were destroyed in the riots. The NCC's board of directors, composed of inner-city residents from the Central Ward, decided that the goal of the NCC would be "to develop safe, decent, and attractive housing for poor residents in a new community within the Central Ward." The NCC identified a forty-five-acre tract of land—fourteen city blocks—in the center of the community to build the new housing units. Forty-five years later, the NCC owns and operates over 2,000 housing units for low-income families and seniors. Yet, the NCC realized it had to do more than build housing if it was to solve the social problems caused by poverty. Reflecting upon those early days of the NCC, Monsignor Linder states, "We looked at the whole person and knew that housing was basic, but certainly not enough to sustain someone and help them get ahead in life. . . . That is where things like job training, education, and health care came into play." Thus, the NCC developed a workforce development center to train residents to be automobile mechanics and health care workers. In addition, the NCC developed two charter schools (K–5 and K–8) for 800 students, child day care facilities, a 180-bed nursing home that serves Medicaid patients, a credit union, and youth programs.[33]

Chicanos Por La Causa is another CDC that builds housing, as well as provides a host of other services. Currently, it manages 4,000-plus units of affordable housing in Arizona. Chicanos Por La Causa has a variety of housing services, which include counseling services on how to buy a home, building of single-family homes for low-income families, and renting an apartment to low-income seniors and families from the eighteen complexes that it owns. Chicanos Por La Causa also helps families with a down payment to buy a home. Tillie Arvizu, a staff member for Chicanos Por La Causa, argues, "Home ownership is one of the best financial decisions a person can make, and that is why it is so important for us to assist families that may not have been able to afford to own a home." In addition, Chicanos Por La Causa owns a construction company and a credit union with over 2,000 members, operates three charter schools, runs a domestic violence shelter, provides elderly services, and produces a Spanish-language radio program focusing on issues facing the community. In total, Chicanos Por La Causa employs 750 people and serves 100,000 people a year.[34]

As impressive as this work is, a criticism of CDCs is that they spend their time competing with each other for limited government funding, which takes away from the larger question that there is not enough money to fund all of the necessary housing projects. In order to solve this problem, advocates have worked to create a dedicated revenue source to fund the construction of affordable, decent housing for all. In 2008, housing advocates convinced Congress to create the National Housing Trust Fund with the goal of providing grants to states to rehabilitate and build rental housing for extremely low- and very low-income households, including the homeless. The National Housing Trust Fund is designed to support financially the forty state trust funds and 625 city trust funds that have been developed over the past two decades. Together, these state and city trust funds have dedicated $1 billion each year to affordable housing. However, these trust funds would be able to build even more units, and get closer to providing affordable housing for all, if they had sufficient funds. Unfortunately, Congress has yet to fund the National Housing Trust Fund. From 2010 to 2013, President Obama requested $1 billion for the fund, but each year Congress has rejected his request. In 2014, Obama once again has proposed $1 billion for the National Housing Trust Fund; Congress has yet to take action.[35]

At the same time, there are even more ambitious plans than Obama's proposal for the National Housing Trust Fund. For example, the National Low Income Housing Coalition is supporting the Common Sense Housing Investment Act (House Resolution [HR] 6677), which would provide over $15 billion a year annually to the National Housing Trust Fund. Introduced by Rep. Keith Ellison (D-MN) in December 2012, HR 6677 would fund the trust fund by changing the mortgage income deduction to a 20 percent tax credit, and capping the deduction at $500,000 instead of $1 million, which it is presently at. This reform would expand the rewards of the mortgage income deduction from 43 million to 60 million households, with 92 percent of the people to receive an increase making below $100,000. Supporters of HR 6677 also point to the fact that an expanded trust fund would lead to the creation of thousands of new construction jobs. Ellison's bill died in committee and was reintroduced into Congress in 2013 as HR 1213.[36]

Whether the United States creates a dedicated revenue source to fund affordable housing will largely depend on community activism. Dr. King once said that *power* is getting one's opponents to say "yes" when they want to say "no." In the case of housing, there are many powerful interest groups, such as businesses, developers, and residents, who oppose affordable housing. It is up to civically engaged residents and housing organizations to develop enough power by bringing together enough community stakeholders to overcome this opposition. Today, community groups around the nation are doing this. For example, Housing LA, a coalition composed of tenants, a local CDC, social service organizations, nonprofit organizations, and faith communities, is advocating to restore funding of the city's Housing Trust Fund to $100 million a year, which Housing LA had helped create in 2000 to build low-income housing. In the past five years, public funding for affordable housing in Los Angeles has been cut $72 million. In January 2013, this coalition held a forum for candidates running for mayor to address these demands, and it drew a standing-room only crowd of 500 people. The struggle to publicly finance low-income housing continues today in Los Angeles, as well as in almost every city and state throughout the nation, and successes will only occur when these housing advocates develop enough community power.[37]

The same housing advocates pushing for the building of more affordable housing units through trust funds are also involved in protecting units from conversion to high-priced condominiums and stopping demolitions. Every year, 200,000 housing units are either converted to market rents or demolished. In San Francisco, tenants, many of them elderly, attended a January 2013 county supervisor hearing to oppose new legislation to convert 2,000 rental units into high-priced condominiums; happily, the seniors and housing advocates were successful at defeating this plan. In Illinois, the Chicago Housing Initiative (CHI), which was formed in 2007 to preserve and expand low-income housing, held a news conference in October 2012 to ask Mayor Rahm Emanuel to stop the planned demolition of 1,800 public housing units. With nearly 60,000 low-income people on the Chicago Housing Authority (CHA) waiting list, CHI argued that it was wrong to destroy the limited public housing units already built.[38]

As part of this struggle, CHI held a protest in December 2012 in front of the public housing units to be demolished and replaced with a mixed-income community. CHI was opposed to the small number of units that were to be made available to the public housing tenants, which was specified at 400 out of 1,200 units. When Kerry Dickson, a spokesperson for the developer, was asked why 800 units were for sale at market rates, she responded, "It's the development team's opinion that this is the best income mix to create a successful mixed-income community." However, the tenants and advocates disagree with this low number of units for the current residents and are pushing for more low-income housing to be included. Generally, what tenants and housing activists want is a one-for-one replacement of the public housing units. Rep. Maxine Waters (D-CA) introduced a bill into the House of Representatives for a one-to-one replacement, but it died in committee. The National Housing Law Project is currently working on this one-for-one replacement of public housing units.[39]

A third approach to bring the United States closer to a constitutional commitment for decent housing for all is to increase rent subsidies to meet the need. Today, the United States spends $29 billion—75 percent of HUD's budget—on housing assistance, which is just one cent out of every dollar spent by the federal government. This investment to house the nation's most vulnerable citizens covers only one out of four households eligible for assistance. Clearly, this amount needs to be increased. The two main housing assistance programs are Section 8 Housing Choice Vouchers, which serves approximately 2 million households, and the project-based rental assistance program, which serves 1.3 million. Vouchers can be used with any landlord that accepts them, whereas the project-based rental assistance program provides subsidized housing at apartment complexes designated for affordable housing.[40]

This need for rental assistance appears whenever local housing authorities make available the possibility of new Section 8 vouchers. In May 2012, the local housing authority in Dallas offered residents the opportunity to be added to a waiting list for vouchers. It was the first such offer in five years, and 21,000 people applied for 5,000 vouchers. In that same year in Plano, Texas, 8,000 people applied for 100 housing vouchers. In Oakland, California, the local housing authority offered vouchers in 2011 for the first time in five years, and 55,000 people applied for 10,000 vouchers. In Atlanta, Georgia, the local housing authority offered vouchers in 2010 for the first time in eight years, and 30,000 people, some waiting for two days in line, lined up at a shopping center for a chance to get on the waiting list.[41]

One solution would be to increase the amount of rental assistance to cover the other four-fifths of the people eligible for it. However, there is no political will to do this presently, so once again, it will take greater public action to increase the funding to even get close to the need. Unfortunately, the opposite has been occurring recently, as funding remained flat in the first decade of the twenty-first century, even though the need for housing assistance has gone up by 40 percent. In 2010–2012, the funding for these housing assistance programs was even cut by $2.5 billion, or about 6 percent. In reality, housing advocates are just trying to maintain the level of funding rather than move closer to any commitment to housing for all. Yet, there are some new initiatives, like the one put forward by the Center on Budget and Policy Priorities to create a federal renter's credit. As noted earlier, home owners in the top income bracket receive over 50 percent of all federal spending on housing benefits. To change this policy so that federal housing support goes to those who are rent burdened rather than to those who can afford housing without subsidies, the Center on Budget and Policy Priorities is promoting a plan to revise the tax code so that renters would receive a tax credit, just as home owners receive a credit on their home mortgage interest payments. It is estimated that a renters' credit capped at $5 billion would lift 250,000 renters out of poverty since it would cut their rent payments by $400 a month. It would also reduce the number of very low-income households who are paying more than 50 percent of their income on housing by 700,000.[42]

A fourth approach to bringing the nation closer to decent housing for all is to stop foreclosures. Some are calling for a New Deal–like mortgage relief program, while others are blocking foreclosures through nonviolent action and demanding banks provide principal reduction; still others are occupying foreclosed homes. Today, 5 million homes have been repossessed in the past six years, with over 5 million more households still in the foreclosure process. President Obama's response has been the Home Affordable Modification Program (HAMP), which is a voluntary effort that provides incentives to lenders to modify mortgages. In the first three years of the program, HAMP has helped to modify 802,000 loans and has used only $3.2 billion of the $30 billion the 2008 financial rescue package provided. In light of the 5 million houses foreclosed on, and the 5 million still in process, some have criticized Obama's plan as too tepid and have called for stronger action. One of the groups calling for a stronger response is the Roosevelt Institute. David Woolner, a senior fellow at the institute, has called for a New Deal response to the foreclosure crisis, whereby the federal government would provide direct assistance to home owners who were threatened with foreclosure. This program would work like Roosevelt's Home Owners' Loan Corporation (HOLC), which was introduced in 1933 and within three years had refinanced 20 percent of all urban mortgages at the cost in today's dollars of $750 billion. The new HOLC would acquire the delinquent mortgages from the banks, and in return provide government bonds. The HOLC would then work closely with the home owners who own the mortgages and design a case-by-case solution. In 2008, Rep. Mark Kirk (R-IL) proposed a new HOLC that would offer refinance options so that home owners could remain in their homes rather than be foreclosed on. Kirk called this $25 billion investment a win-win position, since the lenders would be paid and the home owners would remain in their houses. In addition, the taxpayers will be repaid at the end of the crisis. However, this proposal died in committee. Currently, the advocacy group DEMOS is promoting the HOLC as a solution. Importantly, DEMOS argues that a new HOLC will be able to help the home owners that have strong credit ratings refinance, while helping those who do not have strong credit ratings to obtain significant principal reduction of their mortgage, something that the federal government has been unwilling to support.[43]

Other groups are calling for principal reduction and a stop to post-foreclosure evictions, and they are using nonviolent action to take their demands directly to the banks. In nine cities across Massachusetts and Rhode Island, tenants and home owners have created local bank tenant associations (BTAs) to fight back against the banks that are evicting them at the end of the foreclosure process. The BTAs argue that the banks, which caused the housing crash to occur, received a bailout, but the home owners who have been foreclosed on and evicted from their houses have received little help. The Boston BTA has been working with City Life/Urbana Vida, a grassroots social justice organization with a forty-year history in Boston, and together they have helped hundreds of families remain in their homes by negotiating with the lender for principal reduction. To convince the bank to negotiate with the owner who is about to be evicted, they use a nonviolent strategy of window signs, a letter writing campaign to the bank, and eviction blockades. The eviction blockades are the most dramatic, as fifty-plus tenant members gather at the house at the time of eviction and stand in front of the doorways in order to block the police as they attempt to carry out the eviction. At the same time, they are in communication with the bank, asking them to stop the eviction and to negotiate with the home owner. In addition, the Boston BTA works with Boston Community Capital, a community development financial institution, and they attempt to buy the foreclosed home and sell it back to the original owner. In 2012, Alma Harris, a second-grade teacher for thirty years, had her mortgage reduced 37 percent when Boston Community Capital bought her foreclosed home for $197,000 and then sold it back to her. Alma's original mortgage was a sub-prime loan at $324,000, and she states, "I tried to pay, but I couldn't afford $3,000 a month."[44]

The Occupy movement has also been involved in resisting foreclosures by "occupying" homes when owners have been foreclosed on and faced eviction. In 2012, Occupy activists in Minnesota helped Monique White renegotiate her mortgage with US Bank, camping outside of her home as well as moving into her home to physically stop an eviction. Occupy Minnesota, which up to this point had been a largely white, college-educated movement, gained more credibility in the African American community when its members supported White on the north side of Minneapolis, a predominantly black community that has suffered 40 percent of the foreclosures in the city despite comprising just 13 percent of the population. White, a single mother who works two jobs, had her house sold secretly by the bank at a sheriff's sale while she was in the process of attaining a loan modification. In addition to occupying Monique White's home, Occupy activists collected 6,500 signatures opposing her eviction, and picketed in front of the home of US Bank CEO Richard Davis and at US Bank branch offices. After a six-month struggle, US Bank agreed to renegotiate White's loan at a rate that was equal to the price of housing in her neighborhood post–Great Recession. Nick Espinosa from Occupy Minnesota reflected, "It is amazing that how when we shine a light with the attention that we have been getting on cases like Monique's ... how quickly these banks are actually able to negotiate with home owners, when across the country with people who are facing this crisis, they are completely unwilling." Currently, Occupy Minnesota is working with dozens of families in Minneapolis and throughout the state to renegotiate mortgages with their lenders. However, Nick believes that in order to solve this problem, a grand bargain is necessary with the banks. As Monique White pointed out, "The banks got bailed out. . . . So why aren't they willing to work with home owners and bail them out and rewrite their loans?"[45]

This focus on who got bailed out and who got left out and evicted is a central concern of these housing activists. They are outraged that the banks and lenders have provided loan modifications for only one in four home owners that have applied for them. At the start of the Home Affordable Modification Program, the Obama administration made available $75 billion, but in the first three years of the program it had only spent $1 billion on loan modifications. According to Nell Myhand from Causa Justa/Just Cause, the behavior of the banks and lenders has caused "a devastating transfer of wealth from black and brown communities to the 1%."[46]

In response to this frustration that the banks and lenders are foreclosing and evicting both home owners and renters (40 percent of all evictions happen to renters), local organizations have created a network under the banner of "Take Back the Land." Organizations that are part of this national network are "dedicated to elevating housing to the level of a human right and securing community control over land." Securing the land means that they work to put houseless families into foreclosed homes that are empty, essentially occupying or squatting on the land. However, Take Back the Land sees it as "liberating homes" from the banks.[47] J. R. Fleming from the Chicago Anti-Eviction Campaign recognizes that these actions, which have put numerous families into homes in Atlanta, Chicago, and New York, are illegal, but he believes they are justifiable. He states, "The banks have taken so much from people that it is about time that the people take something from the banks. It was illegal for blacks and whites to eat together, to dine together, to sit together, to walk together, to talk together, but it was something that was morally right. So people tell us that it is illegal for us to occupy our homes, it is illegal to take back our land. They are right, it is illegal, but it is morally right."

Fifth, decent housing for all would mean that homelessness in the United States would no longer exist. Homelessness, at its root, is the inability of a person to afford housing. Clearly, the best way to prevent homelessness is public works, a guaranteed income, and a living wage. However, until the first two constitutional commitments are enacted, other solutions must be explored. Some of these solutions have been discussed earlier in this chapter, such as building enough low-income housing units, providing enough Section 8 housing vouchers, and stopping foreclosures. If these were done, homelessness could be ended. Homelessness could also be ended if more money were budgeted. Mark Johnston, a top HUD official, recently asserted it is possible to end homelessness if the United States spent $20 billion a year rather than just the $1.9 billion that is currently budgeted for homelessness. He also stated that one of the most effective ways to end homelessness is through a Rapid Re-Housing model.[48]

Rapid Re-Housing, also known as Housing First or permanent supportive housing, was developed in 1988 in Los Angeles by Beyond Shelter and is based on the simple idea of getting homeless people into housing immediately before solving any other problems. The other problems that may have led to the person's homelessness—whether it is lack of job training, financial illiteracy, a criminal record, mental illness, or drug addiction—are to be solved later, after the person or family is placed into housing. Also, there is no precondition to get the housing assistance. After they are in stable housing with a standard lease agreement, a range of services is offered to individuals over the next year, but there is no requirement that they sign up for them. For the people who might need services, it has been found that homeless individuals and families are often more open to them after they regain some control over their lives. And for the majority of homeless who don't need services, Rapid Re-Housing is ideal because they obtain permanent housing.[49]

The goal of Rapid Re-Housing programs is to get homeless individuals or families into housing as quickly as possible. The program develops a relationship with apartment administrators throughout the city, then helps individuals and families identify units in neighborhoods they want to live

in, offers advice on how to deal with a bad credit history, and negotiates with
the landlords. Rapid Re-Housing programs offer temporary rent subsidies
that are based on a person's income, and are funded through a variety of
federal programs including Temporary Aid to Needy Families (TANF), the
Community Development Block Grant (CDBG), the Home Investment
Partnership Program, and the Emergency Food and Shelter Program, as well
as from faith and business communities, private donors, and foundations.[50]

Rapid Re-Housing has been shown to be successful and cost-effective
in comparison to temporary or emergency housing. In study after study,
Rapid Re-Housing has been more effective at keeping people in housing in
comparison to other strategies. A recent study examined fourteen communities comparing Rapid Re-Housing, transitional housing, and emergency
housing programs. The study found that when individuals enter a Rapid Re-
Housing program, 75 percent move into permanent housing. In comparison,
individuals entering a transitional housing program had 42 percent move
into permanent housing, whereas individuals entering an emergency housing
program only had 16 percent move into permanent housing. When seven
of these communities looked at the recidivism rates, emergency shelters had
the highest rates, with 15 percent individuals and 11 percent families with
children returning to homelessness within one year. In comparison, Rapid
Re-Housing programs had 9 percent individuals and 4 percent families
with kids return to homelessness within the year, while transitional housing
had 7 percent individuals and 9 percent families with children returning to
homelessness. In addition to having some of the lowest recidivism rates, it is
also the least expensive option to move someone to permanent housing. In
the fourteen communities in the study, the average cost of Rapid Re-Housing
to move a single adult into permanent housing was $5,575. In comparison,
the average cost of an emergency shelter program to move a single adult
into permanent housing was $8,283, and $18,876 for a transitional housing
program. Similar results were found with families.[51]

SUMMARY

In order to achieve the right to a decent home, the United States needs to
guarantee the right to a job and living wage, as well as build more low-income
housing, create a dedicated revenue source to fund construction, provide
rental assistance, stop foreclosures, and enact Rapid Re-Housing policies.

Chapter 4

The Right to a Good Education

The Fourth Amendment

PROBLEM

Today, all US children have a right to an education, but whether it is "good" or "not good" depends on which school a student attends. Much of the time, what determines whether a good education is provided to our nearly 50 million public school students is the parents' social class. For students whose families make more than $100,000 a year, or the top 20 percent of household income, they are receiving a good education. However, for the 11 million children who come from families who live in poverty, the great concern is that they are not receiving a good education. A 2013 congressional report states it starkly: "While some young Americans—most of them white and affluent—are getting a truly world-class education, those who attend schools in high poverty neighborhoods are getting an education that more closely approximates school in developing nations."[1]

The reality is that in the United States, there is a tiered structure that offers different educational opportunities and produces different results depending upon social class. Three tiers—top, middle, and bottom— correspond to the upper class, middle and working classes, and the poor. The top tier is for the upper class, and it offers a well-funded system with well-qualified teachers who teach in well-maintained buildings with small class sizes, state-of-the-art technology, and a curriculum that includes art, music, and foreign language and challenges the students to be critical thinkers and leaders. The middle tier is for the middle class and some members of the working class, and it offers a moderately well-funded system that seems to always be under pressure to do more with less, with mostly qualified teachers who teach in adequate buildings with some access to the latest technology and a curriculum and pedagogy that tend to focus on asking students to produce the right answer. The bottom tier is for the poor and other members of the working class, and it is underfunded, with less qualified teachers who teach in buildings that are often in need of repair, with large class sizes, outdated technology, and a curriculum that rarely includes art, music, and foreign language and focuses on following the rules. Currently, more than 17,000 school districts in the United States—17 percent of all US public schools—operate in areas with a high concentration of poverty (i.e., where over 75 percent of students receive free or reduced-price lunches).[2]

The key issue that divides the two ends of the spectrum is school funding, and the extreme inequality that occurs because of this unequal funding can be seen across the nation. For example, in Illinois, the ten wealthiest school districts receive three times the level of funding as the ten poorest districts. This difference in Illinois can be seen in north Chicago: Roundout Elementary spends $24,244 per student while nearby Taft Elementary spends just $7,023 per student. In North Carolina, the ten wealthiest counties in 2011–2012 spent over four times the amount per student than the poorest ten counties; that state's Orange County spent an astounding ten times more per student than Swain County. In New York, the 100 wealthiest school districts spend $8,600 more per student than the 100 poorest school districts. Billy Easton, director of the Alliance for Quality Education, notes that the difference in spending creates "two systems of education: one for the wealthy and one for the poor." In Texas, where there has been a several-decades-long attempt to equalize school funding, the top 15 percent of wealthy districts still provide $2,000 more per year to students than the bottom 15 percent of poorer districts. This difference equals out to about $64,000 per classroom per year.[3]

When states have tried to decrease this gap between rich and poor, the wealthier schools still get around it by having the parents raise money for the schools through an educational foundation. In California, most of the 1,000 school districts have overall revenue limits that cap spending (i.e., property tax and state revenue) at approximately $5,000. However, at La Jolla Elementary near San Diego, California, the parents get around these spending caps by privately raising money for the school foundation. In 2008 and 2009, La Jolla Elementary raised an additional $400,000 per year, which added an additional 10 percent to its budget per year. Just eighteen miles away from La Jolla is Horton Elementary, where things are much different. At Horton, where 90 percent of the students live in poverty and most are English learners, there is no school foundation that is funded with parents' support, and therefore there is no special fund to reduce class size or enrich the curriculum. Wealthier school districts in California also get around funding equalization by taking advantage of the law, which allows districts to use local property taxes to go above what most other school districts can generate from both local and state support. This loophole in the law allows for Rancho Santa Fe students to receive up to $5,800 more for each student in comparison to California students who are in nonwealthy districts. These districts are called "basic aid" districts, and in 2012 there were 127 of them. Basic aid districts are generally in wealthy communities, or in areas that have a wealthy business in the district, such as an oil production facility.[4]

As with most things that are considered high quality, a good education costs money. That is why the upper class makes sure that its schools are well-funded. Historically, American schools have been the responsibility of the local school districts and the state. This has led to a system where local property taxes have been the primary source of funding schools. (Over the past forty years, a series of lawsuits against this unequal funding system has made the states become more involved in funding schools; more about this later in the chapter.) Where housing prices are higher, these communities have been able to generate enough money to more than adequately fund their schools. In contrast, poorer school districts actually tax themselves at higher rates than wealthier districts, but since their houses cost significantly less, the poorer districts end up with far less money for their schools. And let's be clear: The United States doesn't have an education funding problem. In fact, the nation spends more money on K–12 education than all other developed nations except Switzerland. What the United States does have is an inequality problem created by our local and state funding system, which has created vast disparities both between states and within states. Unbeknownst to most Americans, most developed nations do not fund their schools in such a manner; generally, their education funding comes largely from the national government (54 percent on average), which distributes the money on an equal basis, with smaller portions coming from regional (26 percent) and local (22 percent) governments. However, in the United States, only 9 percent of school funding comes from the national government, with the vast majority of funding being provided by the states (47 percent) and by local governments (44 percent).[5]

This educational funding system has led to a system of unequal funding, where wealthy schools provide a stronger curriculum, more qualified teachers, and newer buildings. For example, the difference in school funding means that Roundout Elementary students have the opportunity to enroll in art, band, chorus, dance, drama, and Spanish, while a few miles away at Taft Elementary, the curriculum does not include art or Spanish classes. In Rancho Santa Fe, the district uses the extra funding to reduce class sizes from 32:1 to 17:1, and the district hires art and music specialists to teach. And in La Jolla Elementary, the money raised by the school foundation goes to the art and choral program, classroom technology, additional teachers to lower class sizes, new artificial turf, and school beautification projects. Close by, Horton Elementary has no school foundation, so there are no special funds for classroom reduction, music programs, or artificial turf; rather, Horton has holes in the playground as a result of trees that have died.[6]

In addition to a more robust curriculum and smaller class size, teachers teach differently depending on the social class settings. Jean Anyon, in her classic work *Social Class and the Hidden Curriculum of Work,* showed that in wealthy schools, students are asked to reason through their answers logically, produce top-quality intellectual material, connect the various parts and fit them together into larger systems, and apply that knowledge to solving problems. Students at affluent schools are encouraged to go beyond facts and to think critically about the social or natural world. For example, a fifth-grade social studies teacher at a wealthy school in New Jersey asks the students, "What mistakes did Pericles make after the war? What mistakes did the citizens of Athens make? What are the elements of a civilization? How did Greece build an economic empire? Compare the way Athens chose its leaders with the way we choose ours." Moreover, teachers at affluent schools are interested in having the students apply the knowledge they are gaining. A fifth-grade literature teacher in that same New Jersey school reminded the students, "It is not enough to get these right on tests; you must use what you learn [in grammar classes] in your written and oral work. I will grade you on that." At wealthy schools, little attention is given to regulate the physical movement of the students, as students are often allowed to move around the room without asking permission.[7]

In comparison, schools that are composed of students at or below the poverty line receive a different pedagogy. Often, the teachers there focus on rote behavior and mechanical learning, with attention given to facts rather than critical thinking. At a fifth-grade low-income school in New Jersey, a literature teacher asked her students to write an autobiography by addressing the following questions: "Where were you born?" and "What is your favorite animal?" These factual questions don't allow the students to provide depth and complexity or be creative. Similarly, when students in poor schools were doing math, the teacher provided information in a fragmented manner that did not connect the learning to larger concepts. When discussing how to make a 1-inch grid, a teacher did not explain they were going to make such a grid or that they were going to use it to study scales. This fragmented learning is a far cry from the integrated learning of the affluent schools.[8]

Wealthier school districts also have more qualified teachers—as determined by high academic skills, teaching in the field they received training in, years of experience, and participation in professional development programs—due to the hiring of less-experienced teachers and a higher teacher turnover rate. In the United States, schools with the highest poverty rates have nearly double the amount of inexperienced teachers (three years or less in the classroom)—20 percent to 11 percent—than schools with the lowest poverty rates. High-poverty schools have 34 percent of the classes in high school taught by teachers that are out of their field of knowledge, in comparison to 19 percent in low-poverty schools. In a recent study in Ohio, which is seen as a state that offers a "good education," 81 percent of the teachers in low-poverty schools were deemed "highly qualified" versus 63 percent in low-income schools. In Illinois, a study found an inverse relationship between teacher quality and poverty: As the number of students in poverty in a school increased, the teacher quality decreased. The wealthy schools had only 5 percent of the teachers that received a teacher quality index in the bottom 25 percent. If the school had 30–49 percent of the kids in poverty, 20 percent of the teachers received a teacher quality index in the bottom 25 percent. However, if the school had 90–100 percent of the kids in poverty, a whopping 84 percent of the teachers received a teacher quality index in the bottom 25 percent.[9]

Even the buildings for poorer students are of lower quality. And while buildings by themselves do not guarantee success in school, it is difficult to learn when the roof is leaking, the bathrooms and water fountains don't work, and the room is either too hot or too cold. The cost of updating and modernizing our school buildings is $542 billion, and not surprisingly, the areas that need the greatest amount of work are in high-poverty areas that have old, worn-out school buildings. In schools where more than 50 percent of the children were eligible for free or reduced or school lunches, 34 percent of them were built before 1950. In comparison, in schools where less than 20 percent of the children are eligible for free or reduced school lunches, just 20 percent of them were built before 1950. In addition, these older schools also have more students in them, as there is a direct correlation between the age of the building and the student population. In 2013, former president Bill Clinton wrote, "In a country where public education is meant to serve as the 'great equalizer' for all of its children, we are still struggling to provide equal opportunity when it comes to the upkeep, maintenance, and modernization of our schools and classrooms."[10]

On top of all these advantages, upper class children are the most well-prepared to enter school since the affluent parents have provided them with the cultural capital to be successful at school (e.g., language skills that teachers respect). The wealthy parents have also been able to provide better nutrition and health care, as well as offer a safe and secure environment for their children to grow up in, which all lead to greater probability that their kids will be more alert and curious and better able to interact with their social environment. Moreover, upper-class parents are able to afford tutors, after-school programs, and summer experiences—all of which help children advance academically.

With all the advantages that come from more money—a stronger curriculum, smaller class sizes, more qualified teachers, better buildings, and more family economic resources—it should be no surprise that the wealthy schools have higher test scores and graduation rates. Sometimes this point is obscured, as the mainstream press generally talks about America's schooling as mediocre since national scores on reading, math, and science are in the middle or a bit below average when compared to other industrialized nations. According to the Program for International Student Assessment (PISA), the United States is ranked fourteenth in reading—students have an average PISA score of 500—and twenty-fifth in math—students have an average PISA score of 487—out of seventy-five countries. However, if social class is taken into account, students in affluent schools have an average score of 551, compared to 461 for students in poverty schools. If the affluent test scores are compared to ten countries that have low poverty rates (e.g., Finland [3.4 percent], Denmark [2.4 percent], etc.), the United States is ranked number one in test scores. But if we look at the average reading scores for high-poverty schools, the United States ranks at the very bottom, between Chile's 449 score and Mexico's 425 score. What explains our nation's middling scores on international tests is the high child poverty rate in the United States (22 percent), which leads to a lowering of its overall score. As Dr. Martin Carnoy, a Stanford education professor, points out, "Nations with more lower-social-class students will have lower overall scores, because these students don't perform as well academically, even in good schools."[11]

These higher test scores can be seen within the United States as well. Take a look at the SAT scores, where higher income has a strong positive correlation with higher test scores in writing, math, and critical reasoning. For every $20,000 jump in family income, there is on average a twelve-point increase in each test section, and a forty-four-point increase in the overall SAT score. This positive correlation occurs at *every* income jump from $20,000 to $200,000 and above.[12]

Wealthy schools also have higher graduation rates and college attendance rates, and lower dropout rates. Affluent schools have a 91 percent graduation rate, in comparison to 68 percent for high-poverty schools, with middle-class schools falling in between. At the same time, students from low-income families are five times more likely to drop out of high school than students from high-income families. This has huge implications since people who don't finish high school are more likely to get stuck in low-income jobs with little future for economic advancement. Today, non–high school graduates earn on average $20,241 a year, in comparison to $30,627 for high school graduates. Similar results are found when looking at college attendance, as students enrolled at schools with little poverty have a college attendance rate of 52 percent, versus 28 percent for high-poverty schools. Graduation rates follow the same pattern: 54 percent of upper-income students graduate from college while just 9 percent of poor students graduate. Incredibly, even when poorer students have higher college entrance scores coming into college than wealthier students, it is the wealthier students that graduate at higher rates. Sadly, this problem is getting worse, as the graduation gap between the wealthy and poor has increased by 50 percent over the past twenty years. This has huge ramifications since a college degree is a ticket out of poverty, as the average college graduate in 2012 who worked full time and was between the ages of twenty-five and thirty-nine made $46,900 a year, in comparison to $30,000 a year for a high school graduate and just $22,900 a year for those who didn't complete a high school degree.[13]

Another one of the key issues that divides the two ends of the spectrum is racism. The legacy of slavery and Jim Crow segregationist policies, as well as the continuing racial segregation in housing, has created schools that remain highly segregated. Today, 74 percent of black students and 80 percent of Latino students attend schools where the majority of students are people of color (50–100 percent), and 15 percent of black students and 14 percent of Latino students go to schools where white enrollment is 0 to 1 percent. At the same time, the average white student attends a school where 75 percent of their classmates are also white. Not surprisingly, the schools that students of color attend are predominantly low-income schools, particularly in urban areas, since institutional racism, both historically and presently, has denied equal opportunity and rewards to people of color. This historic and present-day racism has led to high poverty rates for blacks (28 percent), Latinos (25 percent), and Native Americans (28 percent), with relatively low poverty rates for whites (10 percent). Thus, schools with high percentages of people of color also tend to have high poverty due to this correlation between race and poverty. This combination of social class and race allows for the average white student to attend a school that has the lowest amount of poverty. In 2010–2011, just 6 percent of white students attended high-poverty schools. At the same time, the average black and Latino student attended a school where nearly 75 percent of their classmates were low-income.[14]

For years, social science researchers have been studying whether social class or race is the most important indicator to determine inequality. Today, some research suggests that social class is now more important. To support this claim, researchers point to the gap in standardized test scores, which over the past fifty years has decreased between white and black students but increased between affluent and poor students. In fact, the testing gap has gone down by nearly 40 percent for reading between white and black students since the 1960s, but the testing gap has increased by 40 percent between affluent and poor students. Currently, the achievement gap is now twice as large for social class than race. Dr. Sean Reardon, a Stanford professor who has been conducting this education research, concludes, "We have moved from a society in the 1950s and 1960s in which race was more consequential than family income, to one today in which family income appears more determinative of educational success than race."[15]

The nation's poverty and extreme inequality have led to far too many of our students not receiving a "good education." The percentage of eighth-grade students meeting basic standards at high-poverty schools is only 53 percent in reading and 49 percent in math, compared to 87 percent in both reading and math at low-poverty schools. Moreover, the percentage of eighth-grade students that are proficient is just 12 percent in reading and 13 percent in math, compared to 47 percent in reading and 50 percent in math at low-poverty schools. As the 2013 congressional report states, "Ten million students in America's poorest communities—and millions more African-American, Latino, Asian-American, Pacific Islander, American Indian, and Alaska Native students who are not poor—are having their lives unjustly and irredeemably blighted by a system that consigns them to the lowest-performing teachers, the most run-down facilities, and academic expectations and opportunities considerably lower than what we expect of other students." And as President Obama's secretary of education declared, the United States has had fifty years of reform, endless studies, and numerous commitments from politicians, but "we are still waiting for the day when every child in America has a high quality education that prepares him or her for the future."[16]

SOLUTION

The solution to the "wrong" of education inequality is the right to a good education for all. This right is based on the fundamental belief that in a democracy, it is unjust to offer a superior education to some and an inferior education to others, whether it is based on your class, zip code, or race.

Following is a discussion of the history behind the right to a good education, as well as modern-day approaches to achieve this constitutional commitment. These modern-day approaches include equalizing school funding at the state and national levels, attracting and retaining qualified teachers to high-need schools, reducing class size, providing a content-rich curriculum for all and teaching it using an active learning approach, offering the option of charter schools, providing universal preschool for four-year-olds, and integrating schools.

THE HISTORY OF THE RIGHT TO A GOOD EDUCATION

Ever since the founding of the nation, Americans have struggled for the right to a good education for all. Before the American Revolution, people in the original thirteen colonies were concerned about education, and both "fee" and "free" schools were implemented throughout the Atlantic seaboard. The fee schools were mostly for the wealthy and provided a robust liberal arts education, while the free schools were for the poor and offered basic reading, writing, and arithmetic skills. Thus, from the founding of the nation, free schools were stigmatized as being for the poor and were not seen as offering as good of an education as the fee schools. At the same time, there was no requirement that children attend fee or free schools, since it was the common belief that a child's education was ultimately the responsibility of the parents, and they could educate their child in the family, church, or some voluntary association of like-minded citizens.[17]

After the American Revolution, the idea of "free" schools continued to generate interest, as working-class people pushed for the same educational opportunities for all social classes. In the early nineteenth century, labor activists such as Wilson Pierson and George McFarlane argued for a national education system that should be made available to all social classes. Frances Wright, another labor activist and editor of the *Free Enquiry,* took it one step further and argued that wealthy and poor children should be in the same classes in state-sponsored boarding schools—a radical idea then, as well as now. Wright argued that these boarding schools would go beyond just the common school's focus on reading and writing and should incorporate the various branches of intellectual knowledge. Robert Dale Owen, a social reformer and a colleague of Wright's, suggested that if rich and poor attended the same schools, studied the same subjects, and even dressed in similar clothing, "the pride of riches or the contempt of poverty" would be removed. These suggestions from working-class advocates were not implemented, but they inspired future generations of education reformers who believed that the right to a good education meant that all social classes had equal opportunities to it.[18]

By the 1830s, the idea of a free common school that offered basic education had taken root across New England, and it would expand over the next thirty years to the midwestern and northern states. Secondary school, in contrast, was primarily for the wealthy, as it was seen as a precursor to attend college. By the time of the Civil War, states across the country had adopted the idea of a "common" or public school.

Yet things were different in the South, where the idea of free elementary education did not take root as quickly. The main two avenues of education were through "fee schools," which were operated by various church groups for whites who could pay the tuition, and through private tutors. For Southern blacks in the sixteen slave states, education was illegal, and this policy was enforced through fines, whipping, and imprisonment. It was not until after the Civil War that the idea of free public education became commonplace. This idea of free public education was promoted heavily by the Freedmen's Bureau, which was set up by the federal government to deal with the desperate conditions facing African Americans. After the war, freed blacks had little to no food, land, or education. In response, the Freedmen's Bureau delivered 21 million meals and provided medical assistance to over 1 million freed people. Moreover, the Freedmen's Bureau built over 1,000 free schools, and spent over $400,000 on teacher training. By 1870, over 100,000 black children were in free, public elementary schools in the South. In addition, the Freedmen's Bureau built or funded the construction of over fifteen black colleges. Much of the white community opposed these efforts; in the words of W. E. B. Du Bois, the white community viewed "an educated Negro to be a dangerous Negro ... for education among all kinds of men always has had, and always will have, an element of danger and revolution, of dissatisfaction and discontent."[19]

By the late nineteenth century, there were many forces pushing more and more students into the classroom. Importantly, large factories had supplanted agriculture, as industrial capitalism became the dominant economic system. Capitalism created great wealth, but it also created dire poverty. As a result, the poor and working class lived in substandard housing and received inadequate education. Many of these workers were among the 22 million immigrants who had come to the United States from 1890 to 1910 in a great wave of migration. Initially, both the adult immigrants and their children worked in the factories. However, a variety of competing interests moved the children out of the factories and into public schools. First, citizens were concerned that these new immigrants needed to learn American values and speak English, and the public schools became the site where this Americanization process could occur. Second, progressive reformers wanted to end child labor as they thought it was harmful to children's development. Julia Lathrop, the first director of the federal government's Children's Bureau, made this connection between public school and ending child labor when she stated, "The best way to abolish child labor is by compulsory education. We now can take the greatest forward step in our educational history—we can abolish rural child labor and stop the increase of illiteracy by the same measure—a universal compulsory measure for elementary education." With the abolition of child labor, first in states in the late nineteenth and early twentieth centuries and then nationally in 1935, public schools became *the* place for kids to be during work hours. With the parents now in the factory (rather than on the farm as in previous generations), schools ensured that the immigrant children were properly Americanized, and that they would have adult supervision so that they would avoid hanging out all day and getting into trouble with their parents away.[20]

These cross-currents of reform encouraged the development of requiring students to be in class. By 1900, thirty-four out of forty-five states had compulsory education laws, and thirty states required schooling up to fourteen years of age. Initially, the time required in school differed by state. For example, New Jersey required that all students of ages seven to fourteen be in school twenty weeks a year, whereas Kentucky required only eight weeks of school attendance. Even so, the die had been cast; as the nation moved into the mid-twentieth century, attending public school was no longer an option.[21]

The expansion of education advocated by progressive reformers led to a huge increase in the number of schools built and students served in the first part of the twentieth century, particularly in the fast-growing urban centers. By 1940, one-half of all American youth were receiving high school diplomas. Yet, some were arguing that a good education meant more than just having students in school. These progressive educators believed that a good education required a new pedagogy and curriculum. Educators such as John Dewey challenged the idea that all students should learn the same material at a certain time and that it should be done through rote memorization. Rather, Dewey argued that teachers should teach the various course material when the student was emotionally and intellectually ready for it. This child-centered learning strategy focused on students' interests and developmental stages rather than just covering the material that was designed for that specific age. In addition, Dewey thought that education should rely not on rote memorization but on experiential learning. These changes in the classroom meant that the teacher was no longer the "sage on the stage" who dispensed knowledge but "a guide on the side" who facilitated and supported the child's learning process. As Dewey stated, "The teacher is not in the school to impose certain ideas or to form certain habits in the child, but is there as a member of the community to select the influences which shall affect the child and to assist him in properly responding to these. Thus, the teacher becomes a partner in the learning process, guiding students to independently discover meaning within the subject area." Dewey's ideas for a new pedagogy had a major impact on the schools of education that had been set up to teach the new teachers, but they had a limited effect on public schools, which had already developed a bureaucracy that resisted change.[22]

Another progressive idea that did have an influence in the classroom was the idea for a new curriculum that focused on social reform. The Great Depression led to a major rethinking of our institutions, and education was no different. In the field of education, some educators pushed to make the classroom material more socially relevant to its students. George Counts, an education professor at Columbia University, advocated for the development of a curriculum focusing on the improvement of the general welfare of society so as to develop a "strong sense of social obligation." Inspired by his colleague at Columbia, Harold Rugg went on to develop a series of K–12 textbooks examining issues of civic action, class conflict, poverty, and racism. In the early 1930s, Rugg's textbooks were released under such titles as *The Conquest of America* and *Changing Governments and Changing Cultures: The World's March toward Democracy.* Rugg's books were initially well received and by 1939, 5.5 million textbooks were used in over 5,000 school districts. However, conservative groups launched a withering assault against these books, and by the mid-1940s most school districts had abandoned Rugg's socially relevant curriculum.[23]

From the 1950s to the end of the twentieth century, there were several major attempts to provide a good education for all—including the movement to integrate schools, the development of supplemental educational programs as part of the War on Poverty, the campaign to equalize school funding, and the standards and accountability movement. And while some of these have had their share of victories, they have also had limited gains. From the Civil War into the twentieth century, it was the law of the land in many states to segregate black students, as well as Latinos and Asians, in separate schools. And when segregation was not codified into state law, the social norms of the community ensured that schools were segregated by race. The status quo changed in 1954 when the Supreme Court ruled in *Brown v. Board of Education* that it was unconstitutional for local school districts to segregate students by race. While African Americans and supporters of equality and integration cheered the decision, believing that white schools would offer people of color access to schools with better resources, many whites were displeased. In 1955, in what has been called *Brown II,* the Supreme Court issued an enforcement decree to integrate "with all immediate speed." In the South, many states, school districts, and schools decided to resist this ruling in order to delay and even stop integration. Their methods included closing down public schools rather than integrating them, allowing for "token" integration by selecting only a few hand-picked black students to attend the schools while denying entrance to the vast majority of black students, and providing public money for private schooling. In Prince Edward County, Virginia, officials closed down the public schools for four years. The white students moved to private schools, which of course denied admittance to black students. Thus, black students either had to leave the county to enroll in school or were provided no education at all. These private schools came to be known euphemistically as "segregation academies."[24]

Ten years after the *Brown* decision, little progress had been made in integrating schools. In 1964, only 1.2 percent of black students in the South were attending schools with white students. However, with the passage of the Civil Rights Act of 1964, there was a strong commitment to enforcement. The federal government began threatening the state and local authorities that they were going to cut funding to schools that did not integrate. This strategy was successful, as the percent of black students in the South attending schools with a majority population of white students rose to 32 percent by 1968, and to 45 percent by 1976. The South now had the most integrated schools in the nation, as the percent of black students in the Northeast attending schools with a majority population of white students was just 28 percent, while the Midwest had 30 percent. As the federal courts continued to press schools to integrate throughout the mid-1960s and into the 1970s, some white parents abandoned public education altogether, leaving for private schools. From 1964 to 1972, hundreds of these "segregation academies" were created, and today, many still survive, with thirty-five of them in the state of Mississippi alone.[25]

Another strategy the federal courts began to use to quicken integration was busing students to different schools. In the north and west, where segregation was by custom and not law, the federal courts ordered busing programs in hundreds of cities, including Boston, Cleveland, Detroit, Las Vegas, Los Angeles, Kansas City, San Francisco, San Jose, and Wilmington. While most communities grudgingly accepted busing, some white parents resisted, with the strongest opposition coming from Boston, where a series of protests against busing turned violent. As the community protested at school meetings and in the streets, several racially motivated incidents took place, including the stabbing of a white student by a black student at South Boston High School. In response, administrators closed the school for a month, and when it reopened, South Boston High had over 500 police officers guarding it.[26]

As a result of busing, 44 percent of black students in the South attended majority-white schools by 1988, and the impact on these students was positive. A large-scale study conducted for the US Department of Education showed black children in the South had experienced major educational gains in the 1970s, right at the time of large-scale desegregation efforts. The Citizens Commission on Civil Rights has reported that there was "striking evidence of progress in the performance of black children," with the achievement gap between black and white students narrowing by almost 50 percent from 1970 to 1990. In addition, studies have consistently shown that black students who attended integrated schools during this time did better academically, were more likely to graduate from high school and college, and earned more than students who attended segregated schools. Moreover, the longer black students attended integrated schools, the more positive the impact of integration. At the same time, white children did not suffer any negative outcomes. Importantly, this narrowing of the achievement gap did not occur because blacks and Latinos had the opportunity to sit next to whites, but because they were getting more access to highly qualified teachers and advanced courses. At the same time, parents of all races didn't like busing because it resulted in the loss of neighborhood schools and could be a hassle to have your child bused to another part of town. However, the price was highest for blacks, as their kids generally spent more time on the buses, black teachers were most likely to be fired when schools merged, and black schools were most likely to be closed.[27]

By the 1980s, conservative activists and the Reagan administration were working to end busing, arguing for "color-blind policies" that returned local control to the school districts. Earlier, in 1972, President Nixon had tried to convince Congress to ban busing but was unsuccessful. Two years later, the Supreme Court severely restricted busing by blocking a Detroit plan that was designed to bus city kids across district lines to suburban schools. The attacks against busing culminated in the 1991 Supreme Court decision to allow federal judges to more easily terminate their supervision of school systems and to end busing if judges determined that a school board had eradicated "vestiges of past discrimination ... to the extent practicable," even if it meant that some neighborhood schools would remain segregated. This Supreme Court decision began the process of judges releasing school districts from desegregation court orders. By 2012, more than 200 school districts out of the almost 500 school districts under the jurisdiction of federal judges had been released. Surprisingly, research shows that many school districts were released even though they had high levels of segregation. Not surprisingly, once released from court oversight, 85 percent of the school districts became even more segregated. However, some schools, like Jefferson County Public Schools in Louisville, Kentucky, decided to continue desegregation policies voluntarily, while others adopted to integrate voluntarily, like the Seattle School District. Then, in 2007, the Supreme Court ruled that these voluntary plans were unconstitutional under the Fourteenth Amendment's Equal Protection Clause because they had categorized individual students by race when making individual school assignments. However, the Supreme Court left open the door for future desegregation plans that would allow for race to be one of the considerations of a voluntary diversity plan but which avoided classifying individual students by race.[28]

The result of all of these social forces—white flight from public schools, the decline of busing, the narrowing of voluntary desegregation plans, the expanding Latino population, and the persistent but slowly declining residential segregation for African Americans—has led to a shocking outcome: today, public schools are more segregated than before the 1954 Supreme Court decision to integrate schools. Forty percent of all black and Latino students attend public schools where there are few to no white students. In California, the most diverse state in the nation, 50 percent of all blacks and Asians, and 25 percent of all Latinos, attend highly segregated schools. In rural America, 73 percent of white students attend schools that are almost all white. The South, which led the nation in integration from the 1970s through the late 1980s, has resegregated once again. In 1988, 44 percent of black students in the South attended majority-white schools; today, less than 27 percent do, whereas nearly 50 percent of white students attend all-white schools. And in

Boston, the epicenter of northern white resistance to busing, 85 percent of the students are now black or Latino, with only 15 percent being white. In fact, Latinos attend the most highly segregated schools in the nation. Currently, there is little energy for a second attempt to integrate American schools, with most education advocates pushing for "equity" rather than integration.[29]

Another attempt to provide a good education for all in the second half of the twentieth century was the education programs started during the War on Poverty. As the civil rights movement turned its attention to economic justice, President Johnson also changed focus from ending legal segregation to ending poverty. Interestingly, Johnson's strategy for the War on Poverty focused primarily on education. According to Sargent Shriver, the first director of the Office of Economic Opportunity (OEO), the goal of the War on Poverty was "to offer the poor a job, an education, a little better place to live." Shriver and the other War on Poverty architects argued that poverty was not caused by a defect in the economy but was instead the result of blocked opportunity. Thus, the cure for poverty was to remove barriers that blocked opportunity, such as racism and a lack of education. Not surprisingly, one of the main strategies of the War on Poverty was through education since the Johnson administration held that poor people were culturally deprived and, as a response, had developed a "culture of poverty."

The solution to this perceived deficit of cultural skills and weak family support structure was to increase educational opportunities. Thus, the War on Poverty started such programs as Head Start, Follow Through, Upward Bound, Job Corps, and VISTA. Head Start focused on getting children "school ready" and offered a so-called comprehensive preschool program, which included intellectual stimulation, nutritious food, and health care. Follow Through built on the work of Head Start by providing similar services through the first three years of school. For teenagers, Upward Bound was created to prepare the youth for college, while Job Corps was designed for young adults who did not complete high school and needed a vocational training program. Lastly, for college graduates, Volunteers in Service to America (VISTA) was established, which was a domestic Peace Corps program. Several of these programs have been very successful and are still in operation, such as Head Start, which has demonstrated that students who complete this early childhood education program are more likely to complete high school, have lower crime rates, and have fewer teenage pregnancies. Head Start has been particularly effective when it has been well funded and the interaction between teachers and students has been intense.[30]

With the passage of the Civil Rights Act of 1964 and Voting Rights Act of 1965, which removed institutional racist barriers, and with the additional education obtained through the War on Poverty's new programs, the vision was that everyone would now be allowed to compete equally for the rewards of society. The Johnson administration and other liberal advocates argued that this was the best strategy to create equality of opportunity and to end poverty. However, President Johnson's "unconditional war on poverty" did not end material want. First, not enough money was spent on Johnson's War on Poverty programs to end poverty. For example, full funding for Head Start has never been provided, and even today, still about 60 percent of all preschoolers, or over 1 million children, that qualify for this program do not receive it because of a lack of funding. Second, Johnson's focus on education is a long-term strategy to reduce poverty, not a short-term strategy. There are other strategies, such as public works, that could have been chosen to reduce poverty in a speedier manner. However, it is inaccurate to say that the "unconditional war on poverty" was a failure. From 1964 to 1970, poverty was cut by 37 percent—from 36 million to 24 million people—with much of that reduction coming from large benefit increases to the elderly through Social Security and to poor women with kids through Aid to Families with Dependent Children (AFDC). This large expansion in benefits, along with the development of such programs as Medicare and Medicaid, were part of Johnson's overall vision of a Great Society.[31]

A third attempt in the mid- to late twentieth century to provide a good education for all was the movement to equalize school funding. In 1968, during the tumultuous year when Dr. King and Robert Kennedy were assassinated, Mexican American parents in Texas and California turned to the courts to attempt to remedy the inequality in school funding. In Edgewood, Texas, the parents filed suit in federal court against several local school districts and the state of Texas, arguing that Texas's "method of school financing violated the equal protection clause of the Fourteenth Amendment to the US Constitution" since their children's schools were receiving one-third the amount of funding of the wealthier, mostly white districts surrounding them. In *San Antonio Independent School District v. Rodriguez*, the parents argued that this inequality, which was caused by the way schools were funded by local property taxes, led to the wealthier school districts having small classes, more counselors, larger classrooms, more library books, and ultimately, unequal educational results. In 1971, a federal district court agreed with the parents, ruling that education was a "fundamental right" protected by the US Constitution, and ordered Texas to design a funding system that was not dependent on community wealth. However, in 1973, the Supreme Court ruled in a 5–4 decision that education was not a "fundamental constitutional right," and therefore the state was not required to ensure equal funding to all students.[32]

In Los Angeles, California, in 1968, Mexican American parents filed suit against the state of California, arguing that the local school funding, which had produced inequalities similar to the Texas case, did not meet the requirements of the equal protection clause of the Fourteenth Amendment of the US Constitution *and* the California Constitution. In 1971, the California Supreme Court ruled in *Serrano v. Priest* that unequal school funding had violated both constitutions' guarantee of equal protection. Thus, although the Supreme Court decided two years later in the *Rodriguez* case that unequal funding did not violate the US Constitution, the *Serrano* case still applied in California. However, the intent of the California equalization plan, which stated that there could be no more than a $100 difference in per-pupil spending between school districts, has been undermined both by the private education foundations and by loopholes in the law that allow local districts to use property taxes if they are above the revenue. Back in Edgewood, Texas, the parents again filed suit to equalize school funding, but this time in the Texas state court system. The parents won in 1987, and after much legal and political wrangling, a plan was put in place in 1993 where wealthier school districts began transferring funds to poorer school districts to provide more equity in school funding. However, this "Robin Hood" plan has not produced equal funding, and in 2013, a Texas state court ruled that the present funding plan is unconstitutional since the money is still not distributed fairly. Currently, the Texas legislature is designing a remedy.[33]

By the end of the twentieth century, parents, community organizations, and school districts from forty-four states had sued, charging that the unequal funding of public education had violated their states' constitutions. Twenty state supreme courts agreed with the plaintiffs, and these states were forced to restructure their school finance system to comply with state constitutional standards of equality. Some of these cases focused on equal funding, and others focused on school districts not providing an adequate education, raising the issue that too little of an equal share is unconstitutional. These victorious lawsuits have brought some positive results. For example, within two years of Kentucky's 1989 Supreme Court ruling that the state's funding system was unconstitutional, there was a 15 percent decrease in the funding gap between rich and poor school districts and a 14 percent increase in the average per pupil spending. Also, in five states where the plaintiffs had won in their state Supreme Courts, they have closed the funding gap by an average of 29 percent. However, many of the state legislatures' plans have not gone far enough, and today, unequal funding is still a major issue. According to the 2012 National Report Card on Public School Funding, there are still a significant number of states that do not provide equal funding due to their school finance system. The report concludes, "Most states continue to neglect growing student poverty by failing to direct resources to the students and schools most in need. In some states and regions, the shortfalls in school funding are reaching crisis levels."[34]

A fourth attempt in the latter part of the twentieth century to provide a good education for all was the movement to hold schools accountable through standardized testing. This educational reform effort had its roots in the 1983 report entitled *A Nation at Risk*, which claimed that "the educational foundations of our society are presently being eroded by a rising tide of mediocrity that threatens our very future as a Nation and a people."

This report, written by a group convened by President Reagan's secretary of education Terrel Bell, stated in Cold War terms that the United States had allowed for "unilateral educational disarmament" and that this was threatening the nation's economic development. To turn back this "rising tide of mediocrity," the report made recommendations about course content (e.g., more English, math, and science), higher expectations (e.g., for students to develop a mastery of the subject matter through grades and standardized tests), more school days, and attracting more science and math teachers. Yet, the cause of the crisis, according to the report, was not unequal school funding, racial segregation, or the impact of poverty; rather, the crisis was the result of poor school curriculum, the lack of accountability on student learning, and inadequate teachers. Ironically, the report's solutions went against President Reagan's stated educational goals, which included school vouchers and tuition tax credits to support private schools, a reduction in federal education spending, and the abolishment of the US Department of Education.[35]

With school accountability moving to center stage, school reformers at the federal, state, and local levels began to develop a standards-based curriculum with a focus on math, science, and English, and standardized testing as a way to determine if students were mastering these standards. This work culminated in 2002 with the passage of the No Child Left Behind Act, a signature legislative victory of President George W. Bush. No Child Left Behind fundamentally changed education in every school across the nation and greatly expanded the federal role in education, as it called for all students, regardless of income, race, disability, or language spoken at home, to be proficient at math and reading by 2014. To reach this stated goal, No Child Left Behind requires all public schools to conduct annual testing in math and reading for grades three through eight and at least once in high school, to make adequate yearly progress, to provide annual school report cards, and to hire more qualified teachers.[36]

The key component of No Child Left Behind is that schools are given specific targets every year, which are constantly going up and moving closer to 100 percent proficiency, with the students assessed through state-administered standardized tests to determine if the schools have met their targets. For example, in 2011, the target was for 85 percent or more of the students in a school to demonstrate proficiency, which was up from 78 percent in 2010. When a school does not meet the target, the school is labeled "in need of improvement" and it is offered technical assistance and the students are given the choice of attending another school. If the school does not meet its target for a third year in a row, it is offered additional support, including private tutoring for the students. If the school continues to not meet its targets, the principal and teachers can be fired, and the school can be taken over by the state. A school can also fail to make its adequate yearly progress if one of the subgroups—which include Asian, black, Latino, Native American, multi-racial/ethnic, white, limited English proficient, special education, and low-income—does not meet the target for that year.[37]

Some educators have applauded No Child Left Behind's focus on subgroups since schools that are educating some students well can no longer hide the achievement gaps that exist within the subgroups of their schools. In addition, surveys of teachers and principals show that No Child Left Behind has motivated them to come up with creative new ways to encourage higher achievement. At the same time, many educators have great concerns about No Child Left Behind, including (1) its overemphasis on annual standardized testing as the method to determine student learning, which has encouraged teachers to teach to the test rather than on critical thinking; (2) the adequate yearly progress targets, which have been set in such a manner that makes it difficult for schools to meet their improvement targets; and (3) the idea that by 2014, every third- to eighth-grade student in every state would be 100 percent proficient in math and reading. These concerns have led nearly one-half of superintendents and principals to conclude that No Child Left Behind was meant to undermine public education or was politically motivated.[38]

Today, the number of public schools that are not making their adequate yearly progress continues to rise. In 2011, 48 percent of public schools did not make their annual yearly progress, which was an all-time high, up from 38 percent in 2009 and 29 percent in 2006. Soon after these results were announced, Secretary of Education Arne Duncan reported that the federal government would offer states waivers from the 100 percent proficiency requirement. As of this writing, Secretary Duncan has given over thirty waivers to states, each of which has agreed to some of President Obama's education agenda (e.g., evaluating teachers in part by using standardized testing). In response, some are calling for a rewriting of No Child Left Behind to make it more realistic, while others are calling for it to end, saying that this law has moved the federal government away from its sixty-year role of ensuring that local school districts with large numbers of impoverished children are given supplemental resources, and toward a model that punishes schools that are underachieving.[39]

THE RIGHT TO A GOOD EDUCATION: CURRENT APPROACHES

When talking about the right to a good education, Dr. King reminds us that "we are likely to find that the problems of housing and education, instead of preceding the elimination of poverty, will themselves be affected if poverty is first abolished." Thus, when exploring solutions to education, let's not lose sight of the fact that it will be difficult, if not impossible, to provide a good education for all when 22 percent of US children are living in poverty. Children cannot succeed in school if their housing is too insecure, their health is too fragile, and their minds cannot fully focus on education because their stomachs need food. Our collective efforts must go toward ending poverty in the wealthiest country in the world.[40]

At the same time, this does not mean that we should abandon efforts at improving public schools. The reality is that the similar policies that led to economic inequality and poverty have also led to educational inequality and poverty. Not surprisingly, people in the higher income levels have used their economic and political clout to create policies that support their social class interest, and they have been very successful, as can be seen from the earlier discussion in this chapter. Thus, any attempt to create social policies that challenge their social control of institutional power can be seen as supporting the larger struggle to provide a job, a living wage, and decent housing.

The key social policy that the upper class—and to some extent the middle class—has created and promoted is to procure appropriate funding for their schools, while low-income schools have not been able to do the same. Education has become even more crucial to economic success, and the upper class has created policies that result in quality buildings, fully accredited teachers, small class sizes, a robust curriculum, counselors, a librarian and well-stocked libraries, and all the other accoutrements necessary for a "good education." As discussed earlier, the poor and working class have been trying to level the playing field. This struggle continues today.

Presently, poor and working-class schools continue to use the courts to attempt to equalize school funding. In 2012, a group of Illinois taxpayers brought a case to the state Supreme Court arguing that the financing system violated the equal protection clause of the Illinois constitution since residents in low-income areas were paying higher tax rates than high-income areas in order to fund the public school system. The Illinois financing system is seen by advocates as one of the most unequal in the nation, but that didn't prevent the Illinois Supreme Court from dismissing the case, stating that the alleged injury of paying higher taxes was "not a direct result of the enforcement of the education funding statute." In 2013, the Colorado Supreme Court heard a case filed by parents and school districts in 2005 that all schools in that state were not adequately funded, particularly for Latino, Native American, and rural students. The decision is currently pending.[41]

In Minnesota, sixty-one school districts, representing over 250,000 children, have come together to form Schools for Equity in Education, with the goal of encouraging state legislators to equalize school funding. And in California, Governor Jerry Brown stepped forward in 2013 and proposed a new funding strategy that would provide a large increase of funds to school districts where 50 percent or more are poor (i.e., eligible to receive subsidized lunches), English learners, or in foster homes, while funds for middle- and upper-class kids who are English speakers would grow more slowly. As Brown said,

> Our future depends not on across-the-board funding, but in disproportionately funding those schools that have disproportionate challenges. . . . Aristotle said treating unequals equally is not justice. . . . Growing up in Compton or Richmond is not like it is to grow up in Los Gatos or Beverly Hills or Piedmont. . . . If you look at a classroom in Piedmont and you look at one in Compton, it's a lot different. The Piedmont families have far more money, far more access to the better things in life. And the extent to which we can offset that by putting more funding into those school districts, like Compton, we're going to do that.[42]

In June 2013, Governor Brown and the California legislature came to a compromise agreement, which will ensure that all schools, including those that teach the middle and upper classes, will receive an increase of $537 per student, while at the same time providing school districts an additional $1,470 for each "high-need" student (i.e., supplemental money), plus extra money if a school district has a concentration of high-need students of higher than 55 percent of the student population. Thus, San Ramon Unified, a school district with just 8 percent high-need students, will go from $5,794 per student in 2012–2013 to $9,111 in 2020–2021, whereas Fresno Unified, a district with 92 percent high-need students, will go from $6,544 per student to $12,264.[43]

The fight for equal and adequate funding at the state level goes on; however, there are rumblings from some education advocates and scholars that school funding should be federalized. Michael Lind and Ted Halstead from the New America Foundation argue that while state efforts to reform school funding are important, they will not solve the problem and can lead to "tax revolts," like in California, where local property taxes were capped in the same year the plan to equalize school funding was implemented. Lind and Halstead believe that schools should be primarily funded by the national government: "The federal government, like the central governments in virtually all other advanced nations, should pick up most or all of the tab for K–12 education—on the condition that state and local governments reduce their taxing and spending on education commensurately." They argue that education should be funded by a simple and progressive national consumption tax, which would be calculated by taking a person's annual income and subtracting annual savings. What is left is what the person consumed, and this would be taxed progressively, with the states receiving an equal share of this money on a per-pupil basis. While this would be a fundamental shift from the historic local and state control, it is not without precedent in light of the federalization of education as states have come into alignment with federal goals and standards set out in the No Child Left Behind Act.[44]

Tied to the idea of equal funding is the ability for schools serving working-class and low-income students to be able to attract and retain qualified teachers, to have smaller class sizes, and have a robust and engaging curriculum. Luckily, there is improvement in all of these areas. Throughout the country, states are acting to attract and retain highly qualified teachers to teach in high-need schools. In March 2013, West Virginia enacted legislation to provide loan forgiveness for college students who are willing to teach in high-need communities. A month later, New Mexico's state legislature passed a loan forgiveness bill for new teachers. Earlier in that same year, Arkansas enacted a bill to encourage educators to teach in high-need schools through a new teacher corps program. The Arkansas Teaching Corps provides financial rewards (a $5,000 stipend per year plus salary), but it also offers an accelerated pathway for college graduates to obtain a teaching license, as fellows accepted into the program are not required to go through a standard two-year teaching program but rather are enrolled in an intensive two-month training program before they enter the classroom. In addition, these new teachers receive extensive training and support for the first two years in the classroom. Similar accelerated teaching programs to encourage talented college graduates to become teachers in low-income schools have been developed in Mississippi and North Carolina.[45]

At the national level, the Coalition for Teaching Quality, an association of eighty-two organizations representing civil rights, education advocates, nonprofit and parent organizations, and ninety-plus partner organizations have supported the Equal Access to Quality Education Act. Introduced by Rep. Judy Chu (D-CA) and Rep. Rubén Hinojosa (D-TX), this federal bill is designed to create a pipeline to develop high-quality teachers by providing stipends or other financial incentives for would-be teachers if they participate in (1) a year-long teaching residency program in their first year of teaching, (2) ongoing professional development, and (3) continuous mentorship. The residency program, professional development, and mentorship will be overseen by a partnership between colleges and local school districts. At the time of the bill's introduction, Representative Chu stated, "A student's ability to reach their academic potential should not be determined by the school they attend. But today, we have the most inexperienced teachers being thrown into the highest needs schools. Every student, no matter their background, deserves a fully prepared and qualified teacher." Unfortunately, no action has been taken on this bill, and it languishes in committee.[46]

Another imbalance between wealthy and low-income schools has to do with class size. As described earlier, wealthier schools have lower class sizes than low-income schools. There is a fairly strong consensus among social science researchers that lower class size increases achievement. In the definitive study conducted in Tennessee in 1985–1989, 7,000 K–3 students from seventy-nine schools were randomly assigned to small (fifteen to seventeen) and regular classrooms (twenty-two to twenty-five). The results showed that the smaller classrooms led to higher high school graduation rates, students taking more advanced courses in high school, and more students taking the college entrance exam. Importantly, the Tennessee study concluded, "Poor, minority, and male students reap extra benefits in terms of improved test outcomes, school engagement, and reduced grade retention and dropout rates." Low-income students who had four years of the smaller class size doubled their chances of graduating from high school, while low-income students who had at least three years of the small class size increased their graduation rates to match those of higher income students.[47]

Inspired by the Tennessee study, other states began to call for the reduction of class size. Class size reduction gained even more prominence in 1999 when the federal government created a $1.2 billion program to help reduce class sizes to eighteen students for grades K–3. By 2007, twenty-one states had enacted class-size reduction policies, and by 2010, thirty-five states had enacted a policy limiting the number of students in math, English, or science in at least some grades. Other states showed improvement with class size reduction, particularly if it was a large reduction, like in California where classes were reduced from thirty to twenty in K–3; the result was that third-grade test scores increased by 9 percent in reading and 14 percent in math in five large school districts serving mostly low-income students. In fact, class size reduction has been designated as one of the few reforms by the Department of Education that have actually been shown to work when rigorously tested scientifically. However, the Great Recession caused states to cut their budgets, and nineteen states either relaxed or abolished their class-size reduction policies. Class sizes are again on the rise in the United States, with the average class size estimated to be twenty-five students. However, in low-income communities, it can rise to thirty-five and beyond. This has caused a response by teachers and parents. In Clark County, Nevada—which is home to 2 million people, or three-quarters of the state's residents—hundreds of school teachers and parents gathered at a state building in the spring of 2013 to bring attention to the state legislature and governor about the large class sizes. Addressing the crowd, Ruben Murillo, the president of the Clark County Education Association, argued, "It doesn't take a genius to figure out that the quality of education goes down with an increase in class size. We need the proper funding and resources to educate our kids." Ramona Morgan, a kindergarten teacher at Manch Elementary School, attended the rally, and she decried that she has thirty-five five-year-olds in her class, stating, "These babies need my attention and I can't get to all of them." Rita Morris, a sixth-grade teacher at Hyde Park Middle School, has forty students in her pre-algebra class; at the rally, she said, "Just getting to know the kids is difficult. . . . It's almost near impossible."[48]

Nationally, a group of activist parents has formed Parents Across America, a grassroots organization that wants to connect parents so that they can work together to reduce class size, as well as work for equal school funding, robust curriculum, and evaluations that go beyond standardized testing. Parents Across America has challenged President Obama to work for the type of education that his two daughters are receiving. After the president's reelection in November 2012, Leonie Haimson, founder of Parents Across America, challenged Mr. Obama and the nation to "educate all kids like Sasha and Malia" rather than "cramming kids into classes of 30." Haimson argues, "Just witness the sort of education Obama's own daughters receive: (i) small classes with plenty of personal attention from experienced teachers, (ii) a well-rounded education with art, science, and music, and (iii) little or no standardized testing. By instituting these reforms in the 1970s, Finland was able to turn around its school system and now outranks nearly all other nations in student achievement. If it's good enough for Malia and Sasha, it should be good enough for inner-city public school students in New York City or Chicago."[49]

Another reform that is a part of a good education is to ensure that all students have access to a well-rounded curriculum, which includes art, music, history, geography, and civics in addition to the three R's. Since the passage of No Child Left Behind, many educators have complained about a narrowing of the curriculum to reading, writing, math, and science. Secretary of Education Arne Duncan expressed this concern when he stated that

> President Obama, the First Lady, and I reject the notion that the arts, history, foreign languages, geography, and civics are ornamental offerings that can or should be cut from schools during a fiscal crunch. The truth is that, in the information age, a well-rounded curriculum is not a luxury but a necessity. In America, we do not reserve arts education for privileged students or the elite. Children from disadvantaged backgrounds, students who are English-language learners, and students with disabilities often do not get the enrichment experiences of affluent students anywhere except at school. President Obama recalls that when he was a child "you always had an art teacher and a music teacher. Even in the poorest school districts, everyone had access to music and other arts." Today, sadly, that is no longer the case.[50]

In response, some schools have responded by creating content-rich curriculum. As part of developing content-rich curriculum, schools have learned to create courses that respond to student interests, provide exposure and opportunities for mastery, harness outside expertise to develop teachers' skills, and extend the class day. At Kuss Middle School in Fall River, Massachusetts, a sixth–eighth grade school serving 650 students with 84 percent receiving free lunch, students are allowed to take two elective courses each term from a course offering of over thirty courses (e.g., art, band, foreign language, theater, and video production). These courses are offered at the beginner and more advanced levels. Xavielys Perez, a Kuss student, feels that this content-rich curriculum has changed her life: "Being involved in the Kuss theater program helped me find something I want for my major in college and my future career. I think more people are coming to our school because they know that there is at least one thing that will make their middle school years memorable." Importantly, Kuss students have shown that they can also perform on standardized tests, as their scores are higher than schools in their surrounding district.[51]

Some charter schools, which are publicly funded but have more flexibility than traditional schools, are also providing a content-rich curriculum. Charter schools can set their hours of operation, create schools around a theme, choose their curriculum, control their budget, and fire teachers more easily. Administrators at Woodland Hills Academy in Turtle Creek, Pennsylvania, a K–7 school serving 300 students with 64 percent receiving free lunches, have developed a content-rich curriculum by asking the teachers to draw on their interests to develop elective courses that explore "big ideas." These "Pathway" courses have kindergartners focusing on how food gets to their tables, third graders examining world health issues, and fifth graders learning how to give a public speech. At another charter school—Amistad Academy in Hartford, Connecticut—the students are surveyed each trimester to determine their interests, and then fifteen "Encore" courses are offered based on the results. Matt Taylor, an Amistad school leader, stated, "We don't want them to be academic automatons, so we want to be able to offer classes they're interested in. Colleges are also looking for well-rounded people. Our students also need to develop non-academic skills and interests to be competitive with their more affluent peers in the college admissions process."[52]

Besides providing a good education, the hope is that a content-rich curriculum will encourage students to stay in school. Currently, 1 million students drop out of school each year, with nearly one-half of all African American, Latino, and Native American students failing to graduate from high school. In a recent study, almost one-half of the students dropped out of school because they thought school was boring and did not engage them, while 81 percent said that if school had presented them with more "real-world" learning opportunities, it would have helped them to remain in school.[53]

In addition to curriculum issues, sometimes the presentation of the course material is the problem. A solution to this pedagogical issue is an active learning environment in opposition to "chalk and talk." While there are many possible active learning strategies, one of the most important strategies developed in the past twenty years has been service learning—the integration of the academic curriculum with real-world social issues. Instead of writing something just for the teacher to see, the students are encouraged to apply their knowledge in the classroom to a social issue. For example,

Crellin Elementary School in Oakland, Maryland, in which 87 percent of the students receive free or reduced school lunch, has adopted a place-based service-learning approach that has transformed it from a struggling school to becoming recognized as one of the best elementary schools in Maryland. As one teacher remembers, "When I first started teaching 30 years ago, the image of Crellin was roughnecks, people didn't have any class, didn't know anything. That is what you hear, those people didn't know anything. But now when you hear people talking, other professionals, about Crellin, they are talking about the kids from Crellin as smart, overcoming any obstacle they have in their lives to be the best people they can be."[54]

The reason for this dramatic change was the adoption of a place-based service-learning approach in 2003. This approach tears down the school walls that separate schoolyard from community, and makes the community a central fixture of the curriculum. No longer is the classroom the only source of instruction, as students use the community to learn about history, science, math, and language arts. In addition, service-learning projects are designed to bring the curriculum alive, to develop critical thinking skills, to learn how to conduct research, and to work in groups. At Crellin Elementary, the students initiated a long-term stream study of the river behind their school after a student wondered why the water in the river was orange. In conducting background research, the students learned that 100 years ago, the area between the river and the school was a coal tailings dump, and that the orange water was a result of the water absorbing acids from the coal, which was polluting the river. The students' exploration engaged the larger community, and with the help of residents, nonprofits, and county and state agencies, they collectively came up with a plan to abate the pollution. Currently, as part of an ongoing stream study, students collect water samples, explore biological concepts such as riparian zones, develop language arts skills through the writing of reports, do mathematical equations, and clean trash from the river. In addition to the stream study, students apply their language arts and mathematical skills to making soup for the local hospital or making bread for seniors. This engaged learning strategy has made Crellin Elementary's standardized test scores skyrocket, and it now has the highest pass rate in the state of Maryland on standardized tests.[55]

Similar results have been obtained at the Young Achievers Science and Math Pilot School, a K–8 public school in Mattapan, Massachusetts, where 80 percent of students receive a free or reduced lunch. At Young Achievers, students learn about the various components that make a community, do an analysis about the needs of the community, and then try to bring about the change that the community needs (e.g., advocate for the development of an ice cream parlor). In second grade, students conduct a professional radio show based on what they have learned from their community analysis, which gets aired on the local public radio station. Working in groups of five to seven, students have created segments on air quality and asthma rates, the difficulties that people face in Chinatown, and the importance of public arts, and have even advocated for the development of more space for their burgeoning student population. Students also study how food gets from the farm to the table. As part of this lesson, students go to an apple orchard, where they pick and clean apples and make apple juice. They also write a book about the food system, which has invariably become the most-read book in the class. In the middle school, students conduct water studies in a nearby stream similarly to the Crellin students. Young Achievers Science and Math Pilot School realizes that these studies are more than academic, as they will give the children the necessary tools to understand how communities like theirs are short-changed when it comes to clean drinking water and clean air, as well as to do something about it. Carl Alleyne, a parent of a student at Young Achievers, has noticed the difference that this student-engaged strategy has made. Alleyne states, "It helped change a lot of people's paradigm. They have changed the parents' paradigm. And most importantly, it is changing the kids' paradigm. They are dreaming again. I want to be an astronaut, I want to be a scientist, I want to be an innovator."[56]

Some educators argue that the best way to deliver content-rich curriculum and engaged classrooms is through charter schools. Since their development in the late 1980s, 6,000 charter schools have been created in the United States, serving 2 million students—about 5 percent of the K–12 student population. Supporters argue that charter schools provide innovation and fresh ideas to public education, particularly in high-need areas. However, the charter school movement has not lived up to its promise that it will outperform traditional K–12 schools. A recent extensive study showed that 46 percent of the charter schools performed the same on standardized tests as traditional public schools, and 37 percent of the charters actually did worse. Only 17 percent of the charter schools received higher test scores than their traditional counterparts. These disappointing results are of particular importance since charter schools serve disproportionately the poor and students of color.[57]

Mixed findings also can be found with the standards and accountability movement. Its crowning achievement, the No Child Left Behind Act, promised to reduce significantly the achievement gap between the poor and students of color, and their wealthier and whiter counterparts, by raising standards and holding schools accountable. As was discussed earlier in the chapter, the gap was to be narrowed by raising standards, monitoring standardized test scores, and taking action against schools that do not meet their adequate yearly progress. As was stated earlier, No Child Left Behind has led to several positive accomplishments, such as acknowledging the achievement gaps according to social class, race, and ethnicity within schools, as well as motivating educators to explore new strategies to advance student achievement. Another positive accomplishment has been that No Child Left Behind led to a $25 billion increase in education funding from the federal government.[58]

Overall, No Child Left Behind appears to have achieved a small increase in overall math and reading scores in the nation. For the fourth grade and eighth grade, average math scores on the National Assessment of Educational Progress increased from 235 in 2003 to 241 in 2011, and average reading scores increased from 278 to 284. However, No Child Left Behind has done very little to decrease the achievement gap. For example, students eligible for free lunch had their math scores increase eight points (from 228 to 234) from 2003 to 2011, while kids who were ineligible for free lunch also had their scores increase eight points (from 244 to 252). For eighth graders, the score on the math tests between poor and nonpoor students actually widened by one point. As for fourth-grade reading, overall scores increased from 218 to 221 from 2008 to 2011, and eighth graders increased from 263 to 265. Yet once again, there was little impact on the achievement gap, as students eligible for free lunch and ineligible for fourth-grade reading increased by one point, while the eighth-grade scores decreased by two points. Looking at the racial and ethnic achievement gaps, minimal progress has been made from 2001 to 2011 in reducing black-white and Hispanic-white achievement gaps. The achievement gap for blacks and Latinos is on average more than twenty points for both the math and reading assessments, which is approximately equivalent to two school years. Thus, we need to look to other solutions to decrease the achievement gap than the standards and accountability movement.[59]

In addition to changing what goes on inside schools and classrooms during school hours, there is a movement to get students better prepared for school. Only 48 percent of students in poverty enter kindergarten "school ready," compared to 75 percent from moderate and high incomes. Moreover, low-income children are less likely to have access to high-quality preschool. In order to close this 27 percent gap, President Obama has put forward a ten-year, $75 billion universal preschool proposal for four-year-olds, whereby the federal government provides grants to the states to ensure that children from low- to moderate-income households have access to high-quality preschool. There would also be an incentive for the states to provide high-quality preschool for the middle class. As the Equity and Excellence Commission reported, "If we know anything about learning, it is that the years from birth to age 5 are crucial in every child's life. Nowhere is achieving educational equity more important than at the earliest stages of a child's physical and cognitive development."[60]

Finally, to address the extreme inequality that exists as a result of school segregation, educators and advocates are considering a "second generation" of school desegregation plans. However, these plans have become more complicated in light of the 2007 Supreme Court's decision to limit the use of race as a category to make individual school assignments for voluntary desegregation plans. At that time, approximately 10 percent of all school districts had such plans. In response, school districts have developed two different strategies to integrate schools. One strategy is to create a diversity score for the neighborhoods in a school district, using a variety of characteristics, such as family income, concentration of poverty, parental education, and race. The diversity score is then used to give priority to students whose score would improve a school's diversity. The Berkeley Unified School District plan in California, which survived a court challenge in 2009, uses this type of diversity score to promote integration among its 9,400-student body, which is 8 percent Asian, 21 percent Latino, 24 percent black, 32 percent white, 15 percent multiethnic/other, and 44 percent who receive free or reduced lunch.[61]

A second strategy is to encourage integration by using characteristics such as family income, concentration of poverty, parental education, and English-language learner status, but not to use race. While family income and race are positively correlated, and therefore, there may be some racial integration promoted, this strategy is fundamentally based on the idea that students who come from low-income families will benefit greatly by having access to the good teachers, resources, and facilities that generally come with predominantly white, wealthier schools. After having its desegregation plan ruled unconstitutional by the Supreme Court case in 2007, Jefferson County Public Schools moved to a "class-based" strategy in 2008. In 2012, the Kentucky Supreme Court upheld Jefferson County's "class-based" plan, which allowed parents to choose their local school as one of their four possibilities, but with no guarantee they would receive it. Similarly, Wake County in North Carolina changed over from a race-based strategy to class-based in 2000. Wake County's voluntary segregation policy states that no school will have more than 40 percent of its student population below-income (as determined by free and reduced lunches) or more than 25 percent below grade level in reading. This economic design has achieved nearly as racially integrated schools as under the previous race-based integration plan; it has also achieved higher test scores, as Wake County students have outscored other North Carolina districts with similar students.[62]

SUMMARY

In Chapter 4, eight ideas have been discussed to achieve this constitutional commitment of a right to a good education: equalizing school funding at the state and national levels, attracting and retaining qualified teachers to high-need schools, reducing class size, providing a content-rich curriculum for all, using an active learning approach, developing charter schools, providing universal preschool for four-year-olds, and encouraging integration. These eight policy recommendations will most likely be at the forefront of the effort to guarantee the right to a good education.

Chapter 5

The Right to Adequate Medical Care

The Fifth Amendment

PROBLEM

The right to adequate medical care and the opportunity to achieve and enjoy good health is not yet a reality in the United States. Americans don't have the right to adequate medical care because not everyone can afford it and the United States has not figured out a way to provide health coverage for all. At the same time, the poor and working class face social factors—such as contact with environmental hazards (e.g., air pollution, lead, unsafe water), inability to provide good nutrition, hazardous work conditions, increased stress that comes from living day-to-day financially, and poorly heated and ventilated housing—that make it difficult to achieve and enjoy good health. These social factors make the poor more likely to suffer from diabetes, hypertension, infectious diseases (e.g., influenza and tuberculosis), and lung and cervical cancer. In addition, the poor are 1.6 times as likely to die in infancy, 2.7 times as likely to have no regular source of medical care, and 8 times more likely to not have enough food to eat, when compared to the nonpoor.[1]

Currently, the average cost of health care to cover one person is $468 per month, or $5,615 per year, while the average cost for a family is $1,312 per month, or $15,745 per year. For tens of millions of Americans, this high cost makes it impossible to purchase health care insurance, which denies them the right to adequate medical care. And the lack of this right literally costs human lives, as nearly 45,000 people die each year since they don't have access to health care. The denial of this right makes the United States an outlier, as all other industrialized nations guarantee health care for all by providing some form of national health insurance.[2]

In many ways, the United States is a paradox, as it spends more money than any other industrialized nation on health care yet does not provide universal access and has mediocre results on many health indicators. In 2012, the United States spent $2.6 trillion on medical care, or 18 percent of its gross domestic product (i.e., 18 cents of every US dollar spent), which works out to $8,233 a person. The next closest industrialized nation is the Netherlands, which spends 12 percent of GDP on health care, or $5,388 per person. The average amount spent by industrialized nations is $3,268, or two and one-half times less than the United States. At the same time, the United States is ranked at the bottom of industrialized nations when looking at many health indicators. In a 2013 study that ranked sixteen developed nations according to health indicators, the United States was ranked dead last. The United States has the highest chance for a child to die before age five, the highest rate of death among women due to complications in pregnancy and childbirth, and the second-highest rate of death for both coronary heart disease and lung disease. When comparing the United States to all other nations, the American health care system is ranked thirty-seventh out of 191 nations. More specifically, the United States is ranked thirty-sixth in life expectancy, thirty-ninth for infant mortality, and forty-second and forty-third for adult male and female mortality, respectively.[3]

This health care paradox exists because of the high cost of medical care in the United States and the inability of millions to afford it. The reasons for the high costs are many. First, the American health care system is based primarily on the profit motive, which has led to ever-increasing costs as insurance companies and Health Maintenance Organizations (HMOs) try to maximize profit. In 1960, health care costs were just 5 percent of GDP. By 1985 they were 10 percent, and in 2002 they were 15 percent. Currently, health care costs are 18 percent of GDP, and by 2020, it is estimated that health care spending will consume 20 cents of every dollar spent in the United States, or $4.6 trillion. This rise in health care costs is much higher than the rate of inflation. From 2000 to 2010, the consumer price index rose 26 percent, but health care costs rose 48 percent. This increase in health care spending is evident in the increase in profits of insurance companies, as the top five insurance companies had revenues of $255 billion in 2012 and made $12.3 billion in profit, an increase of $4.5 billion from 2008.[4]

Second, the American hodgepodge system of private insurance companies, HMOs, hospitals, and drug companies has led to unnecessary and excessive administrative costs—by some measures, $190 billion annually. For example, the administrative costs for the public Medicare plan are less than 2 percent, in comparison to the 11 percent spent on the Medicare Advantage plan, which covers the same benefits and population but is operated by private insurers. These administrative costs, which include high-end salaries for upper management, contribute to the high cost of medical care. Third, health care costs are high in the United States since doctors practice defensive medicine in order to protect themselves from malpractice lawsuits. It is estimated that as much as one-third of all medical care delivered can be classified as defensive medicine, at a cost of $650 billion a year.[5]

Fourth, the US system incentivizes doctors to specialize, which has led to a shortage of primary doctors and the underutilization of preventive care. Today, 40 percent of adults are receiving primary care from doctors with specializations. This overuse of specialists increases the cost of health care significantly. It is estimated that the nation could save $67 billion if Americans visited a general practitioner on a regular basis. In addition, studies show that patients have better overall health results when treated first by a primary care doctor. Unfortunately, there is a current shortage of 9,000 primary care doctors in the United States, and this shortage will continue to grow, reaching 66,000 in the next fifteen years. This lack of primary care doctors is cost ineffective.[6]

Last, the high price of prescription drugs, which cost Americans $326 billion in 2012, has led to the high price of health care. In addition to driving up the overall costs of medical care, the high price of drugs means that many Americans can't afford them. In a recent study, 18 percent of low-income and uninsured people did not buy their prescribed medicine because the cost of the drug was prohibitive, while 40 percent asked the doctor to prescribe a lower-cost drug rather than the doctor's first choice. While waiting for his high–blood pressure medication at a Louisville clinic, James Whitlock, a sixty-five-year-old African American who is a retired cobbler, stated, "Medication is so high that people can't afford their medicine."[7]

Taken together, these reasons have made health care unaffordable and inaccessible to many Americans. With 100 million American households making just two times the poverty rate, it is no surprise that 50 million Americans, or 16 percent of the nation's population, do not have health insurance, and 29 million more adults possess insurance but have inadequate benefits (i.e., they are underinsured). People who are uninsured either go without health care or utilize overcrowded emergency rooms, which must by law provide services even if patients cannot pay.[8]

Social class is a powerful lens through which to look at health inequality. As one goes up the income ladder, there is a positive correlation between income and health coverage. When looking at workers who are eighteen to sixty-four years old and are covered through an employment-based plan, it is found that for those making under $10,000 annually, 12 percent have coverage, whereas for those making $10,000–$20,000, 23 percent have health coverage. This positive correlation between social class and health coverage continues up the income ladder: for those making $20,000–$29,999, 41 percent have health coverage; $30,000–$39,999, 56 percent have health coverage; $40,000–$49,999, 61 percent have health coverage; $50,000–$74,999, 76 percent have health coverage; and for those making $75,000 and over, 86 percent have health coverage.[9]

Race is another powerful lens through which to examine health care inequalities. For example, Latinos and Native Americans have the lowest health care coverage—68 percent—while whites have the highest health care coverage—88 percent. African Americans and Asian Americans fall in between with 79 percent and 82 percent coverage, respectively. At the same time, African Americans and Latinos have lower birth weights, receive less prenatal care, and have lower life expectancy rates than whites. Similarly, blacks and Latinos have higher death rates for cancer and heart disease and are more likely to develop infectious diseases and vision problems (as a result of diabetes and glaucoma). Incredibly, the black infant mortality rate is three times that of other races, and blacks have twice the rate of diabetes of whites.[10]

In a speech to the Medical Committee for Human Rights in 1966, Dr. Martin Luther King Jr. stated, "Of all the forms of inequality, injustice in health care is the most shocking and inhuman." The question before us is, what solutions will eradicate the "most shocking and inhuman" of inequalities?[11]

SOLUTION

In 2008, presidential candidate Barack Obama made universal health care a key component of his campaign. With his victory, President Obama made health care the signature issue of his first term, and within just fourteen months, he had done what no president had done before him, and that was to usher through Congress a near universal health care bill. With the passage of the Affordable Care Act in 2010, new policy solutions are being tried to expand health insurance to nearly all people. Modern-day examples to be explored include the implementation of the Affordable Care Act; state efforts, such as in Vermont, to provide universal health care; and Medicare for All.[12]

THE HISTORY OF THE RIGHT TO ADEQUATE MEDICAL CARE

In 1854, one of the first federal legislative bills for health care was introduced, calling for the development of mental asylums to be built for the mentally ill in poverty. The bill for the "Benefit of the Indigent Insane," which was proposed by social reformer Dorothea Dix, also allowed the blind and deaf to get treatment. The House of Representatives and the Senate voted in favor of the bill, but President Franklin Pierce vetoed it. In Pierce's precedent-setting veto, he argued that it was the states' responsibility for social welfare and the not the federal government's. In his veto message, Pierce stated,

> I readily and, I trust, feelingly acknowledge the duty incumbent on us all as men and citizens, and as among the highest and holiest of our duties, to provide for those who, in the mysterious order of Providence, are subject to want and to disease of body or mind; but I can not find any authority in the Constitution for making the Federal Government the great almoner of public charity throughout the United States. To do so would, in my judgment, be contrary to the letter and spirit of the Constitution and subversive of the whole theory upon which the Union of these States is founded.[13]

Pierce's veto gave voice to the perspective that liberty was the defining characteristic of the United States, and that freedom meant holding private property as sacrosanct, individual initiative as paramount, and that a small, decentralized government was the best way to guarantee it. And while this perspective of a limited role for the federal government guided the nation for the next seventy-nine years, until the New Deal, there were several other efforts to have the federal government provide health care, including the Freedmen's Bureau and the Sheppard-Towner Act.

The Freedmen's Bureau was started by the federal government at the conclusion of the Civil War to lift more than 4 million African Americans out of destitution and despair. Between 1865 and 1869, the Freedmen's Bureau constructed sixty hospitals, and doctors working for the bureau provided medical assistance for one-half million black people. In addition, the Freedmen's Bureau provided 21 million meals, built over 1,000 public schools, and constructed several black colleges. Yet, the Freedmen's Bureau's success in providing health care, food, and education to African Americans had no impact on overall federal social welfare policy.[14]

In the early twentieth century, a group comprised mostly of women advocates successfully lobbied for a national infant and maternal health program. At that time, the infant mortality rate in the United States was extremely high, with 111 babies dying for every 1,000 births. After a four-year effort by Julia Lathrop and others from the progressive "child saving" movement, Congress passed the Sheppard-Towner bill, which provided over $2.7 million for new clinics to conduct preventive health examinations for pregnant women and children at no cost. The new law also provided matching funds for states in order to set up state agencies to coordinate its health programs with the Children's Bureau, which was also created during that era. Female doctors and nurses, who had been discriminated against at most hospitals, operated 3,000 maternal and child health clinics. Their collective efforts proved to be very successful, as US infant mortality dropped from 76 deaths per 1,000 births in 1922 to 68 per 1,000 in 1929. However, the male doctors argued that the female doctors were offering substandard health care and that this effort would lead to socialized medicine. The male doctors petitioned Congress, and they were successful in shutting down the funding for the maternal and child health clinics, as the Sheppard-Towner Act was not renewed in 1929.[15]

In the late nineteenth and early twentieth centuries, new advances in medicine and technology made health care much more effective, as well as more expensive. In order to allow regular people to afford this more advanced health care, industrialized nations began to develop national health insurance programs, first in Germany in 1883 and then in England in 1911. And while national health insurance plans may differ in how the services are provided (public or private) and how the money is collected (through general taxation or contributions from employers and employees), they offer affordable health care to people who could not normally afford it.

In the United States, the progressive movement was one of the main groups pushing for national health insurance. Progressives were not confined to a political party but were united in the belief that social structures were at the root of social problems and that public policy could solve societal ills. Thus, progressives proposed national health insurance as a logical response to the affordability question of health care. In 1912, Theodore Roosevelt took up the progressives' call for national health care, becoming the first national politician to advocate for it. Roosevelt failed to win the Republican nomination, so he helped create the "Bull Moose" Party, and together they made national health care a major part of the platform and campaign. Roosevelt finished second, ahead of the Republican candidate, William Taft, but behind Woodrow Wilson. With this defeat, progressives turned to the states to enact health care legislation.[16]

A few years later, progressives put forward a health insurance plan in several state legislatures that resembled the German health plan. The plan called for the coverage of all medical and hospitalization costs, the replacement of income for up to six months for time off work, and a $50 funeral benefit. The cost of the plan would be $2 per worker per month and would be split among workers (40 cents), employers ($1.20), and the state (40 cents). The insurance plan would be required for all workers making less than $100 per month. However, state legislators rejected the plan as doctors, employers, and insurance companies opposed it. It didn't help that the plan was modeled after Germany's, which the United States was at war with. In addition, after the Russian Revolution began in 1917, the plan was seen as communistic, and therefore "un-American."[17]

At the start of the Great Depression in 1930, President Herbert Hoover created the Veterans Administration to provide medical services to the nation's soldiers after they returned from their service. The nation has had a long commitment to providing health services to veterans, dating back to the Naval Home, created in 1812 to provide medical care to disabled veterans, and this commitment continued through the Civil War and World Wars I and II. In 1989, the Department of Veterans Affairs (VA) was created, elevating its director to a cabinet-level position with access to the president. Ironically, the VA provides veterans not just with a single-payer system of funding but with a model of health care that is "socialized." Today, the VA is a nonprofit that owns its facilities (e.g., 153 hospitals, 909 outpatient clinics, 135 nursing homes) and employs its own staff of 13,000 doctors and 55,000 nurses. Importantly, the VA provides health care based on the needs of the 23 million veterans rather than on their ability to pay or their preexisting conditions. Furthermore, the decision on whether to conduct a medical procedure is dependent on the VA doctors and not an insurance company. The VA is also considered a single-payer system since the American taxpayers fund its $53 billion health care budget and the federal government is both the provider of health care and the payer, with veterans paying little to nothing. The VA provides high-quality health care to 5 million veterans annually. As ABC News reports, "Study after study puts the VA system at the very top for fewer medical errors, for effective treatments, for lower costs and for patient satisfaction. And the VA delivers all of this for at least $1,500 less per year per patient than Medicare." These results demonstrate that socialized medical care in the United States can be superior to the private sector, and is particularly impressive since veterans are more likely to have low incomes and lower levels of education, higher rates of disability and psychiatric illnesses, and poor health overall, all of which are associated with receiving substandard care.[18]

While a single-payer, government-run health care system is provided for all veterans, the rest of the population has been provided with other options. From the time of the Great Depression to the end of the twentieth century, there have been numerous efforts to move the nation toward affordable care for all through national health insurance. For example, after the 1936 landslide reelection of President Franklin Roosevelt, FDR shifted leftward and put forward the Social Security Act, which provided for old-age and unemployment insurance, as well as aid to dependent children and workers' compensation. Originally, Roosevelt's proposal included national health insurance, but the American Medical Association (AMA) vehemently opposed it, and it was removed from the legislation in order to not scuttle the overall bill. Several years later, Sen. Robert Wagner, Sen. James Murray, and Rep. John Dingell introduced a bill providing for a national health care and hospitalization fund that would provide unlimited access to doctors, hospitalization for thirty days, lab tests, and X-rays. Money for the health care and hospitalization fund would be collected through employee contributions of 4.5 percent of wages and would be matched by employers, much like the plan that funds Social Security, and people would be able to freely choose their doctors from the ones participating in the program. However, Congress never took a vote on the Wagner-Murray-Dingell bill.[19]

Ironically, one of Roosevelt's wartime policies—that of wage and price controls—gave rise to the modern-day employer-based health insurance system that now serves over 170 million Americans. During World War II, employers were not allowed to offer high wages to workers, so as a job induce-ment, employers offered health insurance. This benefit has mushroomed into hundreds of different plans sold by numerous insurance companies, who are all doing the same thing: evaluating an applicant for coverage, adjudicating and denying claims, marketing, lobbying, and paying their CEOs very high salaries. Today, the median pay for a health care CEO is $10 million.[20]

In 1945, President Roosevelt died, and his successor, Harry Truman, attempted to implement several key constitutional commitments of the Eco-nomic Bill of Rights, including the right to adequate medical care. Just four months after becoming president, Truman sent a special message to Congress, where he restated Roosevelt's idea for an Economic Bill of Rights, calling for the right to a job, a living wage, decent housing, a good education, and adequate medical care. Two months later, Truman sent another special mes-sage to Congress focusing on health care inequality. At that time, 40 percent of the counties in the country did not have access to either a local hospital or one that met the basic minimum standards. Truman stated,

> In the past, the benefits of modern medical science have not been enjoyed by our citizens with any degree of equality. Nor are they today. Nor will they be in the future—unless government is bold enough to do something about it. People with low or moderate incomes do not get the same medical attention as those with high incomes. The poor have more sickness, but they get less medical care. People who live in rural areas do not get the same amount or quality of medical attention as those who live in our cities. Our new Economic Bill of Rights should mean health security for all, regardless of residence, sta-tion, or race—everywhere in the United States.[21]

Truman argued that the health of the nation is a national concern, and it was up to the country to remove financial barriers that blocked people from attaining medical services. He believed that all Americans should have easy access to medical and hospital services, and he called on Congress to distribute the costs "through expansion of our existing compulsory social insurance system." The following year, Truman made national health insurance a central part of his successful election campaign of 1946. With opinion polls showing 60 percent to 70 percent of Americans in support of national health insurance, Truman went on to lead a four-year fight with Congress to develop a modified version of the Wagner-Murray-Dingell bill. Many believed that Truman's policy was an improvement over Roosevelt's original proposal, since it was a single, egalitarian system that covered all people. It was also a "single-payer" health insurance system. In other words, there would be a single fund that pays for health care services. Importantly, *single payer* does not specify a single provider, or whom the physicians work for, or how the service is delivered. And while the single fund is generally operated by the state, as it was in Truman's bill, a single-payer model can also use a mixed public-private model (as will be discussed later with Vermont's single-payer proposal).[22]

Truman knew that the AMA and other opponents would label his proposal "socialized medicine," so he did everything possible to make it clear that he was not proposing this, repeating this denial several times in his special message. At one point he stated, "Socialized medicine means that all doctors work as employees of government. The American people want no such system. No such system is here proposed." In his letter to Congress, Truman stated that under his proposal, people would still be able to choose their own doctors and decide on which hospital to go to, while doctors and hospitals would still be able to accept or reject patients, as well as decide on whether to participate in the insurance program fully, partly, or not at all. The American Medical Association would have nothing of it, and they argued that Truman's national health insurance proposal was socialized medicine, and that it would damage the quality of health care and take away the professional independence of doctors. The AMA, along with the American Hospital Association and the American Bar Association, mustered all their forces to defeat Truman's proposal. In Congress, they found friends among conservative legislators; Sen. Robert Taft, an anti-union conservative, declared that Truman's proposal came directly from the Soviet Union's Constitution, stating, "I consider it socialism. It is to my mind the most socialistic measure this Congress has ever had before it." In the end, the AMA, along with its supporters, defeated Truman's national health insurance proposal. With the defeat of Truman's national health insurance program, the insurance companies jumped at the opportunity to increase their businesses. By 1958, almost 75 percent of Americans had some type of private health insurance plan, and by the 1960s, there were over 700 private insurance companies selling health coverage. However, the price of health care was continuing to increase, with hospital care doubling in the 1950s, which made it extremely difficult for people outside the workplace, particularly seniors, to afford health care insurance.[23]

In 1964, President Johnson's Great Society and War on Poverty increased services to the poor, with a major focus on health care. In a break from Truman's universal policy, Johnson and the Democrat-controlled Congress put forward health care proposals to increase medical care for certain disadvantaged groups. This incremental approach proved successful, as there was great support to cover the hospital costs for seniors. Starting in the late 1950s, a grassroots campaign of concerned citizens encouraged the nation to explore solutions for senior health care. By the 1960s, the poverty rate for seniors was at 30 percent, while 50 percent had no health insurance. This campaign paid off, as in 1965 Congress enacted Medicare, a health insurance program for seniors, and Medicaid, a low-income health care assistance plan. Within the first three years of the program, Medicare enrolled 20 million seniors. In 2013, Medicare provided universal health care to all seniors, as well as disabled beneficiaries, covering nearly 39 million people while Medicaid covered 67 million low-income kids, women who were pregnant or had young children, and disabled people with no work history.[24]

While they may seem like similar programs, Medicare and Medicaid are quite different. Medicare is a federally run insurance program available to all seniors regardless of need. Moreover, Medicare is a "single-payer" system, meaning that the payment for seniors comes from a single fund within the government. Funding for the program comes from federal payroll taxes that all Americans contribute to. At the same time, Medicare is not totally free, as seniors do pay monthly premiums (i.e., $105 a month in 2014). Medicaid, in contrast, is a federal-state government insurance program that serves low-income people and is funded by federal (on average about 57 percent), state, and local governments. Importantly, Medicaid is a decentralized system, where the states determine eligibility, payments, and benefits. This decentralized system has led to great variability between Medicaid programs depending on the state, with some states providing low-income people generous programs and other states providing miserly programs.[25]

The War on Poverty also started the Neighborhood Health Centers program, which provided comprehensive health care services to the poor. These health centers were innovative in that they included poor people in the planning and operating of this community service. To improve the health of the people, the War on Poverty also provided a sixfold increase in the food stamp program, from $36 million to almost $1.9 billion, between 1965 and 1972. This increase in food stamps, along with other War on Poverty programs (e.g., school lunch programs and nutritional supplements for women and young children), nearly eliminated hunger and malnutrition in the nation. The Neighborhood Health Centers, nutrition programs, and Medicaid also had a direct impact on the infant mortality rate, reducing it by 33 percent.[26]

By this point in US history, the major components of the American health care system were in place: (1) employment-based health insurance, (2) Medicare, (3) Medicaid, and (4) Veterans Affairs. What this means for today is the following: For the 170 million Americans (55 percent of the population) who are working, the United States depends on employment-based health insurance, which is paid jointly by employees and employers through payroll deductions. For the 40 million–plus seniors and 8 million young people with certain disabilities, the United States provides a universal single-payer model of health care through Medicare. For the poor, the United States provides Medicaid, which provides health insurance to 62 million people. For the 24 million veterans and their families, the United States provides a publicly run, socialized model of health care, where the clinics and hospitals are run by the government, the doctors and nurses are employed by the government, service is provided free or at little cost, and where the government is the single payer. Last, for the 49 million Americans (or 16 percent of the population) without health insurance, they either pay out of pocket for medical care, go to the emergency ward at a hospital, or go without receiving medical attention. The people without insurance include 22 million whites, 16 million Latinos, and 8 million blacks; it also includes 7 million children.[27]

The question from the 1970s to the present has been what to do about this last group: the uninsured. Throughout the 1970s, there were several unsuccessful attempts to enact a national solution to provide affordable health care for all. In 1971, Sen. Ted Kennedy (D-MA), with the support of organized labor, went back to President Truman's idea and put forward a universal, single-payer health insurance plan, to be funded through payroll taxes. Three years later, President Nixon offered a counterproposal, which called for universal coverage that would be attained through a voluntary employer program and a separate program that would cover the unemployed and working poor. In summarizing the Nixon plan, Senator Kennedy stated, "It's really a partnership between the administration and insurance companies." However, both of these proposals failed to gather enough support, as the war in Vietnam and the resignation of Nixon over the Watergate scandal distracted the nation's attention.[28]

Yet, one proposal that Nixon put forward has left a lasting legacy, and that was the Health Maintenance Organization Act of 1973. This legislation allowed for the development and expansion of health maintenance organizations (HMOs) as it required employers that had twenty-five or more employees to offer an HMO option if the employer offered a traditional health insurance plan. This HMO plan, which was based on the Kaiser Permanente model, defined HMOs as a plan that listed the various benefits to its member, charged a monthly premium that was the same for all members, and was a designed as a nonprofit. Nixon supported the HMO legislation because he saw it as a way to expand health care while at the same time limiting health care costs. John Ehrlichman, one of Nixon's key domestic advisors, put it this way in a conversation he had with the president the day before Nixon announced his support of HMOs: "All the incentives are toward less medical care, because ... the less care they give them, the more money they make ...

and the incentives run the right way." However, some HMOs have been more successful at managing costs by limiting health care than managing health care. Yet, what started small, with fewer than 4 million people enrolled in forty HMOs by the mid-1970s, has expanded to hundreds of HMOs covering almost 60 million Americans. By the 1980s, most HMOs dropped their nonprofit status and became for-profit enterprises once the government cut off the federal aid they had been receiving to support their operations.[29]

Twenty years later, President Clinton made universal health coverage one of his top policy initiatives, but his plan failed to gather enough support in Congress. Clinton's plan called for individual and employer mandates through a competitive private insurance market. However, conservatives opposed it since they believed that it would lead to overregulation by the government. The now famous TV commercials by "Harry and Louise," which showed an average American couple discussing their deep concerns over the Clinton plan, helped to derail it. While the camera focused on Harry and Louise sitting at their kitchen table, a foreboding voice stated, "The government may force us to pick from a few health care plans designed by government bureaucrats." Louise then said, "Having choices we don't like is no choice at all." Harry followed with, "If they choose …" with Louise concluding "… we lose." Liberals also attacked the Clinton plan since they felt that it left too much power and control in the hands of insurance companies. With the right and the left opposed, Clinton's health plan failed.[30]

With the nation seemingly unable to pass a national health care plan, states looked for solutions to access and affordability. In 1994, Oregon, which had been developing a new health care initiative since 1987, began enrolling residents in the Oregon Health Plan, which offered health coverage to every resident in the state below the poverty line. Oregon did this by obtaining a federal waiver from the normal Medicaid requirements (e.g., rules overseeing eligibility and services), which allowed it to enroll more people by limiting the services it offered. A public commission created a list of 745 services that was rank-ordered based on the effectiveness of treatment, the impact on health, and as a tiebreaker, cost. The state legislature then examined the priority list to determine where to draw the line on services. In the first year, the line was drawn at 606; in other words, any illness above 606 was covered under the Oregon Health Plan while any illness below 607 was not covered. As one doctor put it, "Most things at the top are important, and most things at the bottom are not so important." On the positive, Oregonians overwhelmingly supported the plan, as it provided health coverage for 100,000 additional low-income people in the first four years of the program, dropping the number of uninsured from 18 percent to 11 percent. While some criticized the plan as "rationing" health care, others pointed to the fact that Oregon's plan had increased access, while other states were eliminating thousands of families from Medicaid and cutting services.[31]

Many heralded the Oregon approach as a great success, and Minnesota and Tennessee soon followed with their own statewide health programs that expanded services for low-income people, with Minnesota adding 100,000 people and Tennessee adding 500,000 to its Medicaid programs in the late 1990s. Unfortunately, the economic downturn in 2003 caused a decline in state revenues, while the cost of medical care costs continued to increase. These two competing pressures caused a budget shortfall within these state plans. In order to provide the necessary funds for the Oregon Health Plan, the state raised co-payments on various services, charging patients $50 to visit the emergency room and $250 for a hospital visit. These higher costs forced low-income people to leave the Oregon Health Plan in droves, with the numbers enrolled plummeting from 88,874 to 18,000 over a five-year period. Similarly, Tennessee had to cut 200,000 from its Tenn-Care program in 2005.[32]

These setbacks did not stop other states from looking for ways to control costs and expand health coverage to the uninsured. In 2006, Massachusetts passed legislation that provided residents near-universal health care coverage. The Massachusetts model achieved near-universal coverage by mandating that all residents obtain health insurance by July 1, 2007. Employers with more than ten workers were required to provide insurance coverage or they paid annually up to $295 per employee into a "fair share" fund. Within four years, the number of uninsured had been cut from 6.4 percent to 1.9 percent, which was the lowest in the nation in 2010. It is noteworthy that during this same time period, the United States uninsured rate continued to climb, from 15.2 percent to 16.3 percent.[33]

Other states have also tried to pass universal health coverage. In the same year Massachusetts passed its near-universal coverage, California attempted to pass a universal health care bill. In 2006, California's Assembly and Senate passed a health care bill that would have provided universal coverage through a single-payer, publicly funded system. The bill, which was vetoed by Governor Arnold Schwarzenegger, would have pooled all the money the state spends on health care (from the federal and state governments) and combined it with the employer contribution and a new state tax. This single-payer system would have eliminated the need for insurance programs, thus reducing the amount paid by individual and employer. As State Sen. Sheila Kuehl, the bill's sponsor, explained, "Employers pay about 7 percent of payroll, compared to what they pay now if they are providing any plan, which is 10 or 11 percent with no control of the fact that the prices rise every year. . . . Individuals would pay about 3 1/2 to 4 percent of their income, which is a lot less than they pay now because they're paying huge deductibles and there would be no deductibles or co-pays in this plan." The bill, which was similar to the health care systems in Sweden and Finland, passed both state houses again in 2008, but was once again vetoed by Governor Schwarzenegger.[34]

In Vermont, a broad-based coalition of nonprofit, labor, and the faith communities came together to push their state legislature to consider a state solution to the health care crisis. Operating under the banner that health care is a human right, Vermont enacted a bill in 2010 to explore three designs to achieve universal coverage, as well as cut health care costs, and create a preventative health care system that is integrated, rather than fragmented. Currently, 7 percent of Vermont residents are uninsured and 15 percent are inadequately insured. The results of Vermont's efforts will be discussed in the next section.[35]

People have also been working at the local level to find solutions to health care in their communities. In Silicon Valley, a group from Working Partnerships USA and People Acting in Community Together (PACT) encouraged the Santa Clara County Board of Supervisors to develop a comprehensive health care program for all county children (less than one year to eighteen years old) with family income below 300 percent of the poverty line ($62,000). Congress had passed the State Children's Health Insurance Program (SCHIP) in 1997 to provide grants to states to cover health care coverage for children above the eligibility levels of Medicaid, but SCHIP did not cover the kids of undocumented workers, nor was it being fully utilized by low-income families. In response, Working Partnerships USA and PACT put forward the Children's Health Initiative, with the goal of providing health care for all children in Santa Clara County. Using funds from the state's tobacco settlement, Santa Clara County created a new locally funded health insurance program entitled Healthy Kids, which provided health care to all children in the county, and also developed a mass education effort led by community-based advocates to inform low-income residents about eligibility for Healthy Kids, Medicaid, and SCHIP (or Healthy Families in California).[36]

The Children's Health Initiative proved to be a success, as it greatly enhanced comprehensive health care for Santa Clara County kids. Within three years, 71,000 children, who had been previously uninsured, were now receiving health coverage, with Healthy Kids providing insurance for 13,000 children. Funding for Healthy Kids came from the county, local cities, private foundations, and corporate sponsors. Parents also contributed a small amount, as they paid from $4 to $21 a month per child, with a maximum cost of $63 per family and a $5 co-payment for some medical, dental, and vision services. With this success, San Francisco, San Mateo, and Los Angeles Counties replicated the Children's Health Initiative, and in 2007, a statewide organization was created to represent the twenty-four California counties that had developed children's health programs. Collectively, these programs were serving more than 150,000 previously uninsured children in Healthy Kids and had signed up 175,000 more for Medicaid and Healthy Families.[37]

Of course, there were some policy changes at the national level during the 1970s to the early 2000s. In 2002, President Bush greatly expanded the number of community health centers as part of his "compassionate conserva-tism" philosophy, and 1,297 centers had been either constructed or expanded by 2008. This new federal funding for nonprofit community health centers allowed for basic health services to be provided to over 16 million uninsured people, an increase of 60 percent over a six-year period. This was followed by President Bush's prescription drug plan, which allowed 40 million seniors to purchase medicine by paying $35 per month, with Medicare paying up to $2,250 with a $250 deductible. Bush called the prescription drug plan "the greatest advance in health care coverage for America's seniors since the founding of Medicare." However, opponents argued that the $400 billion price tag was underestimated and that without price caps, it was a giveaway to the drug companies.[38]

As the first decade of the twenty-first century was coming to a close, the US health care system was on life support: there were 46 million people with no health care, many people were being denied coverage if they had a preexisting condition, insurance providers were dropping people from coverage in order to avoid paying for procedures, and the overall cost of the overall health care system had increased to $2.3 trillion, or $7,681 per person annually. Health care spending was now 16 percent of the nation's GDP, while medical debt was the cause of over one-half of all bankruptcies. Perhaps the most troubling was the fact that an estimated 45,000 people a year were losing their lives because they did not have access to health care.[39]

The rising costs of health care and its corresponding rise in the unin-sured, along with the practice of insurance companies denying coverage because of a preexisting condition, had made the entire system untenable, and thus helped to create the necessary conditions to allow for a breakthrough at the national level. During the 2008 campaign, candidate Obama stated, "The time has come for universal health care in America," and with his election victory, President Obama made health care the signature issue of his first term. Within fourteen months of becoming president, Obama had done what no president had done before him, which was to usher through Congress a near universal health care bill.[40]

THE RIGHT TO ADEQUATE MEDICAL CARE: CURRENT APPROACHES

The Obama administration and the congressional Democrats attempted to learn from previous failures, and so they offered a bill that mostly kept the existing health care system intact. Obama and the Democrats didn't have the votes or the will to put forward a single-payer system; they also decided that they didn't even have the votes for a government-run "public option" that would compete against the private insurers. So Obama and the Democrats put forward a plan to provide near-universal coverage through the expansion of Medicaid and federal subsidies (i.e., tax credits) and to control costs through the creation of a competitive marketplace that was transparent and to move doctors and hospitals away from a fee-for-service model (i.e., separate fees for every step of each procedure) to paying them in a lump sum for the overall procedure (e.g., for a hip replacement).

Affordable Care Act

When the Affordable Care Act was passed in 2010, some measures took immediate effect, while others took effect over the next four years. What follows is an explanation of the Affordable Care Act, and in particular, a discussion of whether it will achieve the Economic Bill of Rights' constitutional commitment of a right to adequate medical care for all. In addition, other modern-day examples working to achieve this right to adequate health care—for example, Vermont's effort to provide universal health care and the current grassroots movement for Medicare for All—are explored.

The Affordable Care Act had many features that the public approved of, including the requirement that insurance companies provide coverage for people with preexisting conditions, that children under age twenty-six could remain on their parents' health plan, and that seniors received discounts to reduce the costs of the Medicare prescription drug program. At the same time, the Obama plan included the controversial proposal—particularly for conservatives—that all Americans were required to obtain health insurance or be taxed. Ironically, this idea came from the Heritage Foundation, a conservative think tank, in 1989, as an alternative to single-payer health care. One thing that the Obama plan did not include was a government-run "public option" that would compete with insurance companies—to the great disappointment of his liberal supporters—thus leaving the insurance and drug companies in a very strong position to control health care delivery in the United States. Importantly, the public option was a compromise between those that offered a single-payer model—which would stop the 1,200 private insurance companies from offering coverage for essential health services—and those that offered a truly private system that used government subsidies for those who could not afford health care. However, this did not stop conservatives from calling it "socialized medicine" and a "government takeover."[41]

Jacob Hacker, who is now a professor at the University of California–Berkeley, developed the original idea for the public option in 2001, proposing a new public plan that would be similar to Medicare but would cover the nonelderly population. Enrollees would also include people who are currently uninsured, as well as people who are now receiving Medicaid and SCHIP. In addition, employers would have the choice of providing this public option to their employees. The hope was that this would create a pool of enrollees of

130 million people—which would dwarf Medicare's 45 million enrollees—and allow for much lower prices than offered by private insurance programs. This public option would also put downward pressure on health care prices. Due to the affordability of health care, the number of the uninsured would be cut to 2–5 million people. However, by the time the public option was introduced into Congress, it was reduced to just a shell of the original idea, with the plan enrolling just 10 million people, and leaving between 17 and 34 million uninsured. To make it worse, conservative Democrats agreed that the only way they would support a public option was if it would charge 5 percent above the price of Medicare. Even with these changes, conservatives did not support it. With the president wanting to get the legislation passed before his State of the Union address, the idea for a public option was eventually dropped from the legislation. Many liberals believed that without the public option as a part of the Affordable Care Act, the legislation would neither get the nation close to universal care nor be successful at containing costs.[42]

Obama wanted his health care law to have bipartisan support. While he did not achieve this goal—no Republican in the House or Senate voted for the final version—Obama did obtain the support of the powerful interest groups that have historically opposed a national health care plan. The American Medical Association supported the legislation, and the private insurance companies agreed to support it if the plan required that all Americans buy private insurance coverage and it did not include a "public option" to compete against them. And even though Obama campaigned against the employer option and in support of the public option, the private insurance companies got their way in the end. In addition, the large pharmaceutical companies agreed to support the legislation when they got what they wanted, which was to exclude Medicare from being able to negotiate lower drug costs, and to not allow the importation of cheaper drugs from Canada and Europe, both of which Obama had supported in the 2008 campaign.[43]

The Affordable Care Act was signed into law in March 2010, and some parts went into effect that year, including (1) tax credits to small businesses under twenty-five employees to encourage them to provide health coverage, (2) federal matching funds to allow states to cover more people on Medicaid, (3) a one-time $250 rebate check to all seniors in Medicare so as to cover the uncovered costs left by the prescription drug coverage, (4) the ability of children up to twenty-six years of age to remain on their parents' health insurance plan, (5) the stoppage of insurance companies from denying coverage to children who had a preexisting condition, (6) the inability of insurance companies to cancel coverage and deny payment if a customer made an error on an application, (7) the allowance for people to appeal the decisions of insurance companies when they deny services to an external review, (8) the phasing out of lifetime limits on coverage by insurance companies, (9) the inability of companies to make unreasonable rate hikes by requiring them to explain their premium increases in order to receive $250 million of new federal money, as well as to remain eligible for the Affordable Insurance Exchanges, and (10) the funding of new community health centers.[44]

In 2011, more parts of the Affordable Care Act took effect, including additional discounts on senior drugs to make them affordable and free annual wellness visits for seniors, as well as a rule that caps administrative costs by requiring insurance companies to spend a minimum of 85 percent of all premium dollars on health care benefits for large employer plans and 80 percent for small employers and individuals.[45]

As could be expected, the response by liberals and conservatives to these changes varied sharply. On the one hand, liberals argued that the Affordable Care Act was a very good start, but it was not the end of the work; there was still more to be done to get to universal coverage and control costs. On the other hand, conservatives argued that it was a "government takeover" of the health care system, and they hoped that the Supreme Court would overturn the act. However, in 2012, the Supreme Court ruled in a 5–4 decision that the central part of the legislation—i.e., that Americans are required to obtain health insurance or pay a penalty—was constitutional under Congress's power to levy taxes. With this defeat, conservatives turned to the upcoming presidential election, with the hope that Mitt Romney would win and overturn "Obamacare." Even though Romney had signed into law similar legislation when he was governor of Massachusetts, he campaigned aggressively against the legislation, stating, "What the Court did not do on its last day in session, I will do on my first day if elected President of the United States. And that is I will act to repeal Obamacare." With Romney's resounding defeat in the 2012 presidential election, Obamacare was here to stay.[46]

In 2013, more aspects of the Affordable Care Act took effect. Positively, the federal government announced that it was funding 236 new community health care centers, which would serve 1.25 million people. Moreover, to encourage preventative care, states now had to pay no less than 100 percent of Medicare payment rates for primary care services, which was to be fully funded by the federal government. In addition, Health Insurance Marketplaces were created, providing small businesses and individuals the ability to purchase affordable health plans that were transparent in a competitive marketplace. States decided (1) to create a state-based Health Insurance Marketplace or exchange, (2) to develop a Health Insurance Marketplace run in partnership between the state and the federal government, or (3) to do nothing, and default to a federal-run marketplace. By the launch of Obamacare in the fall of 2013, sixteen states (primarily in the West and on the East Coast) had developed state-based exchanges, seven states opted for a federal-state partnership, and twenty-seven states (primarily in the South and Midwest) defaulted to the federal exchange. The goal of the exchanges is to provide citizens with clear information about what type of health care services are being offered, and for the individual to be able to make an informed decision about cost, which will hopefully encourage competition and drive down costs. Advocates of the Affordable Care Act also believe that the insurance marketplaces will improve health care services since to be a part of the exchange, plans must cover certain core benefits; in 2012, over one-half of the individual insurance plans did not meet the new federal minimum standards. Interestingly, within less than a year of implementing their own state exchanges, Nevada, Massachusetts, and Oregon decided to move to the federal exchange due to technical challenges as well as the long-term cost of running an exchange.[47]

In October 2013, Americans began purchasing health care from the state and federal exchanges. The state exchanges, which were set up in the states where Obamacare had more political support, ran fairly well from the beginning; this was in stark contrast to the federal exchange, which has had major computer software problems, making it extremely difficult, and very frustrating, to sign up. This computer glitch led to an extremely slow start for Obamacare, with only 364,682 people signing up for health insurance through the state and federal exchanges in October and November. Following this public relations disaster for the Obama administration, the federal government fixed the computer problems, which allowed 1.8 million people to sign up for health insurance in December. Sign-ups continued throughout the first quarter of 2014, and by mid-April, President Obama reported that 8 million people had signed up for health care through the state and federal exchanges, with 85 percent receiving federal subsidies to help pay for the health care. A recent Kaiser survey suggests that 57 percent of these enrollees were previously uninsured.[48]

In 2014, several other key components of the Affordable Care Act are being implemented. First, companies with more than fifty workers, which is 4 percent of all businesses, must offer health care insurance to employees working thirty or more hours a week. The insurance must be affordable (i.e., no more than 9.5 percent of the worker's income) and cover a core set of health benefits. If the company does not offer employer-sponsored health insurance, it is fined $2,000 per employee (minus the first thirty employees). Almost all big businesses already offer employer-sponsored health coverage, so this new mandate will apply to only 4 percent of large companies. Businesses with fewer than fifty employees, which represent 96 percent of all businesses, are not required to offer insurance; however, they will be offered a tax credit of up to 50 percent of the cost to encourage employers to purchase health insurance. At the same time, individuals are required to purchase insurance or be fined $95 in 2014, with the fine rising to $695 in 2016. Small businesses and individuals will be able to buy health insurance directly from the states' Health Insurance Market. In addition, strong reforms were put into effect that banned insurance companies from not renewing or selling coverage to people who have preexisting conditions, and capping the amount of money spent on administrative services.[49]

In 2014, two other measures—a tax credit and the expansion of Medicaid—have been put into effect in order to expand access to health care. First, the tax credit is made available for people to buy insurance with incomes from 100 percent to 400 percent of the poverty line (400 percent is approximately $43,000 for a person, or $89,000 for a family of four). The goal of this tax credit is to expand health coverage to working-class and middle-class people who are not eligible for Medicaid and other federal programs. Second, the states now have the option to increase their Medicaid program to people making up to 138 percent of the poverty line (i.e., $33,000 for a family of four). The original law stated that the states were required to expand their Medicaid, but the Supreme Court ruled the states could opt out of this provision, and conservative governors and state legislatures have chosen to do so. At the beginning of 2014, twenty-five states had decided to accept the Medicaid expansion, and twenty-five states decided to not accept it. The Obama administration had tried to woo states to participate—with the carrot being that the federal government will cover all costs of the Medicaid increase until 2016, and then gradually move to 90 percent by 2020. The administration thought it had a major victory when the governor of Florida, a strong opponent of Obamacare, announced in February 2013 that he had decided to accept the Medicaid expansion, which would expand coverage to 1.3 million Americans. However, in May, the Florida legislature decided not to accept the funding for the Medicaid expansion. This battle over whether to accept the Medicaid expansion also in Arizona and Michigan, as well as in several other states throughout the nation.[50]

In 2015, another key component will go into effect, and that is how doctors are paid. Much of the 905-page Affordable Care Act is dedicated to changing how doctors and hospitals are reimbursed. This was a primary concern of the legislation because the fee for service model is the main reason behind the meteoric rise in health care spending, from $1,000 per capita in 1962 to over $8,000 today. To control this rising cost, the Affordable Care Act will try to move the health care system away from paying doctors and hospitals for each individual procedure and toward bundling the money and paying them in a lump sum for the overall procedure. If the doctors and hospitals provide the care for less than the lump sum, while also achieving various quality metrics (e.g., not readmitted to hospital after surgery, no infections), they would keep the difference as profit. If the doctors and hospital provide low-quality care, they will receive fewer payments, and thus less profit. The hope is that if the federal government, the largest health care spender in the nation, moves toward value rather than volume, it will also encourage the private health plans to move in this direction, since 78 percent of the plans pay doctors and hospitals in a fee-for-service model.[51]

Questions remain about what will be the effect of the Affordable Care Act on expanding coverage and cost containment. The best estimates are that the Medicaid expansion and subsidies provided to low-income people in the exchanges will cover approximately 30 million more Americans by 2016, while at the same time leaving about 30 million Americans without coverage. Also, some analysts estimate that the various controls built into the Affordable Care Act (i.e., the exchanges, capping of administrative costs, justifying increases in premiums to government regulators, moving away from a fee-for-service model) will contain costs, while others say that costs will expand. What we do know is that health care costs have slowed from 2009 to 2011. In 2003, health care spending grew by almost 9 percent per capita, but from 2009 to 2011, it grew by just 3 percent. It is estimated that about 40 percent of the drop was due to the recession and to people's unwillingness to spend money, but some credit is being given to the Affordable Care Act for shifting the health care system toward cost savings. However, health costs rose by a 9.9 percent annual rate in the first quarter of 2014, as the 8 million people who signed up for health coverage under the Affordable Care Act began utilizing their doctors and hospitals.[52]

Vermont Takes Lead to Provide Universal Coverage

The Affordable Care Act does not provide for universal coverage and thus does not achieve the Economic Bill of Rights' constitutional commitment of a right to adequate medical care for all. People across the country who were committed to this goal were upset that President Obama and Democrats in Congress left intact the current profit system, rather than implement a program that defined health care as a human right, with its belief that health services should be provided to all without consideration of people's ability to pay. As a result, some states are moving toward this goal by working to enact state laws to create a system based on this right. Many progressives believe the best model to guarantee health care for all is the single-payer approach, and Vermont is the first state to approve legislation to do this. As stated above, Vermont passed a bill in 2010 to explore three designs to achieve universal coverage and to cut health care costs: (1) a government-run single-payer system; (2) a public option, which creates a new public plan that would compete against private health care; and (3) a public-private single-payer system.

In June 2011, the Vermont legislature chose a public-private, single-payer model, since it had the largest cost savings and was seen as more politically acceptable. This single-payer system will not allow for private insurance companies to pay for essential medical care, and it will receive its financing from a broad base of taxes, which advocates argue will be less than what Vermonters currently are paying for insurance premiums and deductibles. At the same time, the single-payer system will allow HMOs to operate as long as they are providing health care services in their own facilities and are not just paying for services. In addition, Vermont has decided that a "public-private" board will oversee the single-payer system rather than a governmental agency. The five-person "public-private" board will be composed of patients, doctors and nurses, employers, and representatives from appropriate government agencies, and it will create a budget, define the benefits package, and adjust payment rates. At the same time, the governor has the ability to veto the decisions of this board, while a third-party provider will oversee the claim processing, adjudication, and public relations.[53]

Before implementing "Green Mountain Care," Vermont must still get a waiver from the federal government to bypass some of the Affordable Care Act requirements—something that President Obama said he supports—but under current law, the state must wait until 2017. However, Vermont senators Patrick Leahy and Bernie Sanders and Rep. Peter Welch have put forward federal legislation moving the time frame up to 2014; however, no action has been taken by Congress.[54]

As stated earlier, a broad-based coalition of nonprofit, labor, and faith communities came together in Vermont to work on the "Healthcare Is a Human Right" campaign. For the past five years, the campaign has argued that insurance is not the right way to pay for health care, since insurance manages risk, and medical care is not a risk because it is something that all people need at some point of their life. The campaign considers a visit to a doctor to be similar to going to school, since we all do it and need it. And just as the public has decided that education is a public good for all, and not just a private good for the people who can afford it, the campaign believes that medical care should be available to all and should be publicly financed. In a 2011 op-ed, James Haslam, coordinator of the campaign and lead organizer of the Vermont Workers' Center, stated,

> The health care infrastructure (and services) are public goods that are threatened in the current health care system. In particular, economic incentives distort the provision of quality care, and multiple payers create excessive administrative waste. We do not have to settle for a system that puts profits before health. We can make our health care dollars do what they are supposed to do: enable equal access to care for all. To achieve this, Vermont must provide health care as a public good, readily available to all. Health care belongs to all of us, just like education, and should be publicly financed, with costs and benefits shared equitably by all Vermonters. We can no longer afford the insurance industry that prioritizes private over public interests.[55]

Not surprisingly, Vermont is being heralded as the leader among states trying to achieve universal coverage through a single-payer system, and several state legislatures and health care activists in other states, such as California, Colorado, Hawaii, Illinois, Maine, Oregon, New York, and Washington, are trying to duplicate their success. These health care activists are working to expand the Vermont model; for example, Betty Johnson, co-founder of Health Care for All Oregon, states, "Our ultimate goal would be that this [i.e., single-payer health care] would cover the United States." These activists take solace in the fact that it was the Canadian provinces in the 1940s and 1950s that took the lead in developing a national health care system in Canada.[56]

In addition to states pushing for a single-payer system, there are some who are pushing for a citywide solution. Anthony Weiner, the unsuccessful mayoral candidate for New York in 2013, stated that if he was elected mayor, he would "make New York City the single-payer laboratory in the country." His plan would create a Medicare-like system that covered city workers, retirees, and uninsured immigrants that are excluded from Obamacare. The plan would cover 300,000 city workers, 300,000 retirees, and 500,000 undocumented immigrants. Weiner argued that health care spending in the city of New York, which was at $15.5 billion in 2013 and was expected to rise 40 percent between 2014 and 2017, would be curbed under a citywide single-payer approach. However, his plan would increase payments for the city workers and retirees from nothing to 10 percent of the premiums, and 25 percent if they smoke.[57]

Medicare for All

In addition to pushing a state-by-state approach for the single-payer system, other advocates and politicians support a national approach. As discussed, Obama's Affordable Care Act was both a victory and a defeat for liberals; it was a victory in that it will increase the number of people receiving health care by 30 million and stop some of the worst aspects of private insurance (e.g., the denial of insurance because of preexisting conditions), but it was a defeat in that 30 million people will still be left without coverage. In order to guarantee health care for all, progressives did put forward legislation for a single-payer system in 2009. However, the Obama administration never seriously considered single-payer legislation, even though a single-payer bill had eighty-seven co-signers in the House of Representatives, since the president wanted a bipartisan bill.[58]

This defeat in 2009 has not stopped enthusiasm for a national single-payer system, and several groups, such as Physicians for a National Health Care Plan, California Nurses Association, and HealthCare-Now!, are backing HR 676: The Expanded and Improved Medicare for All Act, which was once again introduced by Rep. John Conyers (D-MI) in 2013. The vision is to replace Obamacare with a national single-payer system by expanding Medicare to cover all Americans. Sen. Bernie Sanders (I-VT), a supporter of this legislation, states, "In my view, while the Affordable Care Act is an important step in the right direction and I am glad that the Supreme Court upheld it, we ultimately need to do better. If we are serious about providing high-quality, affordable healthcare as a right, not a privilege, the real solution to America's health care crisis is a Medicare-for-all, single-payer system. Until then, we will remain the only major nation that does not provide health care for every man, woman, and child as a right of citizenship."[59]

A "Medicare for All" would create a universal health care system that is publicly financed but privately delivered. This legislation would eliminate the private insurance companies, and thus take the profit motive—which leads to the denial of medical care in order to save money—out of the picture. It would leave decisions about what is appropriate care up to physicians and nonprofit health care providers, and not the insurance companies. The overall goal of the system would change to the provision of medical care and promotion of wellness, rather than making a dollar. In addition to universal coverage, this legislation contained costs by reducing administrative waste, provided for regional planning that followed public health needs rather than duplicate services, and lowered the price of prescription drugs through its purchasing power.[60]

Some experts argue that it will be politically difficult to eliminate private insurance companies from providing essential services. However, advocates point to the fact that two-thirds of Americans support a Medicare for All model and that studies have shown that Medicare does a better a job than employer-sponsored private insurance plans at providing access and financial protection. Dr. Andrew Coates, the president of Physicians for a National Health Program, composed of 18,000 doctors, states,

> Health care costs are continuing to rise. . . . At the root of this problem is the private health industry—the big private insurers, drug companies, and hospital chains—whose primary allegiance is to their shareholders and executives, not to patients. The insurers make profits by denying claims and raising premiums, co-pays, and deductibles. They also drag down our health system with the costly paperwork and bureaucracy they inflict on doctors, hospitals, and patients. By replacing the private insurers with a streamlined single-payer system, we can save over $400 billion squandered annually on wasteful paperwork. That's enough money to cover all of the uninsured and to eliminate all co-pays and deductibles.[61]

Jack Bernard, former chair of the Jasper County Republican Party in Georgia, stated in 2013 that a Medicare for All program should at least be considered since it has the ability to contain costs. Bernard states, "Single payer would drive down costs because Medicare (or a utility-like private single-payer insurer) would have leverage to keep costs down. With no other game in town, providers would be forced to operate more efficiently. Drug companies would be pressured to give Americans the same drug pricing that is found elsewhere. . . . The real question is whether either party is willing to stand up to the drug and insurance lobbies and do what is best for America."[62]

SUMMARY

In this chapter, three ideas have been discussed to achieve the constitutional commitment of a right to adequate medical care: the Affordable Care Act, Vermont's single-payer plan, and Medicare for All. These plans are part of the dynamic discussion that is occurring in this nation on how to guarantee the right to adequate medical care.

Chapter 6

The Right to Adequate Protection from Economic Fears of Old Age, Sickness, Accident, and Unemployment

The Sixth Amendment

PROBLEM

Out of all the constitutional commitments in the Economic Bill of Rights, the right to adequate protection from the economic fears of old age, sickness, accident, and unemployment is perhaps the closest to being obtained. Today, senior poverty is 8.7 percent, down from 35 percent in 1960; unemployment insurance has kept 20 million–plus people out of poverty from 1987 to 2009; and 11 million disabled workers and their families are currently receiving disability benefits.[1]

The reason that economic fears among seniors, the unemployed, and the disabled are relatively low, at least in the context of the United States, is due to the changes brought about by the New Deal and the Great Society. In

1935, President Roosevelt signed into law the Social Security Act, which provided old-age assistance and insurance, as well as unemployment insurance, assistance for handicapped children and the blind, workers' compensation, and aid to dependent children. Today, Social Security provides benefits to almost 58 million Americans—over 40 million retirees and their dependents, as well as 8.8 million disabled and 6 million youth whose parents have died. The average check for seniors is $1,262 a month, or $15,144 a year. For most seniors, it is the only source of guaranteed income they will receive; without it, 44 percent of seniors would live below the poverty line. As for the unemployed, 4.5 million receive unemployment insurance, with the average check being $295 a week, or $15,340 a year.[2]

Of course, Social Security can be improved. With 3.5 million seniors (age sixty-five and above) in poverty in 2010, and with 2.3 million more just above it, there is still work to do. Interestingly, new research says that the 9 percent official poverty rate may be too low, as the new Supplemental Poverty Measure puts senior poverty at 15 percent if you take into account variations by region and nonmonetary benefits such as food stamps and tax credits. In addition, the official senior poverty rate varies greatly depending on race, with about 7 percent of whites living in poverty, but with much higher rates among Asians (14 percent), blacks (18 percent), and Latinos (18 percent). Elderly poverty rates also vary by gender, with senior women having almost 40 percent higher poverty rates than men (11 percent vs. 7 percent). With so many people living in poverty or near poverty, 8.3 million adults over the age of sixty face the threat of hunger. These high poverty rates make 9 million Americans who are age fifty and older food insecure.[3]

The primary reason for the increase in elderly poverty is the cost associated with the failing health of our seniors as they age. Almost all seniors below the poverty line (96 percent)—in comparison to retirees who don't live in poverty (62 percent)—have some sort of medical issue, such as arthritis, diabetes, or high blood pressure. Moreover, seniors living in poverty often have a major medical condition, such as cancer, a heart problem, or a stroke. Sudipto Banerjee, a health care researcher, states, "Medical expenditures go up for the elderly as they age and medical expenses have been rising over the past decade very rapidly. . . . A lot of people have to move to nursing homes, and nursing homes are very expensive. People who live there, they lose their income and assets very quickly." Using the federal government's new supplemental poverty measure, which was developed in 2011 to take into account such factors as health care costs, the overall US poverty rate for seniors jumps to 15 percent.[4]

Unemployment insurance can also be improved to get even closer to the constitutional commitment of the right to adequate protection from economic fears. For example, the amount a recipient receives from unemployment insurance varies widely, as each state determines its own level of benefits. In Hawaii, the average unemployment check is $416 a week, which covers on average 54 percent of weekly wages. However, in Arizona, the average unemployment check is $213 a week, covering just 26 percent of weekly wages. Thus, states that offer meager unemployment insurance make it more difficult for recipients to make ends meet.[5]

Today, there are community organizations, policy advocates, and politicians who are working on solutions to strengthen the nation's Social Security system so as to get even closer to the constitutional commitment of the right to adequate protection from economic fear. At the same time, there is a movement to reduce Social Security benefits under the banner of saving the program. It is to these responses that we now turn.

SOLUTION

Currently, conservatives are pushing for a cut to Social Security benefits. In late 2013, Speaker of the House John Boehner (R-OH) announced that he was demanding cuts in Social Security, as well as to Medicare and Medicaid, as part of any agreement with President Obama to increase the debt limit. Boehner and the conservatives argue that in order to reduce the deficit and protect Social Security for the long haul, benefits need to be cut.[6]

At the same time, progressives and liberals are working to stop these cuts in benefits to Social Security. However, these groups are not just content to stop the benefit cuts, but rather are working on a variety of solutions that would strengthen the long-term viability of the program while expanding benefits, and thus get the nation closer to FDR's vision of providing "cradle to grave" security. Groups such as Social Security Works are fighting to increase benefits by $70 per month and to increase benefits to seniors who are most in need. Social Security Works is also working on the revenue side of the issue, promoting a change in Social Security funding so that people making over $113,700 annually would pay Social Security tax. At the state level, groups like the National Employment Law Project are advocating for the strengthening of state unemployment insurance programs by expanding eligibility in order to cover more low-wage workers and part-time workers, and to increase the amount of unemployment benefits, as well as to extend the amount of time they are provided.[7]

THE HISTORY OF THE RIGHT TO ADEQUATE PROTECTION FROM ECONOMIC FEARS OF OLD AGE, SICKNESS, ACCIDENT, AND UNEMPLOYMENT

From the founding of the country until the New Deal era, there was little protection from old age, sickness, accident, and unemployment. The dominant ideology up to the twentieth century was rugged individualism, with its belief that individual initiative was the key to success, private property was sacrosanct, and that a small, decentralized government was the best way to maintain liberty. Yet, from the earliest days of this nation, there were people proposing ideas to provide adequate protection from economic fears.

In 1797, Thomas Paine wrote *Agrarian Justice,* wherein he argued that the new nation should develop a social insurance plan for the elderly, as well as a one-time payment to young adults to ensure a good start in life. Paine had been inspired by the egalitarian society of many Native American tribes, noting that in early human society, all land was held in common. However, with the development of cities and towns, many people did not own land. To reimburse people for their loss of land, Paine believed that people deserved a "natural inheritance." For Paine, this natural inheritance should come in the form of a retirement plan and a one-time payment to be received upon turning twenty-one years of age. Importantly, Paine's proposal was the first US plan for an old-age pension, and it has been credited for inspiring the eventual development of Social Security; however, a retirement plan for all Americans would not be enacted for 138 years following publication of *Agrarian Justice.*[8]

Working against the development of unemployment insurance and old-age pensions was the idea that if people were poor, it was due to some type of immoral conduct, and thus they deserved to be in poverty. This was the dominant thinking in the nineteenth and early twentieth centuries, and the business class and many Christian leaders promoted it. This dominant perspective allowed for two types of poor: the "deserving" and "undeserving" poor. The unemployed fell into the category of the undeserving poor, but many elders escaped this moral branding and were considered part of the deserving poor. As a result, seniors—as well as widows, children, and the disabled—were eligible in the eighteenth and nineteenth centuries to receive "outdoor relief," which was a welfare-like program administered by local Overseers of the Poor, who provided them with wood (for fuel), food, and money.[9]

As cities expanded and poverty grew in the nineteenth century, the nation turned to "the poorhouse" as the collective response to poverty. But while the solution to poverty changed, the analysis of why people were poor remained the same, as the poorhouse continued to distinguish between the worthy and unworthy poor. Poorhouses were built on land next to a farm. Residents were required to work on the farm in exchange for room and board. However, what started as an attempt to provide humane housing for the "worthy, deserving" poor, and strict housing for the "unworthy, undeserving," turned into collective failure, as poorhouses ended up being unsanitary and filthy places to live. In addition, they were unsuccessful at decreasing poverty or limiting outdoor relief. By the early twentieth century, poorhouses were seen as a human dumping ground and a place to be feared. Eventually, they were transformed into "old folks' homes" for senior citizens.[10]

An alternative explanation for why people were poor came from a group of social reformers who argued that the unemployed, as well as seniors that ended up in poverty, were in this condition not as a result of their immorality or lack of work ethic but because of industrialization, low wages, and unemployment. This structural explanation of poverty argued that in this new industrialized society, job loss was the result of the mechanization of agriculture and the reduction of "home manufacturing" due to the new factories in the cities. In addition, because there was an oversupply of labor, with ex-journeymen, immigrants, women, and children competing for these manufacturing jobs, factory wages were kept low—resulting in more poverty.[11]

This alternative explanation also took into effect that senior poverty was caused by changes in the family structure and demography. As a result of industrialization and urbanization, the parents went to the cities for jobs, and the grandparents stayed behind in the farming communities. This exodus led to a decline in the extended family, making it more difficult for seniors to make ends meet. At the same time, the number of seniors grew rapidly due to the progressive movement's successful programs in the field of sanitation and public health. In the first part of the twentieth century, the average lifespan increased by ten years, nearly doubling the numbers of seniors from 3 million to 6 million between 1900 and 1930. With seniors living longer, more of them had a difficult time making ends meet.[12]

In the mid- to late nineteenth century, structural explanations for poverty gained support as a result of a series of economic depressions. The 1893 depression, which was the fourth major economic downturn in fifty-six years, was the largest of the century, lasting five years. The national unemployment rate was 18 percent, and in some states it was much higher—25 percent in Pennsylvania, 35 percent in New York, and 44 percent in Michigan. In the face of massive unemployment, the Charitable Organization Societies, one of the largest charities in the country, abandoned its individualistic approach to poverty reduction (i.e., focusing on the deficits of the individual) and joined forces with the progressive movement, with its belief that the social and economic structures of society were responsible for poverty, and that social reform could greatly reduce social suffering. This progressive perspective, which was popular in the late nineteenth and early twentieth centuries among social reformers, would eventually become the dominant ideology in America from the New Deal through the 1970s. However, it was the Great Depression, during which the national unemployment rate reached 25 percent, that led to the widespread belief that economic structures were responsible for poverty. Mass unemployment challenged the nation's dominant ideology that one's social condition was the result of his or her work ethic and morality, as millions of people wanted to work but few found jobs. The nation was finally ready to adopt a structural approach to unemployment, yet the United States was behind the times, as England in 1910 became the first nation to pass unemployment insurance, and by 1935, ten European nations had already developed such programs. In 1931, Wisconsin became the first state to enact unemployment insurance, basing its program on England's plan. In 1932, Ohio followed, and in preparation of the federal government's passing of the Social Security Act, six more states passed unemployment insurance plans in 1935. By 1938, all forty-eight states had unemployment insurance programs.[13]

As for old-age pensions, the first US program was for military veterans. Since the Revolutionary War in the late eighteenth century, America has provided some type of pension for military veterans. However, it was the Civil War, which left the nation with hundreds of thousands of widows and orphans, as well as 282,000 disabled Union veterans, that led to the creation of pensions. Importantly, the Civil War pensions served as a precursor to Social Security, as the former program had many features that are similar to today's social insurance program. For example, eligibility requirements were determined by law, and the federal government (i.e., the Pension Bureau) decided who actually received the benefits. In addition, all Americans who were entitled to this benefit received it, and there was no shame in getting it since it was considered "earned." Originally, federal pensions were provided to disabled Union veterans with service-related injuries, as well as to widows and orphans. Then, in 1890, legislation was passed that allowed all disabled veterans to receive pensions, regardless if their disability was service-related. Finally, in 1906, all veterans age sixty-five or older were able to receive pensions. Within four years, this easing of the requirements allowed 29 percent of American men who were seniors to receive a Civil War pension. At its peak in 1893, Civil War pensions consumed 43 percent of the federal budget.[14]

In the late nineteenth century, some progressive industries began offering retirement plans. In 1882, the Alfred Dolge Company, which built pianos and organs, offered its workers a company pension, requiring that all workers give 1 percent of their income to a retirement plan, with the company adding 6 percent interest each year. Unfortunately, the Dolge pension plan was short-lived as the company went bankrupt several years later. However, a few other companies took notice, and by 1900, there were five US companies offering pensions to workers. More and more companies began offering pensions, and by 1932, about 15 percent of American workers had a company pension. Unfortunately, that left 85 percent of the nation's workers with no protection from the economic fears of old age.[15]

This lack of protection was brought into focus during the Great Depression, as senior poverty rates rose dramatically. By 1934, over one-half of seniors did not possess enough income to support themselves. President Roosevelt and his wife, Eleanor, were inundated with letters from citizens across this nation, like this one from a South Carolina woman: "Dear Mr. President. I'm 72 years old and have no one to take care of me." Or this letter from a woman in Virginia: "I'm a 60-year-old widow greatly in need of medical aid, food and fuel, I pray that you would have pity on me." This social suffering led President Roosevelt to introduce the Economic Security Bill—soon after renamed the Social Security Act—which included both a retirement and unemployment insurance plan, as well as a plan to aid poor children, handicapped children, and the blind. Another motivating factor to introduce the bill was that Roosevelt was being pushed to act, as several other individuals had put forward far more ambitious plans. For example, the physician Francis Townsend called for a "flat" federal pension for seniors. Under the banner of "Peace and Prosperity Thru Pensions," Townsend called for all citizens age sixty years and older, and retired, to receive $200 a month, with the only restrictions being that they needed to spend the entire amount before the end of each month and they were free from "habitual criminality." Townsend's plan would be financed by a national sales tax of 2 percent on all business transactions. Townsend asserted that his plan would stimulate the economy, abolish old-age poverty, decrease unemployment (since the plan removed seniors from the labor pool), and solve the Great Depression's problem of underconsumption. Townsend's plan gained large public support, and in some districts it was the chief political issue, with several congressmen elected because they supported this plan.[16]

Another more ambitious plan was put forth by Sen. Huey Long (D-LA). His "Share the Wealth" plan proposed an initial redistribution of $5,000 to all citizens, followed by a guaranteed income to all workers of $2,000–$2,500 each year (double the pay for an average factory worker). In addition, Long's plan gave "a pension to all persons above 60 years of age in an amount sufficient to support them in comfortable circumstances" except for the rich. In order to help the unemployed, Long proposed a thirty-hour work week and a four-week vacation, which he argued would greatly decrease unemployment since fewer hours of work means more people must be hired. Long's overall goal was to end poverty in America and provide economic security for all.[17]

A third proposal came from Rep. Ernest Lundeen (Farmer-Labor Party–MN) and also garnered considerable support. The Lundeen bill (House Resolution 2827) provided federal coverage for all workers and utilized national standards to determine benefits. In addition, it provided immediate compensation to unemployed workers at their average weekly wages, and guaranteed coverage until a job was found. It also provided women with sixteen weeks of paid maternity leave. The Lundeen bill was to be funded by an inheritance tax and a tax on the rich and corporations. Support for this bill came from unemployed worker groups, African American and ethnic organizations, women's organizations, and the Communist Party.[18]

These more ambitious plans—along with the continuing economic depression and labor unrest (1.5 million workers went on strike in 1934)—put pressure on President Roosevelt to enact unemployment insurance and old-age assistance. However, FDR's Social Security bill was not as generous as the alternative plans. First, the Social Security Act left the operation of unemployment insurance up to the states, which meant that the states decided the eligibility requirements, as well as the benefit amounts and their duration. This has led to fifty different unemployment programs in the fifty states, with some states offering generous benefits and others providing meager ones. In addition, the federal government said that businesses with eight or more workers were required to offer unemployment insurance, and left it up to the states to determine if they wanted to lower it, with only ten states deciding to cover employers with one or more worker. Second, the unemployment plan limited the length of time of the benefit to sixteen weeks, with most states initially offering between thirteen and sixteen weeks of coverage. Third, the unemployment plan excluded farm workers, domestic workers, and non-profits, which meant that millions of women and people of color would not receive this benefit. Fourth, both unemployment and retirement benefits were based on a person's salary, so what recipients received was based on income rather than need. Fifth, the retirement plan was set up to be jointly funded by employers and workers. And last, the Social Security Act did not blur the lines between social insurance and public assistance (i.e., welfare), as many other industrialized nations had done, but kept social insurance and public assistance separate from one another, which encouraged the American public to accept the unemployment insurance and old-age pension programs since they were defined as social insurance, but continued to stigmatize the poor since public assistance (e.g., aid to poor children) was defined as "welfare" or the "dole," which had a long history of being demonized in this country. Overall, Roosevelt's "cradle to grave" system was a patchwork of programs that left too many people without security since benefits were dependent on the state a person lived in, how much income a person made, how long a person had lived in the state, the length of time the person had worked, and what job a person had.[19]

Not surprisingly, Americans embraced FDR's old-age pension and unemployment insurance plans, as they dealt with two major issues surrounding economic security—elderly poverty and unemployment—and did it in a way that fit nicely into the dominant cultural paradigm of states' rights, limiting benefits for people of color and women, stigmatizing welfare recipients, and providing insurance, albeit social insurance (i.e., people were insured against a future risk, and that risk had a social objective greater than just self-interest). At the same time, it was a victory for the progressive movement, which had been arguing for structural solutions for the past fifty years. FDR's Social Security Act clearly was motivated by the belief that American free-market capitalism was the cause of social suffering and needed to be changed structurally in order to offer working Americans a decent life. In addition, this legislation injected the idea of entitlement into mainstream American society, since all citizens received old-age pensions and unemployment insurance regardless of their income or wealth. Some of these positive changes were felt right away, as unemployment insurance provided immediate help to people without jobs, providing 1 million Americans unemployment benefits of about $10 a week, with most receiving between $5 and $15 a week, depending on their state and level of income. However, other changes, like Social Security, did not begin until 1942, and early on provided only limited payments to seniors.[20]

Over the years, several amendments have been made to the original Social Security Act to expand its benefits. In 1939, retirement benefits were expanded to include not just the worker, but also the worker's spouse and minor children, as well as the spouse and minor children in cases where a worker died prematurely, thus altering Social Security from a workers' retirement program to an economic security program for families.

Another change to Social Security benefits has been the continual increase of the dollar amount received by retirees. To keep up with inflation, Congress increased Social Security benefits by 77 percent in 1950, which was almost the exact amount of the increase in prices since 1940. Three more times throughout the 1950s, Congress increased the dollar amount received by a total of 33 percent. In the 1960s, Congress increased it twice by 20 percent, and in the first three years of the 1970s, Congress increased benefits by 45 percent. These increases to senior benefits reduced senior poverty rates from 32 percent in 1963 to 16 percent in 1973, which was one of the largest drops in poverty in the history of the nation. In 1975, Congress enacted an automatic cost of living allowance (COLA) to raise benefits automatically in order to deal with inflation.[21]

In addition, unemployment coverage has been continuously expanded. Initially, unemployment insurance was offered primarily to private-sector workers who worked in the industrial and commercial industries, and whose companies employed eight or more workers for twenty weeks or more in a year. In 1954, Congress passed a law that amended the Social Security Act to include employers who had four or more employees who had worked for a minimum of one day in twenty weeks. The next year, Congress extended unemployment insurance to all federal workers. In 1970, Congress amended the Social Security Act once again to cover employers with one or more workers, nonprofit organizations with four or more workers, and some additional employer categories (e.g., salesmen paid on commission and agricultural processing workers). In 1974, coverage was extended to state and local government employees, agricultural employers with ten or more employees, domestic workers, and private school teachers. In 2000, unemployment insurance was extended to cover federally recognized Native American tribes. This series of expansions has increased greatly the number of workers covered by unemployment insurance. At the start of the program, the number of American workers covered was about 65 percent, but with the above amendments, it increased to 85 percent by 1972, and to 94 percent of all workers in 2012. Today, the groups that remain uncovered by unemployment insurance include the self-employed, agricultural workers on small farms, and domestic workers who are hired by multiple employers.[22]

Another change to Social Security was in 1961, which lowered the age that men could first receive old-age insurance to sixty-two, albeit it at a reduced rate. In 1965, Congress amended Social Security to include President Johnson's Medicare and Medicaid plan, which created a new social insurance program to provide health coverage to almost all Americans who were age sixty-five or older, as well as a low-income health care assistance plan. In the 1980s, Social Security faced a short-term financial crisis, and action was needed to support the program. Under the leadership of President Reagan, Congress amended Social Security to raise the retirement age for unreduced benefits to sixty-seven in 2027, increase the tax rates slightly to raise more revenue, tax Social Security benefits, and provide coverage for federal employees.[23]

After the reelection of President George W. Bush in 2004, he attempted to partially privatize Social Security in order to "fix" it. Bush claimed that Social Security would be paying out more benefits than it would be collecting in taxes in thirteen years (by 2018), and he claimed that by 2033, Social Security would run a deficit of $300 billion. Bush argued that the best way for Social Security to become financially sound was to allow young workers the ability to put part of their payroll tax contributions into voluntary personal retirement accounts where it would be invested in the stock and bond markets. However, many groups, including the Congressional Budget Office, reported that Bush's idea to privatize Social Security would actually worsen the financial stability of the program, since less money would be coming in to pay for current retirees. In the end, Bush's privatization plan found little support among mainstream Republicans and Democrats, and his plan was scrapped.[24]

The other Social Security program that has greatly expanded is disability insurance. In June 2014, the number of disabled workers and dependents receiving disability was 11 million, up from 3.9 million in 1985. Disabled workers and dependents now receive 16 percent of all Social Security cash benefits ($1,146 a month on average) at a cost of more than $144 billion. This increase in disability benefits could never have occurred without the expansion of the category of who is considered disabled.[25]

Initially, the 1935 Social Security Act provided benefits to handicapped children and the blind. However, in 1950, Congress amended Social Security to create a federal-state program to provide assistance to "permanently and totally disabled persons." In 1956, President Eisenhower signed into law the modern disability insurance program within Social Security, allowing disabled workers age fifty to sixty-four years old who had contributed five years into Social Security over the past ten years to receive cash benefits. In addition, the amendment allowed adults who had been disabled before age eighteen and whose parent was retired or deceased to receive benefits. These new benefits were paid for by a small increase in the tax rate (1.25 percent) on employees and employers, thus increasing the overall rate to 4.25 percent; also, these taxes would now go into a separate disability insurance trust fund. In 1960, Social Security was amended again to allow payments to any disabled worker, regardless of age, and to their dependents. In the early 1980s, President Reagan had asked the Social Security Administration to provide tighter oversight of who was receiving disability, which led to the termination of 1 million people from the disability rolls. There was a public uproar, and Congress responded in 1984 with the Social Security Disability Benefits Reform Act, which replaced the federal government's medical diagnosis with that of the worker's own doctors, and put greater weight on the self-reporting of pain and discomfort by the worker. Upon signing the bill, Reagan stated, "It maintains our commitment to treat disabled American citizens fairly and humanely while fulfilling our obligation to the Congress and the American taxpayers to administer the disability program effectively." This act significantly increased the number of people qualifying for disability benefits.[26]

There have been other factors causing this sharp increase in disability beneficiaries—among them welfare reform, the Great Recession, a decade of military conflict, and an aging population. First, disability beneficiaries have increased sharply due to the 1996 welfare reform law, which put time limits on how long people could receive benefits. The new welfare program—Temporary Assistance for Needy Families (TANF)—was no longer an entitlement to be given to people in need, but rather it was now assistance that had a two-year time limit (or less) during any one stretch and a five-year lifetime limit (or less) on receiving it. Thus, disability insurance became a better option than TANF for those workers with ailments and injuries, as disability benefits are ongoing and have no limits and provide more income ($1,130 for the average monthly disability payment in 2013 vs. $458 for the average monthly TANF payment for a family of three in Ohio or $271 in Texas). In addition, disability beneficiaries receive Medicare after two years, something that is unavailable to those on welfare.[27]

Second, the Great Recession has taken its toll, as 8.4 million jobs were lost in 2008–2009. During this same period, the number of disability claims jumped to 5.1 million; this 19 percent increase was the largest since 1974. As with the previous two recessions in the early 1990s and early 2000s, disability claims increased with rising unemployment. With the unemployment rate holding steady at 10 percent in 2010, some of the unemployed with an injury or ailment turned to disability to pay the bills. As a result, 2.9 million Americans applied for disability insurance in 2010, up from 2.1 million in 2006 and 1.2 million in 1999. In 2012, 5 million people were still unemployed for twenty-seven weeks or more, which was almost twice the rate of the previous high, in 1983. The weak economic recovery in the aftermath of the Great Recession has led to an average of 2.8 million applications a year from 2011 to 2013, with 2.9 million workers added to the disability rolls.[28]

Third, disability beneficiaries have increased as a result of a decade of war in Iraq and Afghanistan. Today, almost 800,000 veterans receive disability benefits from Social Security, and 600,000 younger veterans, many of them with wounds from the recent wars, are waiting to have their claims adjudicated. Fourth, and finally, as Baby Boomers age, there are more people in the age group of fifty to sixty-four, and because of their age, they are more likely to have injuries that prevent them from working. Once on disability, the likelihood of returning to work is very low.[29]

In summary, Social Security started in 1940 as a program serving 222,000 retired workers, and has turned into one of the nation's most effective antipoverty programs, as 59 million people will receive almost $863 billion in 2014, lifting millions out of poverty. Similarly, unemployment insurance, which initially just covered employers working for primarily industrial and commercial companies with eight or more workers, now provides almost all American workers coverage up to twenty-six weeks in all states, with the possibility of extensions if the nation experiences high unemployment. This need for longer unemployment benefits occurred during the Great Recession, when President Obama and Congress in 2009 allowed people to receive unemployment insurance for up to ninety-nine weeks in states with an unemployment rate of 8.5 percent or higher. In 2012, the US unemployment rate was 8.9 percent, and the federal and state governments provided $92 billion in unemployment benefits to about 14 million people. This was up from 2007, when the US unemployment rate was 4.5 percent and the federal and state governments provided $33 billion in benefits to approximately 8 million people.[30]

Retiree and disability benefits, unemployment insurance, and Medicare hospital insurance are all paid for by the Federal Insurance Contribution Act (FICA) taxes. There are two different types of FICA taxes: (1) the Old Age, Survivors, and Disability Insurance (OASDI) tax, which is a 12.4 percent payroll tax on wages split evenly between employers and employees (up to $117,000 on income in 2014), and (2) the Medicare tax, which is a 2.9 percent tax on wages and is split by the employer and employee. Unlike the OASDI tax, the Medicare tax has no wage cap. As of 2013, as part of Obamacare, Medicare tax rates have gone up to 3.8 percent on income over $200,000 for single persons and $250,000 for married couples. This new Medicare tax will also apply to investment income, such as stocks and bonds.[31]

Today, some are calling for strengthening the program through progressive methods, while others are calling for cuts to retirement benefits and dismantling of unemployment insurance. Let us now turn to these current solutions to provide adequate protection from the economic fears of old age and unemployment.

THE RIGHT TO ADEQUATE PROTECTION FROM ECONOMIC FEARS OF OLD AGE AND UNEMPLOYMENT: CURRENT APPROACHES

Before discussing the movement to expand the Social Security system, it is important to examine the latest ideas put forth by conservatives to reduce benefits. In fall 2013, John Boehner, Speaker of the House, was demanding cuts in Medicare, Medicaid, and the Social Security retirement plan as part of any agreement to increase the debt limit, which was at $16.7 trillion at that time. Conservatives argued, as President Bush did a decade earlier, that in order to protect the Social Security system for the long haul and to reduce the overall budget deficit, Social Security benefits needed to be reduced.[32]

The conservatives in Congress were supported by the Business Roundtable, an association of chief executive officers (CEOs) from leading US companies. Earlier in 2013, the Business Roundtable CEOs called for $300 billion of benefit cuts by increasing the age to seventy for full retirement for both Social Security and Medicare and by moving to a "chained consumer price index (CPI)." Many conservative groups have called for an increase in the eligibility age for Social Security from sixty-seven (for those born after 1960) to seventy years of age, but the CEOs' plan went even further, calling for an increase in the age limit to begin receiving Medicare as well. Previously, leading Republicans, such as Speaker of the House John Boehner, had proposed raising the age limit for Medicare from sixty-five to sixty-seven. And for a brief moment, President Obama was reported to have considered this proposal—if the Republicans were willing to accept an expiration of the Bush tax cuts on the top 1 percent and 2 percent of income earners, which they did not.[33]

The CEOs also wanted to substitute a chained CPI for the conventionally used CPI, which conservatives believe is a more accurate measure of inflation. The CPI is important since the government uses it to determine the COLA for various government programs, including Social Security. The traditional CPI is a formula that determines how much the price of goods (e.g., clothes, education, food, housing, medical care, and recreation) rises over time. The chained CPI takes into effect that consumers will change their behavior if the price of something goes up, thus substituting a cheaper alternative in its place.[34]

Medicare and Social Security retirement plans are not the only things on the chopping block. The current official Republican budget, known as the Ryan plan (after Rep. Paul Ryan from Wisconsin), calls for increasing the age eligibility of Medicare and retirement plans, but it also calls for defederalizing Medicaid and unemployment insurance, and giving block grants to the states to take care of the marginalized in the way the state sees fit. Of course, benefits in both plans would be reduced under the Ryan plan. For example, Medicaid funding and the Children's Health Insurance program would be cut by nearly 33 percent by 2023.[35]

Not surprisingly, progressives and liberals have lined up to oppose these benefit cuts and have put forward solutions that would increase the Social Security system. They argue that the system has not cost the taxpayers anything, and has not increased the debt, so why should it be cut? Progressives and liberals also contend that Social Security has been extremely successful at reducing poverty. Any attempt to reduce benefits will result in an increase in poverty. Thus, they maintain that the chained CPI is just a fancy way to reduce benefits, since it would lead to a reduction of benefits by $650 a year for seventy-five-year-olds, and over $1,000 a year for eighty-five-year-olds. For members of Congress, who mostly come from the top income brackets, that might not seem like much, but for people on a fixed income of $17,000 a year, these cuts would be devastating.[36]

At the same time, there is a growing movement among progressives and liberals to not let the conservatives control the agenda, and to fight back by offering a plan to get us closer to Roosevelt's vision of "cradle to grave" security. These groups are not just content to stop the benefit cuts, but rather are working on a variety of solutions that would strengthen the long-term viability of the program while expanding benefits. Over 300 national and state organizations have come together to form Social Security Works, a coalition that represents over 50 million Americans. The coalition encourages its supporters to pressure their congressional representatives to expand Social Security rather than cut it. Social Security Works has been one of the major supporters of the Protecting and Preserving Social Security Act (Senate Resolution 38), which is sponsored by Sen. Tom Harkin (D-IA) and Sen. Mark Begish (D-AK). This proposed act would (1) increase benefits to all Social Security recipients by $800 a year ($70 per month), but would give the largest increases to the middle and lower classes; (2) increase the cost of living adjustments (COLAs) so they take into account the rising costs of food, housing, and health care; and (3) lift the payroll tax cap so that Americans in the top 20 percent and above pay payroll taxes not just on their first $113,700 of income but on anything above this level as well. Ensuring that the top 20 percent of income earners contribute the same share of their income to Social Security as everyone else will extend the life of Social Security for seventy-five years.[37]

SUMMARY

In Chapter 6, I have discussed how the development and expansion of New Deal ideas have brought the nation close to achieving this constitutional commitment of a right to adequate protection from the economic fears of old age, sickness, accident, and unemployment. Currently, the idea that has generated the most interest is an expansion of Social Security, with the payroll tax being increased for high-income earners so as to ensure that all pay their fair share.

Epilogue

This book documents the extremely high levels of poverty and inequality in the United States. Some people say it is impossible to change the current conditions since this is the way it always has been: the rich get richer and the poor get poorer. Others might say it is impossible to change the current conditions because of the political divisions within the United States. They argue that these divisions have caused such a stalemate that it is no longer possible to do great things.

I fundamentally disagree with these arguments. First, as shown in this book, it is possible to make great reductions in poverty and social suffering, as we saw in the early twentieth century and during 1964–1969, when social reforms were implemented. Second, I argue that this nation still has the capacity to achieve great things when it sets its mind on something. This is the nation that fought a war over slavery, and prevailed, and this is the nation that sent a person to the moon. I believe the United States still has the capacity to do great things.

The United States takes pride in being a democratic nation and the leader of the free world. However, I argue that if the United States is to continue on the path of becoming "a more perfect union," it must now turn its attention to implementing the constitutional commitments first set out by President Roosevelt seventy years ago in his 1944 State of the Union address. Otherwise, the United States is destined for plutocracy, where the top 1 percent of income earners controls the vast economic wealth and political power, and the 99 percent are left with the economic scraps and little political power. For as Louis Brandeis, a former Supreme Court justice, postulated, "We may have democracy, or we may have wealth concentrated in the hands of a few, but we can't have both."[1]

Another question that arises when considering an Economic Bill of Rights is how will the nation pay for it, particularly when the United States has a projected deficit of $492 billion (2.8 percent of GDP) in 2014, and an overall national deficit of $17 trillion. It is my belief that once people begin to organize around the implementation of an Economic Bill of Rights, and begin to educate and convince the majority of the US population that this is a necessary step in the country's development, the nation will find the money. And we will find it because we will develop a sound tax policy that has shared responsibility, where corporations and the economic elite pay their share of taxes. Just sixty years ago, corporations paid over 30 percent of all federal taxes, and the 1 percent had a top marginal tax rate of over 90 percent and an effective tax rate of over 60 percent. Today, corporations pay 9 percent of all taxes, and the top 1 percent now has a marginal tax rate of 39.6 percent (up from 35 percent from 2012). When there is more shared responsibility, our nation's deficit will be decreased, and pundits will not be able to claim that the nation cannot afford an Economic Bill of Rights.[2]

So let the great work begin. Now is the time!

Notes

CHAPTER 1

1. Bob Herbert, "The Worst of the Pain," *New York Times,* February 8, 2010, www.nytimes.com/2010/02/09/opinion/09herbert.html?_r=0 (accessed January 5, 2014); Associated Press, "Gap in US Unemployment Rates between Rich and Poor Continues to Widen," *N.J. News,* September 16, 2013, www.nj.com/business/index.ssf/2013/09/gaps_in_us_unemployment_rates.html (accessed January 5, 2014).

2. Analyn Hurtz, "Hiring Is Up in April, Unemployment Down," CNN, May 2, 2014, http://money.cnn.com/2014/05/02/investing/april-jobs-report (accessed July 10, 2104); Chrystia Freeland, "Jobless Recovery Leaves Middle Class Behind," *New York Times,* April 12, 2012, www.nytimes.com/2012/04/13/us/13iht-letter13.html?_r=0 (accessed July 10, 2014); "Employment Situation Summary," Bureau of Labor Statistics, www.bls.gov/news.release/empsit.nr0.htm (accessed July 10, 2014).

3. Dan Diamond, "Why the 'Real' Unemployment Rate Is Higher Than You Think," *Forbes,* July 5, 2013, www.forbes.com/sites/dandiamond/2013/07/05/why-the-real-unemployment-rate-is-higher-than-you-think (accessed July 1, 2014).

4. William Leuchtenburg, *In the Shadow of FDR: From Harry Truman to Bill Clinton* (Ithaca, NY: Cornell University Press, 2001), 214.

5. Nels Anderson, *The Right to Work* (New York: Modern Age, 1938); Nelson Lichtenstein, Susan Strasser, and Roy Rosenzweig, *Who Built America? Working People and the Nation's Economy, Politics, and Society: 1877 to Present,* vol. 2 (New York: Worth Publishers, 2000).

6. Lichtenstein, Strasser, and Rosenzweig, *Who Built America?*; CCC Legacy, "CCC Brief History," www.ccclegacy.org/CCC_Brief_History.html (accessed November 26, 2013).

7. Anne Scitovszky, "The Employment Act of 1946," Social Security Administration, March 1946, www.ssa.gov/policy/authors/ScitovszkyAnne.html (accessed November 26, 2013).

8. Scitovszky, "The Employment Act of 1946."

9. Martin Luther King Jr., "Showdown for Nonviolence," in James M. Washington, *A Testament of Hope: The Essential Writings of Martin Luther King Jr.* (San Francisco: Harper and Row, 1986), 64–72; Martin Luther King Jr., *Where Do We Go*

from Here: Chaos or Community? (New York: Harper and Row, 1967); Martin Luther King Jr., transcription of a speech from video, "The Promised Land, 1967–1968," in *Eyes on the Prize II* (Boston: Blackside, 1990), pt. 4; www.thekingcenter.org/archive /document/showdown-nonviolence# (accessed November 30, 2013).

10.   The American Presidency Project, "Full Employment and Comprehensive Employment and Training Act Bills Remarks on Signing H.R. 50 and S. 2570 into Law," www.presidency.ucsb.edu/ws/?pid=30057 (accessed July 2, 2014).

11.   GovTrack.us, "Text of the Full Employment and Balanced Growth Act," www.govtrack.us/congress/bills/95/hr50/text (accessed July 2, 2014).

12.   GovTrack.us, "Text of the Full Employment and Balanced Growth Act."

13.   GovTrack.us, "Text of the Full Employment and Balanced Growth Act."

14.   Walter Shapiro, "CETA: A '70s Government Jobs Program That Didn't Work," *Politics Daily*, www.politicsdaily.com/2009/11/19/ceta-a-70s-federal-jobs -program-that-didn-t-work (accessed December 1, 2013); Associated Press, "Reagan CETA Jobs," *Spartanburg Herald-Journal*, December 19, 1981, http://news.google .com/newspapers?nid=1876&dat=19811219&id=RIMsAAAAIBAJ&sjid=x80EA AAAIBAJ&pg=3761,4458492 (accessed December 1, 2013).

15.   "The Federal Reserve," Jubilee Initiative, www.jubileeinitiative.org /federalreserveprimer.htm (accessed January 8, 2014).

16.   "History of Cooperatives," Cooperative Development Institute, www .cdi.coop/historyofcoops.html (accessed February 2, 2014).

17.   David J. Thompson, "The Night the Lights Were Lit!" *The Wedge*, www .wedge.coop/history/rochdale-story-lights (accessed December 16, 2013); "The Rochdale Principles," CommunityMarket.org, http://communitymarket.org/wp -content/uploads/2010/04/rochdale.pdf (accessed February 1, 2014).

18.   Thompson, "The Night the Lights Were Lit!"

19.   The Philadelphia Contributionship, www.ushistory.org/tour/philadelphia -contributionship.htm (accessed December 15, 2013); Mondragon Cooperative, Madison Hours, www.madisonhours.org/blog/mondrag%C3%B3n-cooperative (accessed December 16, 2013).

20.   Immanuel Ness, "Worker Cooperatives in the United States: A Historical Perspective and Contemporary Assessment," March 2012, www.workerscontrol.net /authors/worker-cooperatives-united-states-historical-perspective-and-contemporary -assessment (accessed January 11, 2013); Scott Myers-Lipton, *Social Solutions to Poverty: America's Struggle to Build a Just Society* (Boulder, CO: Paradigm Publishers, 2006).

21.   David Herrera, "Mondragon: A Profit Organization That Embodies Catholic Social Thought," http://community-wealth.org/content/mondragon-profit -organization-embodies-catholic-social-thought (accessed December 16, 2013).

22.   Huey P. Newton, "Revolutionary Suicide, on Black Nationalism," quoted in "Notes and Quotes from Huey Newton's Autobiography," February 17, 2012, www.beatknowledge.org/2012/02/17/notes-and-quotes-from-huey-newtons -autobiography (accessed January 4, 2013).

23.   Upton Sinclair, *I, Governor of California, and How I Ended Poverty* (Los Angeles: published by the author, 1934), 22; Ness, *Worker Cooperatives in the United States*.

24.   Federal Reserve Bank of St. Louis, "The Financial Crisis: A Timeline of Events and Policy Actions," http://timeline.stlouisfed.org/index.cfm?p=timeline (accessed July 1, 2014).

25. "The Great Recession," The State of Working America, http://stateofwork ingamerica.org/great-recession (accessed December 1, 2013); Christopher Goodman and Steven Mance, "Employment Loss and the 2007–09 Recession: An Overview," *Monthly Labor Review* 134, no. 4 (2011): 3–12; "The New New Deal," *Time,* November 24, 2008, http://content.time.com/time/covers/0,16641,20081124,00 .html (accessed December 1, 2013); David Demerjian, "Note to Next President: Modern-Day WPA Will Save the Economy," *Wired,* October 19, 2008, www.wired .com/autopia/2008/10/wall-street-bai/ (accessed December 3, 2013).

26. Farhana Hossain, Amanda Cox, John McGrath, and Stephan Weitberg, "The Stimulus Package: Aid to States," *New York Times,* December 17, 2012, http:// projects.nytimes.com/44th_president/stimulus/aid-to-states (accessed December 3, 2013).

27. Thom Patterson, "Will Infrastructure Stimulus Create Jobs?," CNN, February 10, 2009, www.cnn.com/2009/POLITICS/02/10/infrastructure.jobs (accessed December 1, 2013); "ASCE's Infrastructure Report Card Gives Nation a D, Estimates Cost at $2.2 Trillion," American Society of Civil Engineers, February 2009, www.asce.org/pplcontent.aspx?id=2147484137 (accessed December 3, 2013).

28. Michael Shear, "Obama Lesson: 'Shovel Ready' Not So Ready," *New York Times,* October 15, 2010, http://thecaucus.blogs.nytimes.com/2010/10/15 /obama-lesson-shovel-ready-not-so-ready; David Plotz, "The New New Deal," *Slate,* www.slate.com/articles/news_and_politics/interrogation/2012/08/the_new _new_deal_a_book_argues_that_president_obama_s_stimulus_has_been_an _astonishing_success.single.html (accessed December 3, 2013); Jay Hancock, "Prevail- ing Wage Rules Delay Stimulus," *Baltimore Sun,* September 23, 2009, http://weblogs .baltimoresun.com/business/hancock/blog/2009/09/prevailing_wage _requirements_d.html (accessed December 3, 2013).

29. John Dickerson, "Obama's Latest Communication Missteps Open the Door for GOP Criticism," CBS News, October 18, 2010, www.cbsnews.com/news /obamas-latest-communication-missteps-open-the-door-for-gop-criticism (accessed January 5, 2014).

30. Michael Leachman, "New CBO Report Finds Up to 3.6 Million People Owe Their Jobs to the Recovery Act," Center on Budget and Policy Priorities, November 29, 2010, www.cbpp.org/cms/?fa=view&id=3095 (accessed July 1, 2014).

31. Mathew Forstater, "Public Service Job Assurance: A Most Fitting Tribute to Dr. King," Center for Full Employment and Price Stability, January 2001, www .cfeps.org/pubs/sr/sr0101 (accessed January 5, 2014); King, *Where Do We Go from Here.*

32. LaDonna Pavetti, Liz Schott, and Elizabeth Lower-Basch, "Creating Subsidized Employment Opportunities for Low-Income Parents: The Legacy of the TANF Emergency Fund," Center on Budget and Policy Priorities, February 16, 2011, www.cbpp.org/files/2-16-11tanf.pdf (accessed December 5, 2013).

33. Michael Cooper, "In Tennessee Corner, Stimulus Meets New Deal," *New York Times,* July 27, 2009, www.nytimes.com/2009/07/28/us/28county.html?_r=0 (accessed December 5, 2013).

34. Cooper, "In Tennessee Corner, Stimulus Meets New Deal."

35. Elizabeth Lower-Basch, "Extending the TANF Emergency Fund Creates Jobs Now," CLASP, November 19, 2009, www.clasp.org/resources-and-publications

/files/Emergency-Fund-Extension.pdf (accessed December 5, 2013); Heather Knight, "Newsom Steps in as Jobs Now Cash Dries Up," *SF Gate,* September 23, 2010, www .sfgate.com/business/article/Newsom-steps-in-as-Jobs-Now-cash-dries-up-3173798 .php#ixzz2DXj0uLh6 (accessed December 5, 2013); Carolyn Said, "Gloomy Outlook for Summer Youth Employment," *SF Gate,* May 14, 2011, www.sfgate.com/business /article/Newsom-steps-in-as-Jobs-Now-cash-dries-up-3173798 .php#ixzz2DXj0uLh6 (accessed December 5, 2013).

36. Liz Schott and LaDonna Pavetti, "Walking Away from a Win-Win-Win: Subsidized Jobs Slated to End Soon Are Helping Families, Businesses, and Communities Weather the Recession," Center on Budget and Policy Priorities, September 2, 2010, www.cbpp.org/cms/?fa=view&id=3274 (accessed December 6, 2013).

37. Michael Cooper, "Stimulus Jobs on State's Bill in Mississippi," *New York Times,* February 16, 2010, www.nytimes.com/2010/02/17/business /economy/17mississippi.html (accessed December 6, 2013).

38. Heather Hahn, Olivia Golden, and Alexandra Stanczyk, "State Approaches to the TANF Block Grant," Urban Institute, August 2012, www.urban.org /UploadedPDF/412635-State-Approaches-to-the-TANF-Block-Grant.pdf (accessed December 8, 2013); Pavetti, Schott, and Lower-Basch, "Creating Subsidized Employment Opportunities for Low-Income Parents."

39. Andreas Kriefall and Mark Dunlea, "Making New Roads from Welfare to Work: Ramping Up Subsidized Employment and Community Jobs Programs in New York State," Hunger Action Network of NYS, February 2011, www.hunger actionnys.org/Welfare%20Jobs%20Report.pdf (accessed December 6, 2013); Schott and Pavetti, "Walking Away from a Win-Win-Win."

40. Scott Myers-Lipton, *Rebuild America: Solving the Economic Crisis through Civic Works* (Boulder, CO: Paradigm Publishers, 2009).

41. "San Antonio Voters Approve $596 Million Bond Program," City of San Antonio, May 13, 2012, www.sanantonio.gov/2012Bond/NewsReleases /nr20120513.aspx (accessed January 26, 2014).

42. Jeanne Mirer and Marjorie Cohn, "Obama: Create Jobs by Executive Order," Common Dreams, November 8, 2010, www.commondreams.org /view/2010/11/08 (accessed December 6, 2013).

43. "Types of Cooperatives," www.co-oplaw.org/types (accessed February 1, 2014).

44. "Organic Valley Celebrates 25th Anniversary with More Than 575 Farmer-Owners at Co-op's Annual Meeting," Organic Valley, April 11, 2013, www.organicvalley.coop/newsroom/press-releases/details/article/organic-valley -celebrates-25th-anniversary-with-more-than-575-farmer-owners-at-co-ops-annual -meetin (accessed January 10, 2013); Ness, "Worker Cooperatives in the United States."

45. Richard Chamberlain, "The First Twenty Years," www.unioncab.com /History (accessed January 10, 2013); Ness, "Worker Cooperatives in the United States"; Fred Schepartz, "Comments about Union Cab's Bonus Segment in Michael Moore's Movie," *The Worker's Paradise,* April 5, 2010, www .cooperativeconsult.com/blog/?p=276 (accessed January 11, 2013); Fred Schepartz, "The Worker's Cooperative That Should Have Been in Michael Moore's Movie," *The Worker's Paradise,* December 19, 2009, www.cooperativeconsult

.com/blog/?p=185 (accessed January 11, 2013); Jane Burns, "At Union Cab, Co-op Members Earn a Living Wage and Run a Successful Business," August 26, 2009, *American Worker Cooperative,* www.american.coop/node/96 (accessed January 11, 2013).

46. Stephanie Davis, "Green Laundry Service Gives the Less-Fortunate a Chance to Own Their Work," *Cleveland Business Connects Magazine,* 2009, http://cbc magazine.com/index.php?option=com_content&view=article&id=74:fresh-%20 linens&catid=921:magazine (accessed January 12, 2013).

47. Christine Brown, "What Does LEED Certification Mean to the Hotel Industry?," Pinnacle Advisory Group, January 2008, www.pinnacle-advisory.com /leed-certification-jan-2008.html (accessed January 7, 2014); Davis, "Green Laundry Service Gives the Less-Fortunate a Chance to Own Their Work."

48. Emily Barker, "Worker Co-ops Bring Breath of Fresh Air to Ohio," *Co-operative News,* www.thenews.coop/39047/news/co-operatives /worker-co-ops-brings-breath-fresh-air-ohio/.

49. Jose Luis LaFuente and Fred Freundlitch, "The Mondragon Cooperative Experience: Humanity at Work," *Management Exchange,* May 11, 2012, www .managementexchange.com/story/mondragon-cooperative-experience-humanity -work (accessed January 15, 2013).

50. NoBAWC, Network of Bay Area Worker Collectives (NoBAWC) History, June 29, 2002, www.indybay.org/newsitems/2002/06/29/1352121.php (accessed January 15, 2013); Herrera, "Mondragon."

51. Executive Paywatch, AFL-CIO, www.aflcio.org/Corporate-Watch /Paywatch-2014 (accessed July 5, 2014); Jennifer Liberto, "CEOs Earn 354 Times More Than Average Worker," CNN, April 15, 2013, http://money.cnn.com/2013/04/15 /news/economy/ceo-pay-worker (accessed July 5, 2014).

52. "Worker Ownership and Labor Rights, Other Worlds," www.other worldsarepossible.org/worker-ownership (accessed January 15, 2013); LaFuente and Freundlitch, "The Mondragon Cooperative Experience."

CHAPTER 2

1. Rebecca Theiss, "The Future of Work: Trends and Challenges for Low-Wage Workers," Economic Policy Institute, April 27, 2012, www.epi.org/publication /bp341-future-of-work (accessed December 10, 2012).

2. "Union Member Summary," Bureau of Labor Statistics, January 24, 2014, www.bls.gov/news.release/union2.nr0.htm (accessed July 3, 2014); "Facts about Manufacturing," National Association of Manufacturers, www.nam.org /Statistics-And-Data/Facts-About-Manufacturing/Landing.aspx (accessed July 3, 2014).

3. Peter Edelman, "The State of Poverty in America," *American Prospect,* June 22, 2012, http://prospect.org/article/state-poverty-america (accessed December 11, 2012).

4. Mary Kay Henry and Christine L. Owens, "Hardworking Americans Should Not Be Living in Poverty," CNN, July 25, 2012, www.cnn.com/2012/07/25/opinion /henry-owens-minimum-wage/index.html (accessed December 11, 2013); National

Employment Law Project, "$10.74," Raise the Minimum Wage, www.raisethe minimumwage.com/facts/entry/amount-with-inflation (accessed December 10, 2012).

5.   Edelman, "The State of Poverty in America"; Catherine Dodge and Mike Dorning, "Rich-Poor Gap Widens to Most since 1967 as Income Falls," *Bloomberg,* September 12, 2012, www.bloomberg.com/news/2012-09-12/u-s-poverty-rate-stays -at-almost-two-decade-high-income-falls.html (accessed December 12, 2012).

6.   Dodge and Dorning, "Rich-Poor Gap Widens to Most since 1967 as Income Falls."

7.   Adam Smith, *An Inquiry into the Nature and Causes of the Wealth of Nations,* Edwin Cannan, ed. (London: Methuen and Co., 1904), Library of Economics and Liberty, 821–822.

8.   Seth Rockman, *Welfare Reform in the Early Republic: A Brief History with Documents* (Bedford, MA: St. Martin's Press, 2002); Matthew Carey, "A Plea for the Poor, Particularly Females: An Inquiry How Far the Charges Alleged against Them of Improvidence, Idleness, and Dissipation, Are Founded on Truth" (1837), reprinted in David J. Rothman, ed., *The Jacksonians on the Poor: Collected Pamphlets*; Matthew Carey, "Address to New York Ladies," *Miscellaneous Essays* (New York: Burt Frank-lin, 1830), 282, www.nam.org/Statistics-And-Data/Facts-About-Manufacturing /Landing.aspx (accessed December 11, 2012).

9.   Paul S. Boyer, *Urban Masses and Moral Order in America: 1820–1920* (Cambridge, MA: Harvard University Press, 1978); Charles and Mary Beard, quoted in Walter I. Trattner, *From Poor Law to Welfare State: A History of Social Welfare in America* (New York: Free Press, 1979), 71; Nelson Lichtenstein, Susan Strasser, and Roy Rosenzweig, *Who Built America? Working People and the Nation's Economy, Politics, and Society: 1877 to Present*, vol. 2 (New York: Worth Publishers, 2000); Charles Redenius, *The American Ideal of Equality: From Jefferson's Declaration to the Burger Court* (Port Washington, NY: Kennikat Press, 1981).

10.   Michael Katz, *In the Shadow of the Poorhouse: A Social History of Welfare in America* (New York: Basic Books, 1986); Lichtenstein, Strasser, and Rosenzweig, *Who Built America?*; Judith F. Clark, *America's Gilded Age: An Eyewitness History* (New York: Facts on File, 1992); Howard Zinn, *A People's History of the United States: 1492–Present* (New York: HarperPerennial, 1995).

11.   Trattner, *From Poor Law to Welfare State*; Clark, *America's Gilded Age*; Lichtenstein, Strasser, and Rosenzweig, *Who Built America?*, 91; Terrency V. Pow-derly, *Thirty Years of Labor: 1859–1889* (Columbus, OH: Excelsior, 1889), 243.

12.   W. E. B. Du Bois, *The Philadelphia Negro: A Social Study* (New York: Schocken Books, 1967 [1899]).

13.   Gordon Fisher, "From Hunter to Orshansky: An Overview of (Unofficial) Poverty Lines in the United States from 1904 to 1965," US Census Bureau, www.census .gov/hhes/povmeas/publications/povthres/fisher4.html (accessed February 1, 2014).

14.   Pat Garofalo, "100 Years Ago Today, Massachusetts Passed the Nation's First Minimum Wage Law," Think Progress, June 4, 2012, http://thinkprogress.org /economy/2012/06/04/494411/minimum-wage-100-today (accessed February 1, 2014).

15.   Laura Fitzpatrick, "The Minimum Wage," *Time,* July 24, 2009, www.time .com/time/magazine/article/0.9171.1912408.00.html (accessed December 14, 2012).

16.   Myers-Lipton, *Social Solutions to Poverty.*

17. Jason Scott Smith, *Building New Deal Liberalism: The Political Economy of Public Works, 1933–1956* (Cambridge: Cambridge University Press, 2009); Jeannette Gabriel, "A Twenty-First-Century WPA: Labor Policies for a Federal Government Jobs Program," *Social Policy* 38, no. 2 (2007): 38–43.

18. Robert Frank, "The Other Milton Friedman: A Conservative with a Social Welfare Program," *New York Times,* www.nytimes.com/2006/11/23 /business/23scene.html (accessed February 1, 2014).

19. Martin Luther King Jr., "Showdown for Nonviolence," TheKingCenter .org, 1968, www.thekingcenter.org/archive/document/showdown-nonviolence# (accessed December 12, 2012).

20. "What-When-How.com 'Income Maintenance Experiments,'" What -When-How.com, February 2013, http://what-when-how.com/social-sciences /income-maintenance-experiments-social-science (accessed December 15, 2012).

21. "What-When-How.com 'Income Maintenance Experiments.'"

22. "Domestic Politics," *American Experience,* www.pbs.org/wgbh /americanexperience/features/general-article/nixon-domestic (accessed December 1, 2012); Peter Passell and Leonard Ross, "Daniel Moynihan and President-Elect Nixon: How Charity Didn't Begin at Home," *New York Times,* January 14, 1973, www.nytimes.com/books/98/10/04/specials/moynihan-income.html (accessed December 15, 2013).

23. Peter Dreier, "Housing the Working Poor," *Shelterforce,* Fall 2007, http:// nhi.org/online/issues/151/housingtheworkingpoor.html (accessed December 15, 2013).

24. David Welna, "Why Some Are Exempt from Federal Income Taxes," National Public Radio, September 19, 2012, www.npr.org/2012/09/19/161389849 /why-some-are-exempt-from-federal-income-taxes (accessed December 1, 2012); Internal Revenue Service, "Earned Income Tax Credit (EITC) Can Lower Federal Tax" (accessed July 29, 2005); Jonathan B. Foreman, "Earned Income Tax Credit," in Joseph J. Cordes, Robert D. Ebel, and Jane G. Gravelle, eds., *The Encyclopedia of Taxation and Tax Policy* (Washington, DC: Urban Institute Press, 1999), 83–85.

25. Steven Greenhouse, "In Drive to Unionize, Fast-Food Workers Walk Off the Job," *New York Times,* November 28, 2012, www.nytimes.com/2012/11/29 /nyregion/drive-to-unionize-fast-food-workers-opens-in-ny.html?_r=0 (accessed January 4, 2013).

26. Greenhouse, "In Drive to Unionize, Fast-Food Workers Walk Off the Job"; Steven Greenhouse, "Wal-Mart Plays Down Labor Protests at Its Stores," *New York Times,* November 23, 2012, www.nytimes.com/2012/11/24/business/wal-mart -dismisses-labor-protests-at-its-stores.html?_r=0 (accessed January 5, 2013).

27. Steven Greenhouse, "With Day of Protests, Fast-Food Workers Seek More Pay," *New York Times,* November 29, 2012, www.nytimes.com/2012/11/30 /nyregion/fast-food-workers-in-new-york-city-rally-for-higher-wages.html?_r=0 (accessed January 4, 2013).

28. Josh Eidelson, "In Rare Strike, NYC Fast-Food Workers Walk Out," Salon.com, November 29, 2012, www.salon.com/2012/11/29/in_rare_strike_nyc _fast_food_workers_walk_out (accessed January 5, 2013); Ellyn Fortino, "Chicago Fast-Food and Retail Workers Win Victories after April Strike," Progress Illinois, July 10, 2013, www.progressillinois.com/posts/content/2013/07/10/chicago-fast -food-retail-workers-win-victories-after-april-strike (accessed January 5, 2014).

29. Bob Simpson, "Fight for $15, Cuz We Can't Survive on $8.25," *Talking Union,* December 27, 2012, http://talkingunion.wordpress.com/2012/12/27/fight-for-15-cuz-we-cant-survive-on-8-25 (accessed January 5, 2013); "Fight for 15," FightFor15.org, http://fightfor15.org/en/about-us/ (accessed January 5, 2013); Eidelson, "In Rare Strike, NYC Fast-Food Workers Walk Out."

30. Steven Greenhouse, "Walmart Workers Stage a Walkout in California," *New York Times,* October 4, 2012, www.nytimes.com/2012/10/05/business/walmart-workers-in-california-protest.html (accessed January 5, 2013).

31. Greenhouse, "Wal-Mart Plays Down Labor Protests at Its Stores"; Susan Berfield, "Walmart vs. Union-Backed Our Walmart," December 13, 2012, www.businessweek.com/articles/2012-12-13/walmart-vs-dot-union-backed-our-walmart (accessed January 6, 2013); Josh Eidelson, "Over 110 Arrested as Record Black Friday Protests Challenge Wal-Mart, Major Retailers on Low Wages," Democracy Now, www.democracynow.org/2013/12/2/over_110_arrested_as_record_black (accessed January 7, 2014).

32. Catherine Ruetschlin, "Retail's Hidden Potential: How Raising Wages Would Benefit Workers, the Industry and the Overall Economy," *Demos,* November 19, 2012, www.demos.org/publication/retails-hidden-potential-how-raising-wages-would-benefit-workers-industry-and-overall-ec (accessed January 7, 2013); David Moberg, "California Walmart Store Workers Go Out on Historic Strike," *In These Times,* October 4, 2012, http://inthesetimes.com/working/entry/13948/california_walmart_store_workers_go_out_on_historic_strike(accessed January 7, 2013).

33. John Schmitt and David Rosnick, "The Wage and Employment Impact of Minimum Wage Laws in Three Cities," Center for Economic and Policy Research, March 2011, www.cepr.net/documents/publications/min-wage-2011-03.pdf (accessed December 11, 2013).

34. Arindrajit Dube, T. William Lester, and Michael Reich, "Minimum Wage Effects across State Borders: Estimates Using Contiguous Counties," *The Review of Economics and Statistics,* 92, no. 4 (November 2010): 945–964; "States with Minimum Wages above the Federal Level Have Had Faster Small Business and Retail Job Growth," Fiscal Policy Institute, www.fiscalpolicy.org/FPISmallBusinessMinWage.pdf (accessed December 11, 2013).

35. http://data.bls.gov/timeseries/LAUMT064194000000003?data_tool=XGtable, March 4, 2013; Sam Brock, "Reality Check: Hype or Reality? Numbers behind Wage Hike and Jobs," *NBC Bay Area,* February 10, 2014, www.nbcbayarea.com/news/local/Reality-Check-Minimum-Wage-One-Year-Later-244821391.html (accessed March 4, 2013); Janice Shriver, "San Jose-Sunnyvale-Santa Clara Metropolitan Statistical Area (MAS): Seasonal Public Educational Services Led Job Gains over the Month," June 20, 2014, www.calmis.ca.gov/file/lfmonth/sjos$pds.pdf (accessed March 4, 2013); "Average Hours and Earnings of All Employees on Private Nonfarm Payrolls by State and Metropolitan Area, Not Seasonally Adjusted," Bureau of Labor Statistics, http://bls.gov/web/laus/tabled6.pdf (accessed March 4, 2013); Charles Siler, "Berkeley Sets New Minimum Wage; Up to $12.53 by 2016," *Berkeleyside,* June 27, 2014, www.berkeleyside.com/2014/06/27/berkeley-sets-new-minimum-wage-to-reach-12-53-by-2016 (accessed July 2, 2014).

36. Amy Martinez, "$15 Wage Floor Slowly Takes Hold in SeaTac," February 13, 2014, *Seattle Times,* http://seattletimes.com/html/localnews/2022905775

_seatacprop1xml.html (accessed July 4, 2014); Karen Weise, "How Seattle Agreed to a $15 Minimum Wage without a Fight," May 8, 2014, *Bloomberg Businessweek,* www .businessweek.com/articles/2014-05-08/how-seattle-agreed-to-a-15-minimum -wage-without-a-fight (accessed July 2, 2014); Dan McKay, "County Minimum Wage up to $8.50 per Hour," *Albuquerque Journal,* April 24, 2013, www.abqjournal s.com/192045/news/county-minimum-wage-up-to-850-per-hour.html (accessed July 4, 2014).

37. "State Minimum Wages," National Conference of State Legislatures, www.ncsl.org/research/labor-and-employment/state-minimum-wage-chart.aspx (accessed July 4, 2014).

38. Erlend Berg, "Can Large-Scale Public Works Programmes Push Up Wages?" The CSAE Blog, The Center for the Study of African Economies, June 25, 2012, http://blogs.csae.ox.ac.uk/2012/06/can-large-scale-public-works -programmes-push-up-wages (accessed January 6, 2013); "Natural Rural Employment Guarantee Act, Sustainable Development Knowledge Platform," United Nations, http://sustainabledevelopment.un.org/index.php?page=view&type=1006&menu =1348&nr=2032 (accessed January 8, 2013); "A Compilation of Green Economy Policies, Programs, and Initiatives from Around the World," United Nations Conference on Sustainable Development, February 11, 2011, www.uncsd2012.org/content /documents/compendium_green_economy.pdf (accessed January 7, 2013); Carlo del Ninno, Kalanidhi Subbarao, and Annamaria Milazzo, "How to Make Public Works Work: A Review of the Experiences May 2009," World Bank, http://siteresources .worldbank.org/SOCIALPROTECTION/Resources/SP-Discussion-papers/Safety -Nets-DP/0905.pdf (accessed January 7, 2013).

39. Scott Goldsmith, "The Alaska Permanent Fund Dividend: A Case Study in the Direct Distribution of Resource Rent," Institute of Social and Economic Research, University of Alaska, www.iser.uaa.alaska.edu/Publications/2011_01 -PFRevenueWatchPaper.pdf (accessed January 7, 2013).

40. "We Are Not the Beautiful," Idealoblog, October 23, 2013, http://idealo blog.blogspot.com/2013/10/were-facing-shift-in-what-work-means.html (accessed January 8, 2014).

41. Elaine Maag and Adam Carasso, "Taxation and the Family: What Is the Earned Income Tax Credit?" Tax Policy Center, January 12, 2013, www.taxpolicy center.org/briefing-book/key-elements/family/eitc.cfm (accessed January 7, 2013).

42. Davis, "Green Laundry Service Gives the Less-Fortunate a Chance to Own Their Work."

43. Schepartz, "Comments about Union Cab's Bonus Segment in Michael Moore's Movie"; Schepartz, "The Worker's Cooperative That Should Have Been in Michael Moore's Movie"; Burns, "At Union Cab, Co-op Members Earn a Living Wage and Run a Successful Business."

CHAPTER 3

1. NPR Staff, "How America's Losing the War on Poverty," National Public Radio, August 4, 2012, www.npr.org/2012/08/04/158141728/how-americas -losing-the-war-on-poverty (accessed January 21, 2013); Alejandro Lazo, "Rents

Soar as Foreclosure Victims, Young Workers Seek Housing," *Los Angeles Times,* May 5, 2012, http://articles.latimes.com/2012/may/05/business/la-fi-renters -nightmare-20120506 (accessed January 22, 2013); Joint Center for Housing Studies, "America's Rental Housing: Meeting Challenges, Building on Opportunities," President and Fellows of Harvard College, April 26, 2011, www.jchs.harvard.edu /sites/jchs.harvard.edu/files/americasrentalhousing-2011.pdf (accessed January 22, 2013); Editorial, "The Poor, the Near Poor, and You," *New York Times,* November 23, 2011, www.nytimes.com/2011/11/24/opinion/the-poor-the-near-poor-and-you .html?_r=0 (accessed January 21, 2013).

2.   US Census Bureau, "Median Household Income by State: 1984 to 2012," US Department of Commerce, www.census.gov/hhes/www/income/data/state median/ (accessed January 8, 2014).

3.   US Department of Housing and Urban Development, "FY 2013 Budget: Housing and Communities Built to Last," http://portal.hud.gov/hudportal/documents /huddoc?id=CombBudget2013.pdf (accessed January 8, 2014); "Final FY12 Budget Cuts HUD, Rural Housing Programs," Southern California Association of Nonprofit Housing, www.scanph.org/node/3008 (accessed January 8, 2014); Joint Center for Housing Studies, "America's Rental Housing: Meeting Challenges, Building on Opportunities."

4.   Paul Kiel, "The Great American Foreclosure Story: The Struggle for Justice and a Place to Call Home," Pro Publica, April 10, 2012, www.propublica.org/article /the-great-american-foreclosure-story-the-struggle-for-justice-and-a-place-t/single (accessed January 23, 2013); Associated Press, "Fewer Homes Repossessed in 2012," *USA Today,* January 17, 2013, www.usatoday.com/story/money/business/2013/01/17 /homes-repossessed-2012/1841649 (accessed January 23, 2013); Gerald Epstein, "Jon Stewart Was Right," Back to Full Employment, January 4, 2013, http://backtofull employment.org/2013/01/04/jon-stewart-was-right (accessed January 25, 2013); AFL-CIO, "Home Foreclosure Statistics," www.aflcio.org/Multimedia/Infographics /Home-Foreclosure-Statistics (accessed January 24, 2013); Economic Mobility Project, "Weathering the Great Recession: Did High-Poverty Neighborhoods Fare Worse?," Pew Charitable Trust, October 2012, www.pewtrusts.org/uploadedFiles/PCS _Assets/2012/Pew_urban_neighborhoods_report.pdf (accessed January 25, 2013); John Atlas and Peter Dreier, "Public Housing: What Went Wrong?," NHI Shelterforce Online, September/October 1994, www .nhi.org/online/issues/77/pubhsg.html (accessed January 26, 2013); US Department of Housing and Urban Development, "HUD Reports Slight Decline in Homelessness in 2012," December 10, 2012, http://portal.hud .gov/hudportal/HUD?src=/press/press_releases_media_advisories/2012 /HUDNo.12-191 (accessed January 8, 2014); "Experts Predict 2014 Housing Market," *Huffington Post,* January 7, 2014, www.huffingtonpost.com/realtorcom/experts -predict-2014-hous_b_4520120.html (accessed January 27, 2013); Francys Vallecillo, "US Foreclosures Drop 29 Percent, Inventory Falls," *Real Estate News,* January 9, 2014, www.worldpropertychannel.com/north-america-residential-news/us-foreclosures -corelogic-housing-market-florida-nevada-shadow-inventory-mortgages-7863.php (accessed January 12, 2014); Rakesh Kochar, Richard Fry, and Paul Taylor, "Wealth Gaps Rise to Record Highs between Whites, Blacks, Hispanics," Pew Research, July 26, 2011, www.pewsocialtrends.org/2011/07/26/wealth-gaps-rise-to-record-highs -between-whites-blacks-hispanics (accessed January 8, 2014).

5. Kochar, Fry, and Taylor, "Wealth Gaps Rise to Record Highs between Whites, Blacks, Hispanics"; Thomas Shapiro, Tatjana Meschede, and Sam Osoro, "The Roots of the Widening Racial Wealth Gap: Explaining the Black-White Economic Divide," Institute on Assets and Social Policy, February 2013, http://iasp.brandeis.edu /pdfs/Author/shapiro-thomas-m/racialwealthgapbrief.pdf (accessed January 9, 2014).

6. "FDR and Housing Legislation: 75th Anniversary of the Wagner-Steagall Housing Act of 1937," Franklin D. Roosevelt Presidential Library and Museum, www.fdrlibrary.marist.edu/aboutfdr/housing.html (accessed January 28, 2013); G. J. Santoni, "The Employment Act of 1946: Some Historical Notes," in *Review* (St. Louis, MO: Federal Reserve Bank of St. Louis, 1986), 12; "President Truman's Proposed Health Program," Harry S. Truman Library and Museum, www.fdrlibrary .marist.edu/aboutfdr/housing.html (accessed January 28, 2013).

7. Myers-Lipton, *Social Solutions to Poverty.*

8. Silvia Pedraza and Rubén G. Rumbaut, *Origins and Destinies: Immigration, Race, and Ethnicity in America* (Belmont, CA: Wadsworth, 1996); Katz, *In the Shadow of the Poorhouse*; Lichtenstein, Strasser, and Rosenzweig, *Who Built America?*

9. Jacob A. Riis, *How the Other Half Lives: Studies among the Tenements of New York* (Cambridge: MA: Harvard University Press, 1970), 32–33; Katz, *In the Shadow of the Poorhouse*; Zinn, *People's History of the United States*; "Tenements," History, www.history.com/topics/tenements (accessed February 1, 2013).

10. "Government's Role in Low Income Housing," Rental Housing On Line, http://rhol.org/rental/housing.htm (accessed February 3, 2013).

11. "Government's Role in Low Income Housing," Rental Housing On Line; Nikole Hannah-Jones, "Living Apart: How the Government Betrayed a Landmark Civil Rights Law," Pro Publica, October 18, 2102, www.propublica.org/article /living-apart-how-the-government-betrayed-a-landmark-civil-rights-law (accessed January 10, 2014).

12. Gunnar Myrdal and Sissela Bok, *An American Dilemma: The Negro Problem and Modern Democracy*, vol. 1 (New York: Harper and Row, 1944).

13. "The Past: United States Housing Act of 1937," TexasHousing.org, www .texashousing.org/phdebate/past5.html (accessed February 2, 2013); "FDR and Housing Legislation: 75th Anniversary of the Wagner-Steagall Housing Act of 1937," Franklin D. Roosevelt Presidential Library and Museum; Jennifer Stoloff, "A Brief History of Public Housing," US Department of Housing and Urban Development, 2004, http://reengageinc.org/research/brief_history_public_housing.pdf (accessed January 10, 2014).

14. "VA History," US Department of Veterans Affairs, www.va.gov/about_va /vahistory.asp (accessed February 4, 2013); Cyd McKenna, "The Homeownership Gap: How the Post–World War II GI Bill Shaped Modern Day Homeownership Patterns for Black and White Americans," Massachusetts Institute of Technology, June 2008, http://dspace.mit.edu/bitstream/handle/1721.1/44333/276173994.pdf (accessed February 10, 2013).

15. Harry S. Truman, "State of the Union Address Part II," TeachingAmericanHistory.org, January 21, 1946, http://teachingamericanhistory.org/library /document/state-of-the-union-address-part-ii-16 (accessed February 8, 2013).

16. Robert Moroney and Judy Krysik, *Social Policy and Social Work: Critical Essays on the Welfare State* (New York: Aldine de Gruyter, 1998); William

Wunder, "Harry Truman's Fair Deal," Suite101.org, http://suite101.com/article /harry-trumans-fair-deal-a169436#ixzz2IvUBV7QZ (accessed February 9, 2013).

17. Andrew Zimmerman, "Department of Housing and Urban Development," *Zimmerman's Research Guide,* http://law.lexisnexis.com/infopro/zimmermans/disp .aspx?z=1384 (accessed February 8, 2013); Chester Hartman and Rachel G. Bratt, "The Case for a Right to Housing," NHI Shelterforce Online, Winter 2006, www .nhi.org/online/issues/148/righttohousing.html (accessed February 10, 2013).

18. Zimmerman, "Department of Housing and Urban Development"; Hartman and Bratt, "The Case for a Right to Housing."

19. Beryl Satter, "Riots, Real Estate, and Selective Memory," *Black Agenda Report,* October 11, 2009, http://blackagendareport.com/content/riots-real-estate -and-selective-memory (accessed February 11, 2013).

20. Cushing N. Dolbeare and Sheila Crowley, "Changing Priorities, the Federal Budget and Housing Assistance: 1976–2007," National Low Income Housing Coalition, August 2002, http://nlihc.org/sites/default/files/changingpriorities.pdf (accessed February 12, 2013).

21. Dolbeare and Crowley, "Changing Priorities, the Federal Budget and Housing Assistance: 1976–2007."

22. "Statement of the National Council of State Housing Agencies to the House Ways and Means Committee in Support of Preserving and Strengthening the Low Income Housing Tax Credit and Tax-Exempt Housing Bond Programs on the Occasion of the Committee's Hearing on Tax Reform and Residential Real Estate," National Council of State Housing Agencies, April 25, 2013, www.ncsha .org/resource/ncsha-statement-housing-credit-and-housing-bond-programs-hearing -tax-reform-and-residential-real-estate (accessed January 31, 2014).

23. Joint Center for Housing Studies, "American Rental Housing, Homes for a Diverse Nation, Joint Center for Housing Studies," President and Fellows of Harvard College, 2006, www.jchs.harvard.edu/research/publications/americas -rental-housing-homes-diverse-nation (accessed February 25, 2013).

24. Tina Trenkner, "Revisiting the Hope VI Public Housing Program's Legacy," *Governing,* May 2012, www.governing.com/topics/health-human-services/housing/gov -revisiting-hope-public-housing-programs-legacy.html (accessed February 20, 2013).

25. Trenkner, "Revisiting the Hope VI Public Housing Program's Legacy."

26. Michael Grunwald, "The Housing Crisis Goes Suburban," *Washington Post,* August 27, 2006, www.washingtonpost.com/wp-dyn/content /article/2006/08/25/AR2006082501197.html (accessed February 20, 2013); Cushing Dolbeare, "Shifting Fortunes: Trends in Housing Policy and Program," NHI Shelterforce Online, March/April 2000, www.shelterforce.com/online/issues/110 /dolbeare.html (accessed February 20, 2013).

27. Gene Gerard, "Housing Cuts for the Poor, Tax Cuts for the Rich," DemocraticUnderground.com, March 29, 2006, www.democraticunderground .com/articles/06/03/29_cuts.html (accessed January 20, 2014); Patrick Markee, "The Unfathomable Cuts in Housing Aid," *Nation,* December 14, 2011, www.thenation.com /article/165161/unfathomable-cuts-housing-aid (accessed January 10, 2014); Editorial, "The Affordable Housing Crisis," *New York Times,* December 4, 2012, www.nytimes .com/2012/12/05/opinion/the-affordable-housing-crisis.html?_r=1& (accessed January

10, 2014); Will Fischer and Barbara Sard, "Chart Book: Federal Housing Spending Is Poorly Matched to Need: Tilt Toward Well-Off Homeowners Leaves Struggling Low-Income Renters Without Help," Center on Budget and Policy Priorities, December 18, 2013, www.cbpp.org/cms/index.cfm?fa=view&id=4067 (accessed January 10, 2014).

28.   Fischer and Sard, "Chart Book."

29.   Martin Luther King Jr., *Where Do We Go from Here: Chaos or Community?* (New York: Harper and Row, 1967).

30.   US Census Bureau, "Housing Vacancies and Homeownership," US Department of Commerce, www.census.gov/housing/hvs (accessed January 11, 2014).

31.   Karen Ceraso, "Is Mixed-Income Housing the Key?," NHI Shelterforce Online, March/April 1995, www.nhi.org/online/issues/80/mixhous.html (accessed February 22, 2013).

32.   "Expiring Use of Federal Subsidies," Washington Area Housing Partnership, www.wahpdc.org/expiringfed.html (accessed February 19, 2013); "Overview: Community Development Corporations," Community-Wealth.org, http://community-wealth.org//strategies/panel/cdcs/index.html (accessed February 19, 2013); Joseli Macedo, "Housing and Community Planning," in Rhonda Phillips and Robert H. Pittman, eds., *An Introduction to Community Development* (New York: Routledge, 2009).

33.   "New Community Turning 45," *Clarion,* February 2013. www.rayzo .com/portfolio/portfolio_nonProfit_/New%20Community%20Corporation /NCC_Clarion_January_2012.pdf (accessed January 11, 2014).

34.   "New Community Turning 45," *Clarion*; "Chicanos Por La Causa Celebrates 30 Years of Success," *Border Beat,* April 26, 2010, http://borderbeat.net/news/1288 -chicanos-por-la-causa-celebrates-30-years-of-success (accessed February 20, 2013).

35.   Sheila Crowley, "Bill Introduced to Strengthen Affordable Housing for Low and Middle Income Americans through Mortgage Interest Tax Reform," National Low Income Housing Coalition, December 20, 2012, nlihc.org/press /releases/2080 (accessed February 23, 2013); Michael J. Novogradac, "What Is Next for the National Housing Trust Fund?," *Washington Wire,* February 2010, www.novoco.com/journal/2010/02/news_ww_201002.php (accessed February 24, 2013); "What Are Housing Trust Funds?," Center for Community Change, http://housingtrustfundproject.org (accessed February 24, 2013); "President Obama Requests $1 Billion for the National Housing Trust Fund," Southern California Association of Nonprofit Housing, www.scanph.org/node/788 (accessed January 8, 2014); "President's FY14 Budget Request Includes $1 Billion for NHTF; Shows New Estimates for Tax Expenditures," National Low Income Housing Coalition, April 12, 2013, http://nlihc.org/article/president-s-fy14-budget-request-includes -1-billion-nhtf-shows-new-estimates-tax-expenditures.

36.   Sheila Crowley, "Bill Introduced to Strengthen Affordable Housing for Low and Middle Income Americans through Mortgage Interest Tax Reform"; Novogradac, "What Is Next for the National Housing Trust Fund?"; "President Obama Requests $1 Billion for the National Housing Trust Fund," Southern California Association of Nonprofit Housing.

37.   "Leading Mayoral Candidates Debate Housing Issues," *Los Angeles Wave,* January 15, 2013, http://wavenewspapers.com/news/local/article_3d51ebd4-5f4f

-11e2-be35-0019bb30f31a.html (accessed February 20, 2013); "SCANPH's Policy Work," Southern California Association of Nonprofit Housing, www.scanph.org /node/3008 (accessed January 11, 2014).

38. Fernando Martí and Sara Shortt, "Renters Rising," *Shelterforce,* www .shelterforce.org/article/3263/renters_rising (accessed January 31, 2014); Mary C. Piemonte, "Tenants Protest CHA's Plans for Lathrop," We the People Media, December 15, 2012, http://wethepeoplemedia.org/homepage/tenants-protest-chas -plans-for-lathrop (accessed February 24, 2013).

39. Piemonte, "Tenants Protest CHA's Plans for Lathrop."

40. Atlas and Dreier, "Public Housing: What Went Wrong?"; "Section 8 Voucher Funding and Reform," National Alliance to End Homelessness, www .endhomelessness.org/pages/section_8 (accessed January 11, 2014).

41. Mike Morris and Rhonda Cook, "30,000 Line Up for Housing Vouchers, Some Get Rowdy, *Atlanta Journal-Constitution,* August 11, 2010, www.occonnect .com/community/viewtopic.php?f=29&t=10517 (accessed February 24, 2013); Markee, "The Unfathomable Cuts in Housing Aid."

42. Editorial, "The Affordable Housing Crisis."

43. Alan Zibel, "Mortgage-Modification Program (Barely) Beats Critic's Forecast," *Wall Street Journal,* June 6, 2012, http://blogs.wsj.com/develop ments/2012/06/06/mortgage-modification-program-barely-beats-critics-forecast (accessed February 22, 2013); "Foreclosure Crisis," National Low Income Hous ing Coalition, http://nlihc.org/issues/foreclosure (accessed February 12, 2013); "Time to Bring Back the Home Owners Loan Corporation," Roosevelt Institute, www.rooseveltinstitute.org/new-roosevelt/time-bring-back-home-owners-loan -corporation (accessed February 13, 2013); "Mark Kirk Calls for Public Option Bank for Mortgage Loans," *Daily Kos,* March 25, 2010, www.dailykos.com /story/2010/03/25/850639/-Mark-Kirk-R-IL-Calls-for-Public-Option-Bank-for -Mortgage-Loans (accessed February 13, 2013); Amy Traub, Tamara Draut, and David Callahan, "A Homeowners' Loan Corporation for the 21st Century," *Demos,* September 4, 2012, www.demos.org/publication/homeowners-loan -corporation-21st-century (accessed January 12, 2014).

44. "Bank Tenant Leaders Head to Boston," Springfield No One Leaves, March, 17, 2011, www.springfieldnooneleaves.org/?p=402 (accessed February 13, 2013); Cara Bayles, "City Life/Vida Urbana Celebrates Accomplishments at 'We Shall Not Be Moved' Exhibition," Boston.com, February 20, 2011, www.boston.com /yourtown/news/dorchester/2011/02/city_lifevida_urbana_celebrate.html#sthash .kJhlzFbC.dpuf (accessed February 16, 2013).

45. "New Occupy Homes Coalition Links Homeowners, Activists in Direct Action to Halt Foreclosures," Democracy Now, November 11, 2011, www.youtube.com /watch?feature=player_embedded&v=r8tdCUtZLKQ (accessed February 18, 2013); Jacob Wheeler, "Occupy MN Moves into Foreclosed Home in North Min neapolis," *Uptake,* November 10, 2011, www.theuptake.org/2011/11/10/occupy -mn-moves-into-foreclosed-home-in-north-minneapolis/#sthash.w4OSKXXh .dpuf (accessed February 18, 2013); "Victory: Monique White Wins Negotiation to Save Her Home!" Occupy Our Homes, May 3, 2012, http://occupyourhomes .org/blog/2012/may/3/monique-white-victory/#sthash.k3mbsqdO.dpuf (accessed February 18, 2013); "For Sale: The American Dream—Chicago Anti-Eviction

Campaign Featured on Fault Lines," Take Back the Land, September 5, 2012, www
.takebacktheland.org/index.php?mact=News,cntnt01,detail,0&cntnt01articleid=1
82&cntnt01returnid=15 (accessed February 18, 2013).

46. Alan Zibel and Louise Radnofsky, "Only 1 in 4 Got Mortgage Relief,"
Wall Street Journal, February 28, 2011, http://online.wsj.com/article/SB10001424
05274870469290457616698259482812.html (accessed February 20, 2013).

47. Anjali Kamat, "Homeownership: An American Fantasy," *Huffington
Post: The Blog,* September 5, 2012, www.huffingtonpost.com/anjali-kamat/housing
-crisis_b_1859434.html (accessed on January 31, 2014).

48. Annie Lowrey, "Homeless Rates in US Held Level amid Recession, Study
Says, but Big Gains Are Elusive," *New York Times,* December 10, 2012, www.nytimes
.com/2012/12/10/us/homeless-rates-steady-despite-recession-hud-says.html?_r=1y&
(accessed February 22, 2013); Roman and Stand, "Housing First"; "Our Reflections
on Mark Johnston's Remarks at the COHHIO Conference," National Alliance to End
Homelessness, April 23, 2012, www.endhomelessness.org/blog/entry/our-reflections
-on-mark-johnstons-remarks-at-the-cohhio-conference#.UTKSehnSxF8 (accessed
February 24, 2013); Adam Peck, "Infographic: We Could End Homelessness with the
Money Americans Spend on Christmas Paper," Think Progress, December 10, 2012,
http://thinkprogress.org/economy/2012/12/10/1311041/infographic-homelessness
-christmas-decorations/?mobile=nc (accessed February 25, 2013).

49. "Path Beyond Shelter Programs," Path Beyond Shelter, www.epath.org
/site/PATHBeyondShelter/programs.html (accessed February 25, 2013).

50. Roman and Stand, "Housing First."

51. "Rapid Re-Housing: A History and Core Components," National Alliance to End Homelessness, April 22, 2014, www.endhomelessness.org/library/entry
/rapid-re-housing-a-history-and-core-components.

CHAPTER 4

1. Renee Schoof, "Rich-Poor Spending Gap on Schools Hurts Kids, Report Says,"
McClatchy Newspapers, February 19, 2013, www.mcclatchydc.com/2013/02/19/183590
/rich-poor-spending-gap-on-schools.html (accessed March 4, 2013).

2. Mike Green, "Are High-Poverty Schools Educating the Poor to Remain
So?," *Huffington Post,* March 19, 2011, www.huffingtonpost.com/mike-green/high
-poverty-schools_b_862869.html (accessed March 4, 2013); Bruce J. Biddle and
David C. Berlinder, "A Research Synthesis: Unequal School Funding in the United
States," *Beyond Instructional Leadership* 59, no. 8 (May 2002), under "Educational
Leadership," www.ascd.org/publications/educational-leadership/may02/vol59
/num08/Unequal-School-Funding-in-the-United-States.aspx (accessed March 4,
2013); "Census: Income Gap between Rich and Poor Got Wider in 2009," *USA
Today,* October 1, 2010, http://usatoday30.usatoday.com/money/economy/2010
-09-28-census-income-gap_N.htm (accessed March 5, 2013).

3. Jane Stancill, "Gap between Rich, Poor May Be Growing," *News Observer,*
June 19, 2011, www.newsobserver.com/2011/06/19/1283936/rich-school-poor
-school-the-gap.html#storylink=cpy (accessed March 16, 2013); Lisa Black, "Spending

Gap between State's Rich, Poor Schools Is Vast," *Chicago Tribune,* November 7, 2011, http://articles.chicagotribune.com/2011-11-07/news/ct-met-school-funding -gaps-20111107_1_spending-gap-taft-s-district-poorest-schools (accessed March 6, 2013); Emma Lee, "Study Finds Persistent Resource Gap in North Carolina Public Schools," Public School Forum of North Carolina, January 13, 2014, www.ncforum .org/study-finds-persistent-resource-gap-in-north-carolina-public-schools (accessed July 5, 2014); Jessica Bakeman, "School Spending Gap Comes under Fire," *Journal News,* March 3, 2013, www.lohud.com/article/20130303/NEWS/303030087 /School-spending-gap-comes-under-fire?odyssey=tab|topnews|text|Frontpage&ncl ick_check=1 (accessed January 31, 2014).

4.   C. Zawadi Morris, "Report: NY Wealthy School Districts Spend $8,600 More per Student Than Poor Districts," *Prospect Heights Patch,* March 4, 2013, http:// prospectheights.patch.com/articles/report-ny-wealthy-schools-districts-spend -8600-more-per-student-than-poor-districts-f63269c7 (accessed March 8, 2013); Will Weissert, "Expert Says Poor School Districts Tax More, Get Less," Red Raid-ers, November 2, 2012, http://redraiders.com/texas/2012-11-02/expert-says-poor -school-districts-tax-more-get-less#.UTIucBn8tF8 (accessed March 8, 2013); Anthony Cody, "Rich Schools/Poor Schools: The Gap Grows," *Educa-tion Week,* September 23, 2009, http://blogs.edweek.org/teachers/living-in -dialogue/2009/09/rich_schoolspoor_schools_the_g.html (accessed March 8, 2013); Joanne Faryon and Kevin Crowe, "Schools in Rich Neighborhoods Receive More Tax Dollars," KPBS, May 19, 2011, www.kpbs.org/news/2011 /may/19/schools-rich-neighborhoods-receive-more-tax-dollar (accessed March 9, 2013); Isabelle Dills, "Public School Funding Formula Rewards St. Helena, Hurts Napa," *Napa Valley Register,* September 22, 2012, http://napavalleyregister .com/news/local/public-school-funding-formula-rewards-st-helena-hurts -napa/article_df17e378-0514-11e2-b38f-0019bb2963f4.html (accessed March 8, 2013).

5.   Michael Lind and Ted Halstead, "The National Debate over School Funding Needs a Federal Focus," New America Foundation, October 8, 2000, www.newamerica .net/node/5833 (accessed March 11, 2013); Veronique de Rugy, "K12 Spending per Student in the OECD," Mercatus Center, http://mercatus.org/sites/default/files /publication/k-12-education-spending-pdf_0.pdf (accessed March 11, 2013).

6.   Black, "Spending Gap between State's Rich, Poor Schools Is Vast."

7.   Jean Anyon, "Social Class and the Hidden Curriculum of Work," *Jour-nal of Education* 162, no. 1 (Fall 1980), http://cuip.uchicago.edu/~cac/nlu/fnd504 /anyon.htm (accessed March 10, 2013).

8.   Anyon, "Social Class and the Hidden Curriculum of Work."

9.   Michael B. Sauter, Ashley C. Allen, Lisa Nelson, and Alexander E. M. Hess, "America's Richest School Districts," 24/7 Wallstreet, June 6, 2012, http://247wallst.com/special-report/2012/06/06/americas-richest-school-districts /5/ (accessed March 9, 2013); Heather G. Peske and Kati Haycock, "Teaching Inequality: How Poor and Minority Students Are Shortchanged on Teacher Qual-ity," *The Education Trust,* June 2006, http://milwaukeepartnershipacademy.org/ pubs/teach_inequality_rprt-6_06_ed_trust.pdf (accessed September 14, 2014).

10.   Philip Elliot, "School Maintenance Report Shows Need for $542 Billion to Update, Modernize Buildings," *Huffington Post,* March 15, 2013, www.huffing

tonpost.com/2013/03/12/school-maintenance-report_n_2858279.html (accessed March 11, 2013); Schoof, "Rich-Poor Spending Gap on Schools Hurts Kids."

11. Jonathan Rabinovitz, "Poor Ranking on International Test Misleading about U.S. Student Performance, Stanford Researcher Finds," *Stanford News,* January 29, 2013, http://news.stanford.edu/news/2013/january/test-scores-ranking-011513.html (accessed March 10, 2013); Martin Carnoy and Richard Rothstein, "What Do International Tests Really Show about US Student Performance?" Economic Policy Institute, January 28, 2013, www.epi.org/publication/us-student-performance-testing/ (accessed March 10, 2013); Alan S. Brown and Linda LaVine Brown, "What Are Science and Math Test Scores Really Telling U.S.?" *Bent of Tau Beta Pi,* Winter 2007, www.tbp.org/pubs/Features/W07Brown.pdf (accessed March 10, 2013); US Census Bureau, "Poverty," US Department of Commerce, 2012, www.census.gov/hhes/www/poverty/about/overview/ (accessed January 13, 2014).

12. Catherine Rampell, "SAT Score and Family Income," *New York Times,* August 27, 2009, http://economix.blogs.nytimes.com/2009/08/27/sat-scores-and-family-income/ (accessed March 17, 2013); Harold Meyerson, "Richie Rich Aces the SAT," *American Prospect,* September 25, 2012, http://prospect.org/article/richie-rich-aces-sat (accessed March 17, 2013); Daniel H. Pink, "How to Predict a Student's SAT Score: Look at the Parents' Tax Return," www.danpink.com/2012/02/how-to-predict-a-students-sat-score-look-at-the-parents-tax-return (accessed March 17, 2013).

13. Tami Luhby, "College Graduation Rates: Income Really Matters," CNN, November 28, 2011, http://money.cnn.com/2011/11/21/news/economy/income_college/index.htm (accessed March 17, 2013); Jason M. Breslow, "By the Numbers: Dropping Out of High School," PBS, September 21, 2012, www.pbs.org/wgbh/pages/frontline/education/dropout-nation/by-the-numbers-dropping-out-of-high-school (accessed March 18, 2013); "Fast Facts," National Center for Educational Statistics, http://nces.ed.gov/fastfacts/display.asp?id=77 (accessed July 6, 2013).

14. Gary Orfield, John Kucsera, and Genevieve Siegel-Hawley, "E Pluribus … Separation: Deepening Double Segregation for More Students," The Civil Rights Project, March 19, 2012, http://civilrightsproject.ucla.edu/research/k-12-education/integration-and-diversity/mlk-national/e-pluribus … separation-deepening-double-segregation-for-more-students (accessed March 20, 2013); US Census Bureau, "Income, Poverty and Health Insurance Coverage in the United States: 2011," US Department of Commerce, September 12, 2012, www.census.gov/newsroom/releases/archives/income_wealth/cb12-172.html (accessed March 20, 2013); "Health and Social Issues Afflicting Modern Native Americans: An Expose," National Relief Charities, December 9, 2011, http://nationalreliefcharities.tumblr.com (accessed March 20, 2013); Valerie Strauss, "The Achievement Gap, by the Numbers," *Washington Post,* September 9, 2012, http://articles.washingtonpost.com/2012-09-09/local/35498072_1_achievement-gap-high-poverty-schs-black-students (accessed April 18, 2013).

15. Pat Garofalo, "Studies Show Growing Education Gap between Rich and Poor," Think Progress, February 10, 2012, http://thinkprogress.org/education/2012/02/10/422671/education-gap-rich-poor/?mobile=nc (accessed March 20, 2013).

16. Green, "Are High-Poverty Schools Educating the Poor to Remain So?";
Schoof, "Rich-Poor Spending Gap on Schools Hurts Kids"; Stacy Teicher Khadaroo,
"Economic Segregation Rising in US Public Schools," *Christian Science Monitor,* May
27, 2010, www.csmonitor.com/USA/Education/2010/0527/Economic-segregation
-rising-in-US-public-schools (accessed March 15, 2013); Julianne Hing, "Still Separate and Unequal, Generations after *Brown v. Board,*" Colorlines, May 17, 2011,
http://colorlines.com/archives/2011/05/brown_v_board_of_education_feature
.html (accessed March 20, 2013).

17. "Common School Movement: Colonial and Republican Schooling,
Changes in the Antebellum Era, the Rise of the Common School," *Educational
Encyclopedia,* http://education.stateuniversity.com/pages/1871/Common-School
-Movement.html (accessed March 21, 2013).

18. Scott Myers-Lipton, *Social Solutions to Poverty: America's Struggle to
Build a Just Society* (Boulder, CO: Paradigm Publishers, 2006); "Common School
Movement."

19. "The Freedmen's Bureau," http://eh.net/encyclopedia/the-freedmens
-bureau (accessed March 21, 2013); Myers-Lipton, *Social Solutions to Poverty.*

20. Myers-Lipton, *Social Solutions to Poverty.*

21. Jeff Lingwall, "Compulsory Schooling, the Family, and the 'Foreign
Element' in the United States, 1880–1900," Carnegie Mellon University, Heinz
College, www.heinz.cmu.edu/research/372full.pdf (accessed March 21, 2013).

22. John Dewey, "My Pedagogic Creed," *School Journal* 54, no. 3 (January
1897): 77–80.

23. Kathleen Bennett de Marrais and Margaret D. LeCompte, *The Way
Schools Work: A Sociological Analysis of Education* (New York: Longman, 1990); Peter
F. Carborne Jr., *The Social and Educational Thought of Harold Rugg* (Durham, NC:
Duke University Press, 1977); George S. Counts, *The Social Foundations of Educa-
tion* (New York: Charles Scribner's Sons, 1934), 542.

24. "*Brown v. Board*: Timeline of School Integration in the US," *Teaching Tolerance* 34, no. 25 (Spring 2004), www.tolerance.org/magazine/number
-25-spring-2004/feature/brown-v-board-timeline-school-integration-us (accessed
January 14, 2014).

25. Bob Smith, *They Closed Their Schools: Prince Edward County, Virginia,
1951–1964* (Chapel Hill: University of North Carolina Press, 1965); Sarah Carr, "In
Southern Towns, 'Segregation Academies' Are Still Going Strong," *Atlantic,* December 13, 2012, www.theatlantic.com/national/archive/2012/12/in-southern-towns
-segregation-academies-are-still-going-strong/266207 (accessed March 27, 2013);
Leadership Conference on Civil Rights Education Fund, "School Desegregation and
Equal Educational Opportunity," The Leadership Conference, 2001, www.civilrights
.org/resources/civilrights101/desegregation.html (accessed March 27, 2013).

26. David Frum, *How We Got Here: The '70s* (New York: Basic Books, 2000).

27. Leadership Conference on Civil Rights Education Fund, "School Desegregation and Equal Educational Opportunity"; David L. Kirp, "Making Schools Work,"
New York Times, May 19, 2012, www.nytimes.com/2012/05/20/opinion/sunday
/integration-worked-why-have-we-rejected-it.html?_r=0 (accessed March 21, 2013).

28. Daniel S. Levine, "Schools Resegregate after Being Freed from Judicial
Oversight, Stanford Study Shows," *Stanford News,* December 5, 2012, http://

news.stanford.edu/news/2012/december/schools-resegregation-study-120412 .html (accessed March 27, 2013); Aaron Epstein, "Court: Busing Orders Are Not Permanent," *Inquirer,* January 16, 1991, http://articles.philly.com/1991-01-16 /news/25817250_1_school-desegregation-gwendolyn-gregory-single-race-schools (accessed March 27, 2013); Sean F. Reardon, Elena Grewal, Demetra Kalogrides, and Erica Greenberg, "Brown Fades: The End of Court-Ordered School Desegregation and the Resegregation of American Public Schools," Center for Education Policy Analysis, http://cepa.stanford.edu/content/brown-fades-end-court-ordered -school-desegregation-and-resegregation-american-public-schools (accessed March 29, 2013); Sarah Garland, "Was *Brown v. Board* a Failure?," *Atlantic,* December 5, 2012, www.theatlantic.com/national/archive/2012/12/was-brown-v-board-a -failure/265939/ (accessed March 29, 2013); University of Arkansas, "Arkansas Teacher Corps to Address Shortages in State Schools," *Newswire,* January 8, 2013, http://newswire.uark.edu/Article.aspx?ID=19891 (accessed March 29, 2013); Kevin Pieper, "No Experience Needed for This Teaching Gig," *USA Today,* February 25, 2013, www.usatoday.com/story/news/nation/2013/02/24/arkansas-teacher -corps-program/1944129/ (accessed April 8, 2013); Maria Godoy and Mark Walsh, "Parsing the High Court's Ruling on Race and Schools," National Public Radio, June 28, 2007, www.npr.org/templates/story/story.php?storyId=11507539 (accessed April 18, 2013); Leadership Conference on Civil Rights Education Fund, "School Desegregation and Equal Educational Opportunity."

29. Gary Orfield, "US Schools Are More Segregated Today Than in the 1950s," Project Censored, www.projectcensored.org/top-stories/articles/2-us-schools-are -more-segregated-today-than-in-the-1950s-source/ (accessed March 29, 2013); Dan Carsen, "What You Need to Know: The Legacy of School Segregation," Southern Education Desk, February 14, 2012, www.southerneddesk.org/?p=1082 (accessed April 19, 2013); Harvard Graduate School of Education, "New National Study Finds Increasing School Segregation," www.gse.harvard.edu/news_events/features/1999 /orfielddeseg06081999.html (accessed April 19, 2013).

30. Jeanne Ellsworth and Lynda J. Ames, "Hope and Challenge: Head Start Past, Present, Future," in Jeanne Ellsworth and Lynda J. Ames, *Critical Perspectives on Project Head Start: Revisioning the Hope and Challenge* (New York: State University of New York Press, 1998); Janet Currie and Duncan Thomas, "Does Head Start Make a Difference?" *American Economic Review* 85, no. 3 (1995): 341–364; "Head Start Statistical Fact Sheet," US Department of Health and Human Resources: Head Start Bureau, http://eclkc.ohs.acf.hhs.gov/hslc/mr/factsheets/2013-hs-program -factsheet.html (accessed January 30, 2014); Chloe Gibbs, Jens Ludwig, and Douglas L. Miller, "Does Head Start Do Any Lasting Good?" National Bureau of Economic Research, September 2011, www.nber.org/papers/w17452.pdf (accessed March 29, 2013).

31. Myers-Lipton, *Social Solutions to Poverty.*

32. Richard A. Gambitta, "Oxford Companion to the US Supreme Court: San Antonio Independent School District v. Rodriguez," Answers, www.answers .com/topic/san-antonio-independent-school-district-v-rodriguez-1#ixzz2qOm2Lzli (accessed January 14, 2014).

33. Bruce Baker, David Sciarra, and Danielle Farrie, "Is School Funding Fair? A National Report Card," Education Law Center, June 2012, www.school

fundingfairness.org/ (accessed March 29, 2013); Tovia Smith, "Judge Rules Texas' School-Funding Method Unconstitutional," National Public Radio, February 4, 2013, www.npr.org/2013/02/04/171113168/judge-rules-texas-school-funding -method-unconstitutional (accessed March 29, 2013).

34. Michael Ling and Ted Halstead, "The National Debate over School Funding Needs a Federal Focus," New America Foundation, October 8, 2000, www.newamerica.net/node/5833 (accessed April 4, 2013); "Kentucky," *Access,* www.schoolfunding.info/states/ky/lit_ky.php3 (accessed April 4, 2013); Margaret Hadderman, "Equity and Adequacy in Educational Finance," www.ericdigests .org/2002-1/equity.html (accessed April 4, 2013).

35. Greg Toppo, "Nation at Risk: The Best Thing or the Worst Thing for Education," *USA Today,* August 8, 2008, http://usatoday30.usatoday.com/news /education/2008-04-22-nation-at-risk_N.htm (accessed April 1, 2013).

36. "No Child Left Behind," *Education Week,* September 19, 2011, www .edweek.org/ew/issues/no-child-left-behind (accessed April 2, 2013); Vickie Alger, "Time to Retire, Not Reauthorize, No Child Left Behind," Independent Women's Forum, July 18, 2013, www.iwf.org/publications/2791754/Time-to-Retire,-Not -Reauthorize,-No-Child-Left-Behind (accessed January 31, 2014).

37. "No Child Left Behind," *Education Week*; Jamey Dunn, "Set Up to Fail? Sweeping Changes Are Proposed for No Child Left Behind," *Illinois Issues,* June 2011, http://illinoisissues.uis.edu/archives/2011/06/setuptofail.html (accessed April 2, 2013); "Are 82 Percent of Schools Failing?" CNS News, March 15, 2011, http://cnsnews.com/news/article/are-82-percent-schools-failing (accessed April 2, 2013).

38. Adam Gamoran, transcription of a speech from video, *Educational Inequality in the Aftermath of No Child Left Behind,* March 29, 2011, http://vimeo .com/34873705 (accessed April 2, 2013).

39. Alexandra Usher, "No Child Left Behind: Adequate Yearly Prog- ress," Center on Education Policy, November 1, 2012, www.cep-dc.org/index .cfm?DocumentSubSubTopicID=8 (April 15, 2013); Joy Resmovits, "No Child Left Behind Waivers Granted to 33 US States, Some with Strings Attached," *Huffington Post,* August 13, 2012, www.huffingtonpost.com/2012/07/19/no-child-left-behind -waiver_n_1684504.html (April 15, 2013); Diane Ravitch, "It Is Time to Repeal No Child Left Behind," Big Think, http://bigthink.com/videos/its-time-to-repeal -no-child-left-behind-2 (accessed April 2, 2013).

40. King, *Where Do We Go from Here.*

41. "School Funding System Tested in Court: Do State Mandates Usurp Local Control?" Education Justice, February 29, 2012, www.educationjustice.org /news/february-29-2012-school-funding-system-tested-in-court.html (accessed April 15, 2013).

42. George Skelton, "Brown Takes a Page from Aristotle," *Los Angeles Times,* January 13, 2013, http://articles.latimes.com/2013/jan/13/local/la-me-cap -budget-20130114 (accessed April 17, 2013).

43. John Fensterwald, "It's a Deal: Brown, Top Lawmakers Raise Base Fund- ing in Finance Formula," *Ed Source,* June 11, 2013, http://edsource.org/today/2013 /its-a-deal-brown-top-lawmakers-raise-base-funding-in-finance-formula/33350# .UtSOkfb1udL (accessed January 13, 2014).

44. Lind and Halstead, "The National Debate over School Funding Needs a Federal Focus"; Robert H. Frank, "The Progressive Consumption Tax," *Slate,* December 7, 2011, www.slate.com/articles/business/moneybox /2011/12/the_progressive_consumption_tax_a_win_win_solution_for_reducing _american_economic_inequality_.html (accessed January 13, 2014).

45. Hoppy Kercheval, "Tomblin's Education Package Matters," *Charleston Daily Mail,* March 26, 2013, www.charlestondailymail.com/Opinion/HoppyKercheval /201303250097 (accessed April 16, 2013); Suzi Parker, "If Teachers Work at Low-Income Schools, Should Their College Debt Be Forgiven?" Takepart, April 3, 2013, www.takepart.com/article/2013/04/03/student-loan-forgiveness-teachers-low-income -schools (accessed April 16, 2013); Debra Hobbs and Bruce Holland, "An Act to Amend the Teacher Licensure Law for Non-Traditional Applicants; And for Other Purposes, HB 1364," 89th General Assembly of State of Arkansas, February 8, 2013, www.arkleg .state.ar.us/assembly/2013/2013R/Acts/Act413.pdf (accessed April 16, 2013).

46. "Reps. Chu, Hinojosa Bring Quality Educators to Neediest Kids," March 21, 2013, http://chu.house.gov/press-release/reps-chu-hinojosa-bring-quality -educators-neediest-kids (accessed April 17, 2013); Judy Chu and Rubén Hinojosa, "Equal Access to Quality Education Act of 2013," www.govtrack.us/congress/bills/113 /hr1334/text (accessed April 16, 2013).

47. Charles Achilles, "Class-Size Policy: The STAR Experiment and Related Class-Size Studies (National Council of Professors of Educational Administration)," *NCEPA Publication,* October 2012, http://files.eric.ed.gov/fulltext/ED540485 .pdf (accessed April 16, 2013); Paul Gorski, "The Myth of the Culture of Poverty," *Educational Leadership* 65, no. 7 (April 2008), www.ascd.org/publications/educational -leadership/apr08/vol65/num07/The-Myth-of-the-Culture-of-Poverty.aspx (accessed April 16, 2013); Kevin Yamamura, "California Retreats on Class-Size Reduction," *Sacramento Bee,* January 20, 2013, www.sacbee.com/2013/01/20/5126802 /california-retreats-on-class-size.html#storylink=cpy (accessed April 10, 2013); "Why Class Size Matters," Parents Across America, http://parentsacrossamerica .org/what-we-believe-2/why-class-size-matters (accessed April 10, 2013).

48. "Class Size," *Education Week,* August 3, 2004, www.edweek.org/ew /issues/class-size (accessed April 10, 2013); "Descriptive Evaluation of the Federal Class-Size Reduction Program," www2.ed.gov/rschstat/eval/other/class-size/index .html (accessed April 9, 2013); Paul Takahashi, "Clark County Teachers Rally in Campaign for Smaller Class Sizes," *Las Vegas Sun,* March 13, 2013, www.lasvegassun .com/news/2013/mar/13/clark-county-teachers-rally-campaign-smaller-class (accessed April 9, 2013); "Hundreds Rally for Class Size Reduction," Class County Education Association, March 13, 2013, http://ccea-nv.org/index.php/hundreds-rally-for-class -size-reduction (accessed April 9, 2013); Cindy Long, "Does Class Size Really Matter?," NEA Today, April 20, 2011, http://neatoday.org/2011/04/20/does-class-size-really -matter (accessed April 13, 2013); Institute of Education Sciences, "Identifying and Implementing Education Practices Supported by Rigorous Evidence: A User Friendly Guide," US Department of Education, December 2003, www2.ed.gov/rschstat /research/pubs/rigorousevid/rigorousevid.pdf (accessed April 13, 2013).

49. Leonie Haimson, "Educate All Kids Like Sasha and Malia," *In These Times,* November 21, 2012, http://inthesetimes.com/article/14187/educate_all _kids_like_sasha_and_malia (accessed April 10, 2013); "Who We Are," Parents

Across America, http://parentsacrossamerica.org/what-we-believe-2/why-class-size -matters (accessed April 10, 2013).

50. Arne Duncan, "The Well-Rounded Curriculum," April 9, 2010, www2 .ed.gov/news/speeches/2010/04/04092010.html (accessed April 16, 2013).

51. "Engaging Electives at Kuss Middle School," National Center on Time and Learning, www.timeandlearning.org/files/Engaging%20Electives%20-%20 Matthew%20J.%20Kuss%20Middle%20School.pdf (accessed January 31, 2014).

52. "Use Time to Provide a Well-Rounded Education," National Center on Time and Learning, www.timeandlearning.org/files/TWS_Use_Time_to _Provide_a_Well-Rounded_Education.pdf (accessed January 31, 2014).

53. "Most Dropouts Leave School Due to Boredom, Lack of Encouragement, Report Finds," *Philanthropy News Digest,* March 3, 2006, http://foundationcenter .org/pnd/news/story.jhtml?id=133800007 (accessed April 12, 2013).

54. Bob Gliner, transcription of a conversation from video, *Schools That Change Communities,* www.docmakeronline.com/schoolsthatchangecommunities .html (accessed January 31, 2014).

55. "Most Dropouts Leave School Due to Boredom, Lack of Encouragement, Report Finds"; John Bridgeland, "Fight Poverty: Lower High School Drop Out Rates," Spotlight on Poverty and Opportunity, www.spotlightonpoverty.org/news .aspx?id=d7489aaa-8d79-4382-a6a6-fcecbcaa4ada (accessed April 13, 2013); John Bridgeland, John Dilulio Jr., and Stuart Wulsin, "Engaged for Success: Service Learning as a Tool for High School Dropout Prevention," Case Foundation, http:// casefoundation.org/case-studies/engaged-for-success-service-learning (accessed April 13, 2013); David Sorbel, "Swimming Upstream against the Current: Chang- ing the School," *Community Works Journal Online Magazine for Educators,* www .communityworksinstitute.org/cwjonline/essays/a_essaystext/sobeloakland.html (accessed April 12, 2013); Liz Bowie, "Small Garrett County School Ranks No. 1 in Test Scores," *Baltimore Sun,* July 22, 2010, http://articles.baltimoresun.com/2010 -07-22/news/bs-md-schools-rank-20100722_1_maryland-school-assessment -elementary-schools-test-scores (accessed April 12, 2013).

56. Gliner, *Schools That Change Communities.*

57. Christine Armario, "Charter School Student Numbers Soar to More Than 2 Million," *Huffington Post,* December 7, 2011, www.huffingtonpost .com/2011/12/07/charter-school-student-nu_n_1133807.html (accessed April 17, 2013); Center for Research on Education Outcomes, "Multiple Choice: Charter School Performance in 16 States," Stanford University, June 2009, http://credo .stanford.edu/reports/MULTIPLE_CHOICE_CREDO.pdf (accessed April 17, 2013).

58. Elizabeth Harrington, "Education Spending Up 64% under No Child Left Behind but Test Scores Improve Little," CNSNews.com, September 26, 2011, www.cnsnews.com/news/article/education-spending-64-under-no-child-left -behind-test-scores-improve-little (accessed April 17, 2013).

59. Institute for Education Sciences, "Fast Facts," National Center for Educa- tion and Statistics, http://nces.ed.gov/fastfacts/display.asp?id=147 (accessed April 18, 2013); Lyndsey Layton, "U.S. Students Make Gains in Math but Stall in Reading," *Washington Post,* November 1, 2011, http://articles.washingtonpost.com/2011-11-01 /local/35284486_1_naep-scores-eighth-graders-500-point-scale (accessed April 13, 2013); Institute for Education Sciences, "Fast Facts"; "Achievement Gap," *Education*

Week, August 3, 2004, www.edweek.org/ew/issues/achievement-gap (accessed April 18, 2013).

60. Jonathan Schorr, "Obama Administration Budget Makes Major Invest-ment in Early Learning," US Department of Education, April 10, 2013, www .ed.gov/blog/2013/04/obama-administration-budget-makes-major-investment -in-early-learning (accessed April 15, 2013); Equity and Excellence Commission, "For Each and Every Child: A Strategy for Education Equity and Excellence)," US Department of Education, February 2, 2013, www2.ed.gov/about/bdscomm/list /eec/equity-excellence-commission-report.pdf (accessed April 14, 2013); "Fact Sheet: President Obama's Plan for Early Education for All Americans," February 2013, www.whitehouse.gov/the-press-office/2013/02/13/fact-sheet-president-obama-s -plan-early-education-all-americans (accessed April 15, 2013).

61. Keith Kamisugi, "Calif. Appellate Court Upholds Promoting Diversity in Schools," Equal Justice Society, March 18, 2009, http://equaljusticesociety .wordpress.com/2009/03/18/calif-appellate-court-upholds-promoting-diversity-in -schools (accessed April 19, 2013); Tony Favro, "Racially Diverse Schools Harder to Attain after US Court Decision," City Mayors, www.citymayors.com/education /us-desegregation.html (accessed April 19, 2013).

62. Richard Kahlenberg, "The New Look of School Integration," *American Prospect,* June 2, 2008, http://prospect.org/article/new-look-school-integration (accessed April 19, 2013).

CHAPTER 5

1. "Defining Poverty and Why It Matters for Children," Children's Defense Fund, August 2005, www.childrensdefense.org/child-research-data-publications /data/definingpoverty.pdf (accessed February 1, 2014).

2. Carmen DeNavas-Walt, Bernadette D. Proctor, and Robert J. Mills, *Income, Poverty, and Health Insurance Coverage in the United States: 2003, US Census Bureau, Current Population Reports,* 2004, www.census.gov/prod/2004pubs /p60-226.pdf (accessed June 20, 2013); Richard Knox, "US Ranks below 16 Other Rich Countries in Health Report," National Public Radio, January 9, 2013, www .npr.org/blogs/health/2013/01/09/168976602/u-s-ranks-below-16-other-rich -countries-in-health-report (accessed May 2, 2013); Henry J. Kaiser Family Foun-dation, "2013 Employer Health Benefits Survey," August 20, 2013, http://ehbs.kff .org/?page=charts&id=1&sn=6&p=1 (accessed May 2, 2013); Susan Heavey, "Study Links 45,000 US Deaths to Lack of Insurance," Reuters, May 2, 2009, www.reuters .com/article/2009/09/17/us-usa-healthcare-deaths-idUSTRE58G6W520090917 (accessed June 20, 2013).

3. Christopher J. L. Murray and Julio Frenk, "Ranking 37th—Measuring the Performance of the US Health Care System," *New England Journal of Medicine* 362, no. 2 (January 2010), www.nejm.org/doi/full/10.1056/NEJMp0910064 (accessed May 1, 2013).

4. John Commins, "Healthcare Costs Soar above Overall Inflation," Health-Leaders Media, October 22, 2010, www.healthleadersmedia.com/page-1/FIN-258088 /Healthcare-Costs-Soar-Above-Overall-Inflation (accessed June 19, 2013).

5. Paul Krugman, "Administrative Costs," *New York Times,* July 6, 2009, http://krugman.blogs.nytimes.com/2009/07/06/administrative-costs (accessed February 1, 2014); "New Study Puts Defensive Medicine Costs at between $650–$850 Billion Annually," AHIP, October 17, 2011, www.ahipcoverage.com/2011/10/17/new-study-puts-defensive-medicine-costs-at-between-650-750-billion-annually (accessed February 1, 2014).

6. Pauline W. Chen, "Where Have All the Primary Doctors Gone?," *New York Times,* December 20, 2012, http://well.blogs.nytimes.com/2012/12/20/where-have-all-the-primary-care-doctors-gone (accessed May 2, 2013).

7. "National Health Expenditure Projections 2010–2020," Centers for Medicare and Medicaid Services, www.cms.gov/Research-Statistics-Data-and-Systems/Statistics-Trends-and-Reports/NationalHealthExpendData/downloads/proj2010.pdf (accessed May 2, 2013); Elizabeth Wikler, Peter Basch, and David M. Cutler, "Paper Cuts: Reducing Healthcare Administrative Costs," Center for American Progress, June 11, 2012 (accessed May 1, 2013); Annie Lowry, "Study of US Health Care Systems Finds Both Waste and Opportunity to Improve," *New York Times,* May 1, 2012, www.nytimes.com/2012/09/12/health/policy/waste-and-promise-seen-in-us-health-care-system.htm (accessed May 1, 2013); Jeffrey Young, "High Drug Cost Spells Health Risks for Poor and Uninsured: Report," *Huffington Post,* April 9, 2013, www.huffingtonpost.com/jeffrey-young/drug-cost-concerns-spell-_b_3040358.html (accessed May 2; 2013); "Industries," CNN, May 21, 2012, http://money.cnn.com/magazines/fortune/fortune500/2012/industries/223/ (accessed September 21, 2013); Paul Krugman, "The Conscience of a Liberal," *New York Times,* July 6, 2009, http://krugman.blogs.nytimes.com/2009/07/06/administrative-costs/ (accessed June 9, 2013); Katie Thomas, "US Drug Costs Dropped in 2012, but Rises Loom," *New York Times,* March 18, 2013, www.nytimes.com/2013/03/19/business/use-of-generics-produces-an-unusual-drop-in-drug-spending.html?pagewanted=all&_r=0, (accessed June 19, 2013).

8. Christian Nordqvist, "Underinsured Adults Rose from 16 Million to 29 Million in 7 Years," *Medical News Today,* September 9, 2011, www.medicalnewstoday.com/articles/234193.php (accessed June 19, 2013); Emily Jane Fox, "Fewer Americans Uninsured—Census Bureau," CNN, September 12, 2012, http://money.cnn.com/2012/09/12/news/economy/census-bureau-health-insurance/index.html (accessed June 19, 2013).

9. Stephanie Kelton, "An Introduction to the Health Care Crisis in America: How Did We Get Here?" Center for Full Employment and Price Stability, September 2007, www.cfeps.org/health/chapters/html/ch1.htm (accessed June 19, 2013).

10. Lesley Russell, "Fact Sheet: Health Disparities by Race and Ethnicity," Center for American Progress, December 16, 2010, www.americanprogress.org/issues/healthcare/news/2010/12/16/8762/fact-sheet-health-disparities-by-race-and-ethnicity/ (accessed May 3, 2013).

11. Amanda Moore, "Tracking Down Martin Luther King Jr.'s Words on Health Care," *Huffington Post,* January 18, 2013, www.huffingtonpost.com/amanda-moore/martin-luther-king-health-care_b_2506393.html (accessed May 28, 2013).

12. Nedra Pickler, "Obama Calls for Universal Health Care," *USA Today,* January 25, 2007, http://usatoday30.usatoday.com/news/washington/2007-01-25

-obama-health_x.htm?hiddenMacValue=0&hiddenMacPrintValue=0 (accessed May 28, 2013).

13. "The Tragedy of Ten-Million Acre Bill," *Health Matters,* January 29, 2011, http://healthmatters4.blogspot.com/2011/01/tragedy-of-ten-million-acre-bill.html (accessed May 7, 2013); "Veto Message: Franklin Pierce," *The Laws of Nature and Nature's God,* May 3, 1854, www.lonang.com/exlibris/misc/1854-pvm.htm (accessed May 7, 2013).

14. W. E. B. Du Bois, *Black Reconstruction* (Millwood, NY: Kraus-Thomson, 1976).

15. Katz, *In the Shadow of the Poorhouse*; Carolyn M. Moehling and Melissa A. Thomasson, "Saving Babies: The Contribution of Sheppard-Towner to the Decline in Infant Mortality in the 1920s," National Bureau of Economic Research, April 2012, www.nber.org/papers/w17996 (accessed February 1, 2014); J. Stanley Lemons, "The Sheppard-Towner Act: Progressivism in the 1920s," *Journal of American History* 55, no. 4 (March 1969): 776–786, http://kcjohnson.files.wordpress.com/2012/12/shep-towner-act-article.pdf (accessed February 1, 2014).

16. "American President: The Campaign and Election of 1914," University of Virginia Miller Center, http://millercenter.org/president/roosevelt/essays/biography/3 (accessed February 1, 2014).

17. Brian Palmer, "Obama Says Theodore Roosevelt Lobbied for Health Care Reform: Did Insurance Even Exist Back Then?" *Slate,* March 9, 2010, www.slate.com/articles/news_and_politics/explainer/2010/03/obama_says_theodore_roosevelt_lobbied_for_health_care_reform_.html (accessed May 8, 2013).

18. Lynn Petrovich, "The VA Monologue," Green Party of New Jersey, May 5, 2013, www.gpnj.org/is_the_va_socialized_medicine (accessed June 12, 2013); Office of the Under Secretary of Defense (Comptroller)/CFO, "United States Department of Defense Fiscal Year 2012 Budget Request," February 2011, http://comptroller.defense.gov/defbudget/fy2012/FY2012_Budget_Request_Overview_Book.pdf (accessed June 13, 2013); US Department of Veterans Affairs, "VA History," March 14, 2013, www.va.gov/about_va/vahistory.asp (accessed June 13, 2013); US Department of Veterans Affairs, "Facts about the Department of VA," January 2009, www.vacareers.va.gov/assets/common/print/fs_department_of_veterans_affairs.pdf (accessed June 13, 2013); "Potential Costs of Veterans' Health Care," Congressional Budget Office, October 7, 2010, www.cbo.gov/publication/21773 (accessed June 20, 2013); Tim Johnson, "Veterans Affairs Health Care System No. 1," ABC News, December 12, 2007, http://abcnews.go.com/Health/story?id=3991225&page=1#.UcMu9Ovpypp (accessed June 20, 2013); Timothy Noah, "The Triumph of Socialized Medicine," *Slate,* March 8, 2005, www.slate.com/articles/news_and_politics/chatterbox/2005/03/the_triumph_of_socialized_medicine.html (accessed June 20, 2013).

19. "Has a National Health Program Been Put before Congress?," American Historical Association, www.historians.org/projects/giroundtable/Health/Health4.htm (accessed May 8, 2013).

20. "Healthcare Crisis: Healthcare Timeline," www.pbs.org/healthcarecrisis/history.htm (accessed June 1, 2013); "Improved Medicare for All as per the Expanded and Improved Medicare for All Act," Medicare for All, www.medicareforall.org

/pages/HR676 (accessed June 1, 2013); Joe Light, "Health Care CEOs Earn Top Pay," *Wall Street Journal,* November 16, 2010, http://blogs.wsj.com/health/2010/11/16/health-care-ceos-bring-home-the-bacon/ (accessed May 10, 2013).

21. "Special Message to the Congress Recommending a Comprehensive Health Program," Harry S. Truman Library and Museum, November 19, 1945, www.trumanlibrary.org/publicpapers/index.php?pid=483 (accessed May 10, 2013).

22. "Healthcare Crisis: Healthcare Timeline," PBS, www.pbs.org/healthcare crisis/history.htm (accessed May 10, 2013).

23. Harry Truman, "Text of Truman Plea for Public Health Program," in Cynthia Rose, ed., *American Decades Primary Sources, 1940–1949* (Detroit, MI: Gale, 2004); "Special Message to the Congress Recommending a Comprehensive Health Program," Harry S. Truman Library and Museum; "Healthcare Crisis: Healthcare Timeline," PBS; "National Health Expenditure Projections 2010–2020," Centers for Medicare and Medicaid Services.

24. "The Medicare Prescription Drug Benefit Fact Sheet," November 19, 2013, Henry J. Kaiser Family Foundation, http://kff.org/medicare/fact-sheet/the-medicare-prescription-drug-benefit-fact-sheet (accessed July 11, 2014); "Policy Basics: Introduction to Medicaid," *Center on Budget and Policy Priorities,* May 8, 2013, www.cbpp.org/cms/index.cfm?fa=view&id=2223 (accessed January 15, 2014).

25. "A Brief History: Universal Health Care Efforts in the US," Physicians for a National Health Program, www.pnhp.org/facts/a-brief-history-universal-health-care-efforts-in-the-us (accessed May 13, 2013); "What if I Have Medicare?" www.healthcare.gov/using-insurance/medicare-long-term-care/medicare/ (accessed May 13, 2013); Marlo Sollitto, "What's the Difference between Medicare and Medicaid?," www.agingcare.com/Articles/difference-between-medicaid-medicare-142798 .htm (accessed June 21, 2013); "What Is the Difference between Medicare and Medicaid?" US Department of Health and Human Services, http://answers.hhs .gov/questions/3094 (accessed June 21, 2013); Kelly Kennedy, "Medicare Part B Premiums Won't Go Up in 2014," *USA Today,* October 29, 2013, www.usatoday .com/story/news/nation/2013/10/28/doughnut-hole-medicare-part-d/3286733 (accessed January 15, 2014); "How Much Does It Cost Each Month for Me to Have Original Medicare?" Medicare Interactive, www.medicareinteractive.org /page2.php?topic=counselor&page=script&slide_id=1672 (accessed January 15, 2014); Victoria Wachino, Andy Schneider, and David Rousseau, "Financing the Medicaid Program: The Many Roles of Federal and State Matching Funds," Kaiser Family Foundation, January 2004, http://kaiserfamilyfoundation.files.wordpress .com/2013/01/financing-the-medicaid-program-the-many-roles-of-federal-and -state-matching-funds-policy-brief.pdf (accessed January 15, 2014).

26. Katz, *In the Shadows of the Poorhouse*; "US Rep. Ron Kind Says That 'Thanks to Medicare,' 5% Fewer Seniors Are in Poverty, and Most Have Health Coverage," www.politifact.com/wisconsin/statements/2011/aug/25/ron-kind/us-rep -ron-kind-says-thanks-medicare-75-fewer-seni/ (accessed May 10, 2013); "Medicare: Holes in the Safety Net," Kaiser Family Foundation, http://kff.org/medicaid /issue-brief/medicaid-a-primer/www.dhs.wisconsin.gov/guide/pay/medicare.htm (accessed June 5, 2013); Daniel B. Wood, "Census Report: More Americans Relying on Medicare, Medicaid," *Christian Science Monitor,* June 6, 2011, www.csmonitor.com

/USA/2011/0913/Census-report-More-Americans-relying-on-Medicare-Medicaid-VIDEO (accessed June 4, 2013).

27. "Effects of Health Care Spending on the US Economy," http://aspe.hhs.gov/health/costgrowth/ (accessed June 13, 2013); "Health Insurance Highlights: 2011," US Department of Commerce, www.census.gov/hhes/www/hlthins/data/incpovhlth/2011/highlights.html (accessed June 13, 2013).

28. Jennifer Evans and Jaclyn Schiff, "A Timeline of Kennedy's Health Care Achievements and Disappointments," *Kaiser Health News*, September 7, 2010, www.kaiserhealthnews.org/stories/2009/august/26/kennedy-health-care-timeline.aspx (accessed May 13, 2013).

29. Presidential Recordings Program, "Participants: Richard Nixon and John Ehrlichman," University of Virginia Miller Center, February 17, 1971, http://whitehousetapes.net/transcript/nixon/450-023 (accessed June 11, 2013); Phil Galewitz, "Nixon's HMOs Hold Lessons for Obama's ACOs," *Kaiser Health News*, October 21, 2011, http://capsules.kaiserhealthnews.org/index.php/2011/10/nixons-hmos-hold-lessons-for-obamas-acos (accessed June 18, 2013).

30. Wendell Porter, "Echoes of the Past in Anti-ObamaCare Ads," The Center for Public Integrity, July 15, 2013, www.publicintegrity.org/2013/07/15/12967/opinion-echoes-past-anti-obamacare-ads (accessed February 1, 2014).

31. Thomas Bodenheimer, "The Oregon Health Plan—Lessons for the Nation," *New England Journal of Medicine* 337, no. 9 (1997): 651–655.

32. "Oregon Health Plan: An Historical Overview," Oregon Department of Human Services, 2006, www.oregon.gov/OHA/healthplan/data_pubs/ohpoverview0706.pdf?ga=t (accessed May 17, 2013); Bodenheimer, "The Oregon Health Plan—Lessons for the Nation"; Sarah Kliff, "Can Oregon Save American Health Care?" *Washington Post*, January 18, 2013, www.washingtonpost.com/blogs/wonkblog/wp/2013/01/18/can-oregon-save-american-health-care/ (accessed May 17, 2013); "MinnesotaCare at Risk in State's $5B Problem," CBS Minnesota, May 15, 2011, http://minnesota.cbslocal.com/2011/05/15/minnesotacare-at-risk-in-states-5b-problem/ (accessed May 17, 2013); Gordon Bonnyman, "The TennCare Cuts: Plunging into the Unknown," http://capone.mtsu.edu/berc/tnbiz/pdfs/healthcare/bonnyman60906.pdf (accessed May 17, 2013); Elena Conis and Carol Medlin, "Update on Oregon Health Plan (OHP) Restructuring," *Health Policy Monitor*, April 2008, http://hpm.org/en/Surveys/IGH_-_USA/11/Update_on_Oregon_Health_Plan_%28OHP%29_Restructuring (accessed May 18, 2013).

33. Kathleen O'Connor, "How Has Health Reform Affected Businesses in Massachusetts?," *Seattle/LocalHealthGuide*, http://mylocalhealthguide.com/2013/06/18/how-health-reform-affected-businesses-in-massachusetts (accessed February 1, 2014).

34. Umang Malhotra, *Solving the American Health Care Crisis* (iUniverse, 2009); Richard Knox, "Health Care in Massachusetts: 'Abject Failure' or Work in Progress?," National Public Radio, February 13, 2012, www.npr.org/blogs/health/2012/02/13/146701343/health-care-in-massachusetts-abject-failure-or-work-in-progress (accessed May 20, 2013); Steve Hahn, "Does California Have the Cure?" *Metroactive*, www.metroactive.com/metro/04.18.07/senate-bill-840-0716.html (accessed May 20, 2013); "Single-Payer Health Care Coverage," California Alliance for Retired Americans, http://graypanterssf.igc.org/cara_leg/sb_840.htm

(accessed May 20, 2013); "Organizing for Single-Payer Publicly Financed Universal Health Care," http://healthcareforall.org/ (accessed May 20, 2013).

35. William C. Hsiao, "State-Based Single-Payer Health Care—A Solution for the United States?" *New England Journal of Medicine* 364 (March 2011): 1188–1190; Art Edelstein, "Vermont Health Care Bill, S88, Becomes Law without Governor's Signature," *Vermont Business Magazine,* May 28, 2010, www.vermontbiz.com /news/may/vermont-health-care-bill-s88-becomes-law-without-governors-sgnature (accessed June 8, 2013).

36. "Healthy Kids," Santa Clara County Family Health Plan, www.scfhp .com/programs-and-services/healthy-kids (accessed May 21, 2013); Christopher Trenholm, Embry Howell, Dana Hughes, and Sean Orzol, "The Santa Clara County Healthy Kids Program: Impacts on Children's Medical, Dental and Vision Care," Mathematica Policy Research, July 2005, www.mathematica-mpr.com/publications /PDFs/santaclara.pdf (accessed May 20, 2013); Karen de Sá, "Santa Clara County Leaders Push Ballot Measure That Would Rescue Children's Health Care Coverage," *San Jose Mercury News,* July 6, 2010, www.mercurynews.com/news/ci_15444782 (accessed May 20, 2013).

37. "Healthy Kids," Santa Clara County Family Health Plan; Trenholm, Howell, Hughes, and Orzol, "The Santa Clara County Healthy Kids Program"; de Sá, "Santa Clara County Leaders Push Ballot Measure That Would Rescue Children's Health Care Coverage."

38. "Bush Signs Landmark Medicare Bill into Law," CNN, December 8, 2003, www.cnn.com/2003/ALLPOLITICS/12/08/elec04.medicare/ (accessed May 24, 2013); Kevin Sack, "Expansion of Clinics Shapes Bush Legacy," *New York Times,* December 25, 2008, www.nytimes.com/2008/12/26/health/policy/26clinics .html?pagewanted=all&_r=0 (accessed May 24, 2013).

39. "$2.3 Trillion Spent on Health Care in 2008," CBS News, January 5, 2010, www.cbsnews.com/2100-250_162-6057429.html; "Medicare Turns 47: Can Our Nation Be Proud as the Brits with Their New N.H.S.?—Yes," Single Payer Now, August 1, 2012, www.singlepayernow.net/blog/medicare-turns-47-can-our-nation -be-proud-as-the-brits-with-their-n-h-s-yes/ (accessed May 29, 2013).

40. Nedra Pickler, "Obama Calls for Universal Health Care," *USA Today,* January 25, 2007, http://usatoday30.usatoday.com/news/washington/2007-01-25-obama-health_x.htm?hiddenMacValue=0&hiddenMacPrintValue=0 (accessed May 28, 2013).

41. James Mitchiner, "It's Time for Single-Payer," Physicians for a National Health Program, August 7, 2012, www.pnhp.org/news/2012/august/its-time-for -single-payer (accessed June 20, 2013).

42. John Geyman, "The Public Option: Dead by Pen Strokes in Congressional Committees," Physicians for a National Health Program, July 27, 2009, http://pnhp .org/blog/2009/07/27/the-public-option-dead-by-pen-strokes-in-congressional -committees/ (accessed June 10, 2013); Jia Lynn Yang, "The Man Who Invented Health Care's Public Option," CNN, September 4, 2009, http://money.cnn .com/2009/09/04/news/economy/public_option_hacker.fortune/ (accessed June 20, 2013); Kip Sullivan, "Bait and Switch: How the 'Public Option' Was Sold," Physicians for a National Health Program, July 20, 2009, http://pnhp.org/blog/2009/07/20 /bait-and-switch-how-the-%E2%80%9Cpublic-option%E2%80%9D-was-sold/ (accessed June 20, 2013).

43. "Chronology," PBS, www.pbs.org/wgbh/pages/frontline/obamasdeal /etc/cron.html (accessed June 21, 2013); Paul Blumenthal, "The Legacy of Billy Tauzin: The White House–PhRMA Deal," Sunlight Foundation, February 12, 2010, http://sunlightfoundation.com/blog/2010/02/12/the-legacy-of-billy-tauzin-the -white-house-phrma-deal/ (accessed June 21, 2013); Hal Scherz, "After Supporting ObamaCare, Has the American Medical Association Lost Its Way?" Fox News, July 18, 2011, www.foxnews.com/opinion/2011/07/18/after-supporting-obamacare-has -american-medical-association-lost-its-way/ (accessed June 21, 2013).

44. "Key Features of the Affordable Care Act," US Department of Health and Human Services, www.healthcare.gov/law/timeline/#event6-pane (accessed May 31, 2013).

45. "Key Features of the Affordable Care Act," US Department of Health and Human Services.

46. Allen McDuffee, "Ask a Think Tank: Romney's Plan to Repeal Obama-care on Day One," *Washington Post,* July 2, 2012, www.washingtonpost.com/blogs /think-tanked/post/ask-a-think-tank-romneys-plan-to-repeal-obamacare-on-day -one/2012/07/02/gJQAxl0QIW_blog.html (accessed June 4, 2013); "Transcript, Video of Romney's Remarks on Supreme Court Ruling," *Wall Street Journal,* June 28, 2012, http://blogs.wsj.com/washwire/2012/06/28/transcript-of-romneys-remarks -on-the-supreme-court-ruling/ (accessed June 4, 2013).

47. Reid Wilson, "Nevada Will Join Federal HealthCare.gov Exchange," May 21, 2014, *Washington Post,* www.washingtonpost.com/blogs/govbeat /wp/2014/05/21/nevada-will-join-federal-healthcare-gov-exchange (accessed July 6, 2014); Dan Mangan, "One by One, States Shutter Health Insurance Exchanges," May 6, 2014, CNBC, www.cnbc.com/id/101646874# (accessed July 6, 2014); "HHS Awards Affordable Care Act Funds to Expand Access to Care," US Depart-ment of Health and Human Services, November 7, 2013, www.hhs.gov/news /press/2013pres/11/20131107a.html (accessed July 11, 2014).

48. Peter Suderman, "Obamacare's State-Based Insurance Exchanges Are Also Producing Enrollment Errors," *Reason,* December 6, 2013, http://reason .com/blog/2013/12/06/obamacares-state-based-insurance-exchang (accessed June 4, 2013); "ObamaCare: Health Insurance Exchange," Obamacare Facts, http:// obamacarefacts.com/obamacare-health-insurance-exchange.php (accessed June 6, 2013); Tami Luhby, "Most Individual Health Insurance Isn't Good Enough for Obamacare," CNN, April 3, 2013, http://money.cnn.com/2013/04/03/news /economy/health-insurance-exchanges/index.html (accessed June 11, 2013); "State Decisions on Health Insurance Marketplaces and the Medicaid Expansion, 2014," Kaiser Family Foundation, http://kff.org/health-reform/state-indicator /state-decisions-for-creating-health-insurance-exchanges-and-expanding-medicaid/ (accessed January 14, 2014); Don Sapatkin and Robert Calandra, "Obamacare Sign-Ups Soar, but Confirmed Coverage Is an Issue," *Inquirer,* January 15, 2014, http://articles.philly.com/2014-01-14/news/46188769_1_open-enrollment-period -federal-exchange-premiums (accessed January 15, 2014); Liz Hamel, Mira Rao, Larry Levitt, Gary Claxton, Cynthia Cox, Karen Pollitz, Mollyann Brodie, "Sur-vey of Non-Group Health Insurance Enrollees," June 19, 2014, Henry J. Kaiser Foundation, http://kff.org/private-insurance/report/survey-of-non-group-health -insurance-enrollees (accessed July 6, 2014); Eric Whitney, "Obamacare Sign-Ups

Show Wide Variation by State, Ethnicity," May 2, 2014, NPR, www.npr.org /blogs/health/2014/05/02/308775527/obamacare-sign-ups-show-wide-variation -by-state-ethnicity (accessed July 6, 2014); "Nearly 2.2 Million Americans Selected Plans in the Health Insurance Marketplace from October through December," US Department of Health and Human Services, January 13, 2014, www.hhs.gov/news /press/2014pres/01/20140113a.html (accessed July 11, 2014).

49. Sarah Kliff, "You Ask, We Answer: Here's How Obamacare's Employer Mandate Works," *Washington Post,* April 15, 2013, www.washingtonpost.com/blogs /wonkblog/wp/2013/04/15/you-ask-we-answer-heres-how-obamacares-employer -mandate-works/ (accessed June 11, 2013); "Individual Mandate Q&A," Aetna, www .aetna.com/health-reform-connection/questions-answers/individual-mandate .html (accessed June 5, 2013); Karen E. Klein, "Advice for Small Employers Confused by Obamacare," *Bloomberg Businessweek,* March 28, 2013, www.businessweek.com /articles/2013-03-28/advice-for-small-employers-confused-by-obamacare (accessed June 11, 2013).

50. Sarah Kliff, "Obamacare's Five Biggest Challenges," *Washington Post,* March 23, 2013, www.washingtonpost.com/blogs/wonkblog/wp/2013/03/23 /obamacares-five-biggest-challenges/ (accessed June 7, 2013); Sarah Kliff, "Florida Rejects Medicaid Expansion, Leaves 1 Million Uninsured," *Washington Post,* May 5, 2013, www.washingtonpost.com/blogs/wonkblog/wp/2013/05/05/florida-rejects -medicaid-expansion-leaves-1-3-million-uninsured/ (accessed June 7, 2013).

51. Sarah Kliff, "Health Reform at 2: Why American Health Care Will Never Be the Same," *Washington Post,* March 24, 2012, www.washingtonpost.com/blogs /wonkblog/post/health-reform-at-2-why-american-health-care-will-never-be-the -same/2012/03/22/gIQA7ssUVS_blog.html (accessed June 8, 2013).

52. "30 Million to Remain Uninsured under Obamacare," Single Payer Action, June 6, 2013, www.singlepayeraction.org/2013/06/06/30-million-to-remain -uninsured-under-obamacare/ (accessed June 13, 2013); Paul Davidson, "Health Care Spending Surges in First Quarter," May 4, 2014, *USA Today,* www.usatoday.com /story/money/business/2014/05/03/health-care-spending-gdp/8570053 (accessed July 10, 2014).

53. David Himmelstein, Kip Sullivan, and Steffie Woolhandler, "Recom- mendation: HMO Exemption in State Single-Payer Legislation Must Be Specific and Narrow," Physicians for a National Health Program, July 1, 2010, www.pnhp.org /news/2010/july/recommendation-hmo-exemption-in-state-single-payer-legislation -must-be-specific-and-n (accessed June 15, 2013).

54. Hsiao, "State-Based Single-Payer Health Care"; "Health Care Reform Report Recommends Hybrid Single-Payer," *Vermont Business Magazine,* Janu- ary 19, 2011, www.vermontbiz.com/news/january/health-care-reform-report -recommends-hybrid-single-payer (accessed June 13, 2013); "Medicare for All!" *Nation,* June 1, 2011, www.thenation.com/article/161084/medicare-all #ixzz2Uo0AUi5j (accessed May 20, 2013); Edelstein, "Vermont's Health Care Bill."

55. James Haslam, "Beyond the Market: Why We Must Treat Health Care as a Public Good," Vermont Workers' Center, April 19, 2011, www.workerscenter .org/node/835 (accessed June 14, 2013).

56. Jen Matteis, "The Trouble with the US Health Care, and a Possible Solution," *Corvallis Advocate,* April 12, 2012, www.corvallisadvocate.com/2012/the-trouble-with-u-s-health-care-and-a-possible-solution/ (accessed June 14, 2013); John Nichols, "Bernie Sanders, Nurses: We Still Need 'Medicare for All,'" *Nation,* June 28, 2012, www.thenation.com/blog/168649/bernie-sanders-nurses-we-still-need-medicare-all#ixzz2Wm3CHkkg (accessed June 20, 2013).

57. Nina Bernstein, "Weiner Wants City to Test Single-Payer Health Care," *New York Times,* June 20, 2013, www.nytimes.com/2013/06/21/nyregion/weiner-wants-city-to-test-single-payer-health-care.html (accessed June 21, 2013).

58. Ed Weisbart, "A Single-Payer System Would Reduce US Health Care Costs," *American Medical Association Journal of Ethics* 14, no. 11 (November 2012): 897–903; Ken A. Bode, "'Obama's Deal': A Frontline Documentary Worth Watching," CPB, May 4, 2010, www.cpb.org/ombudsman/display.php?id=40 (accessed June 20, 2013).

59. Nichols, "Bernie Sanders, Nurses"; "Medicare Turns 47," Single Payer Now.

60. "Conyers Reintroduces National Single-Payer Health Care Bill," Healthcare-Now!, February 14, 2013, www.healthcare-now.org/conyers-reintroduces-national-single-payer-health-care-bill (accessed June 20, 2013); "Doctors Group Hails Reintroduction of Medicare-for-All Bill," Physicians for a National Health Program, February 14, 2013, www.pnhp.org/news/2013/february/doctors-group-hails-reintroduction-of-medicare-for-all-bill#node-8326 (accessed June 20, 2013).

61. Chris Fleming, "Medicare Beneficiaries Less Likely to Experience Cost and Access Problems Than Adults with Private Coverage," Health Affairs Blog, July 19, 2012, http://healthaffairs.org/blog/2012/07/19/medicare-beneficiaries-less-likely-to-experience-cost-and-access-problems-than-adults-with-private-coverage/ (accessed June 20, 2013).

62. "GOP Hospital Calls for Single-Payer (Medicare for All) As Solution to Health Care Crisis," *Daily Kos,* June 10, 2013, www.dailykos.com/story/2013/06/11/1215275/-GOP-Hospital-Executive-Calls-For-Single-Payer-Medicare-For-All-As-Solution-To-Health-Care-Crisis (accessed June 20, 2013); Jack Bernard, "Single Payer Is Needed Cure," *Charlotte Observer,* June 10, 2013, www.charlotteobserver.com/2013/06/10/4097735/single-payer-is-needed-cure.html#storylink=cpy (accessed June 20, 2013).

CHAPTER 6

1. "Social Security and Elderly Poverty," National Bureau of Economic Research, www.nber.org/bah/summer04/w10466.html (accessed June 25, 2013); Marisol Bello, "As Seniors Climb from Poverty, Young Fall In," *USA Today,* February 16, 2012, http://usatoday30.usatoday.com/news/nation/story/2012-02-16/child-senior-poverty/53107636/1 (accessed June 25, 2013); Mitchell Hirsch, "The Poverty-Fighting Effects of Unemployment Insurance," *Unemployed Workers,* June 10, 2011, http://unemployedworkers.org/sites/unemployedworkers/index.php/site/blog_entry/the_poverty-fighting_effects_of_unemployment_insurance (accessed

June 25, 2013); Steve Hargreaves, "Disability Claims Skyrocket: Here's Why," CNN, April 11, 2013, http://money.cnn.com/2013/04/11/news/economy /disability-payments/index.html (accessed July 18, 2013).

2. Michael B. Katz, *In the Shadows of the Poorhouse: A Social History of Welfare in America* (New York: Basic Books, 1986); Gerald D. Nash, Noel H. Pugash, and Richard F. Tomasson, *Social Security: The First Half Century* (Albuquerque: University of New Mexico Press, 1988); Cynthia Rose, *American Decades Primary Sources, 1930–39* (Detroit: Gale, 2003); Roger Lowenstein, "A Question of Numbers," *New York Times Magazine,* January 16, 2005, 40–47, 72, 76, 78, www.nytimes .com/2005/01/16/magazine/16SOCIAL.htmll (accessed June 24, 2013); "Policy Basics: Top Ten Facts about Social Security," Center on Budget and Policy Priorities, November 6, 2012, www.cbpp.org/cms/?fa=view&id=3261 (accessed June 25, 2013); "More Americans Claim Extended Unemployment Benefits," *Christian Science Monitor,* June 21, 2013, www.csmonitor.com/Business/Paper-Economy/2013/0621 /More-Americans-claim-extended-unemployment-benefits (accessed June 25, 2013); "Can You Live on $330 a Week?" MSN, February 18, 2011, http://money.msn.com /how-to-budget/can-you-live-on-330-a-week-mainstreet (accessed July 15, 2013); "Social Security Basic Facts," Social Security Administration, July 26, 2013, www .ssa.gov/pressoffice/basicfact.htm (accessed July 26, 2013).

3. Administration on Aging, "A Profile of Older Americans: 2011," US Department of Health and Human Services, www.aoa.gov/Aging_Statistics /Profile/2011/docs/2011profile.pdf (accessed February 1, 2014); Becky Squires, "Hunger among Older Americans Spikes," AARP Foundation, August 29, 2011, www.aarp.org/aarp-foundation/our-work/hunger/info-2012/hunger-research-2011 .html (accessed February 1, 2014).

4. Emily Brandon, "Poverty Increasing among Retirees," *US News,* May 21, 2012, http://money.usnews.com/money/retirement/articles/2012/05/21/poverty -increasing-among-retirees (accessed July 1, 2013); "Rising Healthcare Costs Driving Up Senior Poverty Rates, Says Kaiser," *Family Link,* May 21, 2013, www .familylink.net/blog/entry/rising-healthcare-costs-driving-up-senior-poverty-rates -says-kaiser (accessed July 3, 2013).

5. Douglas McIntyre, "The 10 Best States for Unemployment Benefits—and the 10 Worst," *Daily Finance,* May 13, 2011, www.dailyfinance.com/2011/05/12 /unemployment-benefits-best-worst-states (accessed July 3, 2013).

6. Matt Smith, "House Speaker John Boehner Demands Cuts for Debt Limit Increase," CNN, October 7, 2013, www.cnn.com/2013/10/06/politics /congress-budget (accessed December 29, 2013).

7. "Scrapping the Payroll Tax Cap Is the Fairest Way to Make Social Security Solvent," April 16, 2012, Social Security Works, www.socialsecurityworks.org /scrapping-payroll-tax-cap-fairest-way-make-social-security-solvent (accessed July 8, 2014); "Contribution and Benefit Base," Social Security Administration, www.ssa .gov/oact/cola/cbb.html (accessed July 8, 2014); "Strengthen State Unemployment Insurance Programs," NELP, January 2009, www.nelp.org/page/-/UI/UIState Recession.pdf (accessed July 8, 2014).

8. Myers-Lipton, *Social Solutions to Poverty.*

9. Myers-Lipton, *Social Solutions to Poverty.*

10. Myers-Lipton, *Social Solutions to Poverty.*

11. Myers-Lipton, *Social Solutions to Poverty.*

12. Carrie A. Werner, "The Older Population: 2010," US Department of Commerce, US Census Bureau, www.census.gov/prod/cen2010/briefs/c2010br-09 .pdf (accessed July 3, 2013).

13. "A History of UI Legislation in the United States and NYS: 1935–2007," New York State Department of Labor, Division of Research and Statistics, February 2009, www.labor.ny.gov/stats/PDFs/History_UI_Legislation.pdf (accessed July 16, 2013).

14. "Historical Background and Development of Social Security," Social Security Administration, www.ssa.gov/history/briefhistory3.html (accessed July 15, 2013); Timothy S. Jost, *Disentitlement? The Threats Facing Our Public Health Care Programs and a Rights-Based Response* (New York: Oxford University Press, 2003).

15. "Historical Background and Development of Social Security," Social Security Administration, www.ssa.gov/history/briefhistory3.html (accessed July 16, 2013).

16. Francis E. Townsend, *New Horizons: An Autobiography* (Chicago: J. L. Stewart, 1943); Rose, *American Decades Primary Sources, 1930–1939.*

17. Myers-Lipton, *Social Solutions to Poverty.*

18. Myers-Lipton, *Social Solutions to Poverty.*

19. Franklin Folsom, *Impatient Armies of the Poor: The Story of Collective Action of the Unemployed 1808–1942* (Niwot: University Press of Colorado, 1991); Frances Perkins, *The Roosevelt I Knew* (New York: Viking Press, 1946); Katz, *In the Shadow of the Poorhouse*; Ronald Kimmons, "What Taxes Do Employers Have to Match?," eHow Money, www.ehow.com/list_7422630_taxes-do-employers-match _.html (accessed July 15, 2013); "Historical Background and Development of Social Security," Social Security Administration, www.ssa.gov/history/briefhistory3.html (accessed July 15, 2013).

20. Myers-Lipton, *Social Solutions to Poverty.*

21. Katz, *In the Shadows of the Poorhouse*; Nash, Pugash, and Tomasson, *Social Security: The First Half Century*; Arthur J. Altmeyer, "Three Years' Progress toward Social Security," *Social Security Bulletin* 1, no. 8 (August 1938), www.ssa.gov /history/aja838.html (accessed July 6, 2013).

22. Geoffrey Kollmann, "Social Security: Summary of Major Changes in the Cash Benefits Program," *Social Security,* May 18, 2000, www.ssa.gov/history /reports/crsleghist2.html (accessed February 1, 2014); "A History of UI Legislation in the United States and NYS: 1935–2007," New York State Department of Labor, Division of Research and Statistics, February 2009, www.labor.ny.gov/stats/PDFs /History_UI_Legislation.pdf (accessed July 16, 2013); "Unemployment Compensation," *Almanac of Policy Issues,* www.policyalmanac.org/social_welfare/archive /unemployment_compensation.shtml (accessed July 16, 2013); "Social Security Basic Facts," Social Security Administration, July 26, 2013, www.ssa.gov/press office/basicfact.htm (accessed August 2, 2013).

23. Kollmann, "Social Security: Summary of Major Changes in the Cash Benefits Program."

24. "Text of President Bush's 2005 State of the Union Address," *Washington Post,* February 2, 2005, www.washingtonpost.com/wp-srv/politics/transcripts /bushtext_020205.html (accessed July 16, 2013).

25. "Benefits Paid by Type of Beneficiary," Social Security Administration, www.ssa.gov/cgi-bin/currentpay.cgi (accessed July 9, 2014); Veronique De Rugy, "Social Security Disability Insurance Costs Are Exploding," August 8, 2013, *Washington Examiner,* http://washingtonexaminer.com/social-security-disability -insurance-costs-are-exploding/article/2533992 (accessed July 9, 2014).

26. "Historical Background and Development of Social Security," Social Security Administration, www.ssa.gov/history/briefhistory3.html (accessed July 22, 2013); James D. Agresti and Stephen F. Cardone, "Social Security Basics," Just Facts, April 5, 2013, www.justfacts.com/socialsecurity.basics.asp (accessed July 22, 2013); "The Faces and Facts of Disability," Social Security Administration, www .ssa.gov/disabilityfacts/materials/ppt/disability-facts.ppt (accessed July 8, 2014); Avik Roy, "How Americans Game the $200 Billion-a-Year 'Disability-Industrial Complex,'" *Forbes,* April 8, 2013, www.forbes.com/sites/theapothecary/2013/04/08 /how-americans-game-the-200-billion-a-year-disability-industrial-complex (accessed July 10, 2014).

27. Office of Family Assistance, "Characteristics and Financial Circumstances of TANF Recipients, Fiscal Year 2010," US Department of Health and Human Services, August 8, 2012, www.acf.hhs.gov/programs/ofa/resource/character/fy2010 /fy2010-chap10-ys-final (accessed February 1, 2014); "What Is Social Security Disability Insurance?," National Academy of Social Insurance, www.nasi.org/learn /socialsecurity/disability-insurance (accessed July 10, 2014); Ife Floyd and Liz Schott, "TANF Cash Benefits Continued to Lose Value in 2013," October 21, 2013, Center on Budget and Policy Priorities, www.cbpp.org/cms/index.cfm?fa=view&id=4034 (accessed July 10, 2014).

28. "The Great Recession," The State of Working America, http://stateof workingamerica.org/great-recession (accessed July 8, 2014); www.huffingtonpost .com/2010/01/08/unemployment-rate-decembe_n_416008.html; Richard W. Johnson, Karen E. Smith, and Owen Haaga, "How Did the Great Recession Affect Social Security Claiming?," July 29, 2013, Urban Institute, www.urban .org/UploadedPDF/412875-how-did-the-great-recession.pdf; "Unemployment in December 2010," January 11, 2011, Bureau of Labor Statistics, www.bls.gov/opub /ted/2011/ted_20110111.htm (accessed July 8, 2014); John Merline, "The Sharp Rise in Disability Claims," Federal Reserve Bank of Richmond, www.richmondfed .org/publications/research/region_focus/2012/q2-3/pdf/feature3.pdf (accessed July 8, 2014); "Selected Data from Social Security's Disability Program," Social Security Administration, www.ssa.gov/oact/STATS/dibStat.html (accessed July 8, 2014).

29. "Social Security—Serving Those Who Serve Our Nation," Strengthen Social Security, www.strengthensocialsecurity.org/veterans-report (accessed July 22, 2013); "Social Security Beneficiary Statistics," Social Security Administration, www.ssa.gov/OACT/STATS/OASDIbenies.html (accessed July 22, 2013); "Ben- efits Paid by Type of Beneficiary," Social Security Administration, www.ssa.gov /OACT/ProgData/icp.html (accessed July 22, 2013); Mark Nadel, Steve Wamhoff, and Michael Wiserman, "Disability, Welfare Reform, and Supplemental Security Income," *Social Security Bulletin* 65, no. 3 (2003–2004); John Merline, "5.4 Million Join Disability Rolls under Obama," *Investor's Business Daily,* April 20, 2012, http:// news.investors.com/business/042012-608418-ssdi-disability-rolls-skyrocket-under -obama.htm#ixzz2ZtvkaGcL (accessed July 23, 2013); Bill Briggs, "Obama Urged

to Step in to Fix VA Backlog," *US News,* March 21, 2013, http://usnews.nbcnews.com/_news/2013/03/21/17404780-obama-urged-to-step-in-to-fix-va-backlog?lite (accessed August 5, 2013).

30. "Unemployment Insurance Program Description and Legislative History," Social Security Administration, Office of Retirement and Disability Policy, 2012, www.ssa.gov/policy/docs/statcomps/supplement/2012/unemployment.html (accessed July 18, 2013); "A History of UI Legislation in the United States and NYS: 1935–2007," New York State Department of Labor, Division of Research and Statistics, February 2009, www.labor.ny.gov/stats/PDFs/History_UI_Legislation.pdf (accessed July 18, 2013); "Unemployment Insurance in the Wake of the Recent Recession," Congressional Budget Office, November 12, 2012, www.cbo.gov/publication/43734 (accessed August 30, 2013).

31. "Fact Sheet," Social Security Administration, www.ssa.gov/pressoffice/factsheets/basicfact-alt.pdf (accessed August 30, 2013); "FICA—Wage Limits and Tax Rates," University of Minnesota, www1.umn.edu/ohr/payroll/tax/wagelimits; "Policy Basics: Federal Payroll Taxes," Center on Budget and Policy Priorities, March 31, 2014, www.cbpp.org/cms/?fa=view&id=3853 (accessed July 10, 2014).

32. Dan Popkey, "In Idaho, Boehner Vows to Succeed with Entitlement Reform This Fall," *Miami Herald,* August 27, 2013, www.miamiherald.com/2013/08/27/3588598/in-idaho-boehner-vows-to-succeed.html#storylink=cpy (accessed August 30, 2013).

33. Suzy Khimm, "CEOs Want to Raise the Retirement Age to 70," *Washington Post,* January 18, 2013, www.washingtonpost.com/blogs/wonkblog/wp/2013/01/18/ceos-want-to-raise-the-retirement-age-to-70/ (accessed September 14, 2013).

34. Khimm, "CEOs Want to Raise the Retirement Age to 70."

35. Rob Schofield, "Report: Ryan Budget Would Harm NC's Schools, Public Health, and Safety," NC Policy Watch, March 27, 2013, http://pulse.ncpolicywatch.org/2013/03/27/report-ryan-budget-ncs-schools-public-health-and-safety/#sthash.gXuzOu8H.dpuf (accessed September 14, 2013).

36. Sam Stein, "Obama Offered to Raise Medicare Eligibility Age As Part of Grand Debt Deal," *Huffington Post,* September 10, 2011, www.huffingtonpost.com/2011/07/11/obama-medicare-eligibility-age_n_894833.html (accessed September 14, 2013); Paul N. Van de Water, "Medicare in Ryan's 2014 Budget," Center on Budget and Policy Priorities, March 15, 2013, www.cbpp.org/cms/?fa=view&id=3922 (accessed September 14, 2013).

37. Ellen Lockyer, "Begich to Introduce Social Security Legislation," Alaska Public Media, May 2, 2013, www.alaskapublic.org/2013/05/02/begich-to-introduce-social-security-legislation/ (accessed December 29, 2013).

EPILOGUE

1. Louis D. Brandeis Legacy Fund for Social Justice, www.brandeis.edu/legacyfund/bio.html (accessed March 30, 2014).

2. "Updated Budget Projections: 2014–2024," April 14, 2014, Congressional Budget Office, www.cbo.gov/publication/45229 (accessed July 11, 2014); Drew Desilver, "Five Facts about the National Debt: What You Should Know," Pew

Research Center, October 9, 2013, www.pewresearch.org/fact-tank/2013/10/09/5
-facts-about-the-national-debt-what-you-should-know (accessed March 30, 2014);
"The Truth-O-Meter Says: In the 1950s, a Lot of People Got Rich—and They Had
to Pay a Top Tax Rate of 90 Percent," PolitiFact.com, www.politifact.com/truth
-o-meter/statements/2009/oct/02/michael-moore/michael-moores-film-capitalism
-claims-richest-paid (accessed April 16, 2014); David Kocieniewski, "US Business
Has High Tax Rates but Pays Less," May 2, 2011, www.nytimes.com/2011/05/03
/business/economy/03rates.html?_r=0 (accessed April 16, 2014).

Index